"Believe in God and Get Ahead"

A Grandmother's Advice

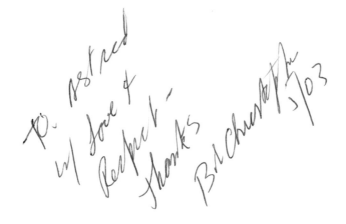

An American Biography
By Robert A. Christopher

~

D E D I C A T I O N

With great appreciation, love, and humility, I dedicate this book to my loving and supportive wife of fifty-two years, Marty, and to our three sons, Robert, James, and John, who, like their mother, have given my life purpose and fulfillment. Without them, I'd be floundering in the wastelands of aimless pursuit.

I also dedicate this book to the memory of my Grandmother Christopher, who raised me and started a headstrong boy on his path of life, with a lasting admonition.

And lastly, I dedicate this book to the millions of my fellow *Silent Generation* men and women, who spoke for us softly, but effectively, and allowed me to tag along on their trek into history.

May God bless them all.

*　　　　　*　　　　　*

Ernest Hemingway, our acclaimed "Truly American Author," and winner of the Nobel Prize for Literature said of his writing, "All you have to do is write one true sentence. Write the truest sentence you know." This is mine, "Never doubt or underestimate the power and beneficence of the Holy Spirit or the love of a caring woman."

~

ACKNOWLEDGMENTS

My deep thanks to:

Marty Christopher, my wife of fifty-two years, for her unflagging love, encouragement, and support.

Rebecca Salome – Berkeley, California, my erudite, stern, but guiding-light editor, who taught me the beauty of never giving up until we had the correct word usage and clear thinking. She is the rudder of my literary ship.

Elizabeth Shaw – Tucson, Arizona, a *grand dame* of editing, who taught her daughter, my editor, the trade, and encouraged me at the start.

Stewart Scott – Olympia Fields, Illinois, for technical help, **Carollyn Hamilton**, for page layout, and design, and **Melinda Roeleveld** and **Kirk Middleton** for illustrations. Scott Communications, Inc.

Sandra Desjardins – Scottsdale, Arizona, a creative writing professor at Scottsdale Community College, who told me not to be afraid to write, and that syntax was not a fee for misbehaving.

The Rt. Rev. William E. Swing – San Francisco, Bishop of the Episcopal Diocese of California for his humane and spiritual work on behalf of all mankind, and for his inspiration to Marty and me.

Kingdon Gould Jr. – Laurel, Maryland, my partner at Globe Industries for broadening my business scope and showing me the highest standards of integrity, generosity and friendship.

Neil K. Bortz – Cincinnati, Ohio, a true friend, who through his visionary and inspirational leadership helped me to put something back into the community that nurtured me in the formative years of my life.

Roger B. Smith – Detroit – Chairman and CEO, General Motors Corporation (ret.) for corporate and industry inspiration and support in the early renaissance of the American automotive industry in its emergence from the dark days of 1980-81.

~

FOREWORD

When a member of the Silent Generation speaks up, the spell is broken. Silence gives way to a strong, clear utterance. In the case of Robert Christopher's *"Believe in God And Get Ahead,"* the reader is in for a treat. Not only are seven decades of life in the United States portrayed in a personal manner, but the bedrock values that under girded that time are movingly revealed. This is no self-indulgent success story. It is Exhibit A of Middle America's humble beginnings, discovery of discipline, repeated failures, enduring faith, and happy endings that bring the duty to give back. And not in isolation! This is the mystery of pragmatic life lived in a genuine religious context. Ultimately this book is not about an age or a sociological insight. It is about a man, an uncommonly honest person, who gives us hope in the human endeavor. I feel privileged to know this man and to have read his book.

The Right Reverend William W. Swing
Episcopal Bishop, Diocese of California
San Francisco

~

PROLOGUE

Browsing through one of today's mega book stores, I came across *Generations* by William Straus and Neil Howe. The title piqued my interest, as I had read a lot about *The Lost Generation* of my literary heroes, Fitzgerald, Dos Passos, and Hemingway.

I was intrigued by the detailed premise offered by Strauss and Howe—that each generation has its own distinguishing complexion, and its own special, time-molded characters that become "the voices of their generation."

The more I perused the book, the more I realized that not only do the generations have their characteristics, foibles, mores, and hopefully, a meaningful legacy to leave behind, but so do you and I. History has its eras, societies have their generations, and we as individuals have our biographies—our own intimate stories. To leave our stories is to leave a legacy that others may learn from…generation after generation.

Before I paid for the book, I gleaned some kernels from the chapter on my generation: The Silent, those born between 1925 and 1942. I was not overjoyed when I read the one-word description: adaptive—with its implication of being followers, conformists, and "silent." So I decided to write this book in an attempt to capture the forces that shaped my generation, through the camera lens of my life, my times, and my fellow man.

It would be arrogant for me to think my story would be considered *belles lettres*, but this biography is from the heart and soul of me and my Silent Generation. I hope it will bring to you memories, associations, a lesson or two, and the deep significance that a grandmother's advice—her legacy to me—had in molding my life. May you leave such a legacy to your loved ones and to our succeeding generations.

Robert A. Christopher
Scottsdale, Arizona
May, 21, 2002

～

C H A P T E R

1

The past creates the present, and the present recreates the past.

"Mr. Christopher, your left carotid artery is over eighty percent blocked. You're a stroke waiting to happen."

"What does that mean, Doctor Fowl?"

"It means only twenty percent of the main artery that feeds blood to the brain is open. It's like this. See how the opening shrinks."

"I see." I watch him make a circle with his thumb and index finger, closing down the circle to a tiny opening, like stopping down the lens of a camera from wide open to f 64. " Not good, huh?"

"It means that any further restriction, or a thickening of your blood, could cause a stroke. One that might induce paralysis."

"What...what can be done?" I feel my pulse rate accelerate and my stomach muscles knot. I haven't been operated on or in a hospital in all my seventy-two years. Not sure I want to hear his answer, I look away trying to get my bearings, fighting for control of myself. I see the adjustable examination table and the stainless steel box used for sterilizing surgical implements. On the wall, I see the medical waste disposal container with its glaring red-lettered warnings. Sensing the doctor's reply, I turn. He looks honest. Hell, I gotta trust him. What else?

"We perform surgery. We clamp off the artery during the operation, take out a layer of artery wall and patch it. Opening up the artery will increase blood flow, probably back to fully normal."

"What's the alternative to surgery?"

"No alternative. Maybe you can live a few years without a stroke, but you are at very high risk. Have you ever had surgery before?"

"No, and that's my problem. I have claustrophobia, and I've always been a control person. In a word, I'm scared. Is the operation done under full anesthesia?"

"Yes. But, Mr. Christopher, I must tell you that during the operation a stroke could occur, or there might be a temporary loss of control over your tongue, as the nerve that controls the tongue is often alongside the carotid, and on rare occasions could be temporarily impaired."

"Is that normal?" God, what is this man saying? I need the operation to prolong my life, yet he's telling me I may have a stroke while he's doing it! My under arms are wet. I feel queasy...trapped.

"No. I've performed three hundred of these procedures, and only experienced one stroke, which was from other causes. You are in good health and a-symptomatic. You should do fine."

I look to my left, into the soft, sincere blue eyes of Marty. After fifty years of marriage, she knows my every thought, fear and question, sometimes even before I do myself. "I can't say what you should do, Chris, but if it were me, I'd do it as soon as possible."

Thinking back to my first meeting with the doctor, six months earlier, I should have gone for the surgery then. He told me that it was a gamble not to. I guess he just didn't sound firm enough. He left that tiny loophole for me to weasel out. The MRI he had me do a month ago cinched it for him...I guess it should for me too. God, I don't want to be a burden on Marty with a stroke. It isn't fair. In a surge of anxious resolve that comes from I know not where, I say, "Okay, Doctor, let's do it."

"Fine, I'll set it up at the hospital. They'll call you as to day and time."

*　　　　　*　　　　　*

On the drive home from the clinic I'm silent. Knowing for the first time I have a physical defect that requires hospitalization makes me realize my life has an end. It would be an end that I cannot predict or control. I am so vulnerable. I am now an older man who is starting to fail. I am going to be completely under someone else's control and at the mercy, no not mercy, but skill, of some person or group I don't know. God, I'm glad my wife is here! My overactive imagination draws the picture of me totally prone, unable to do anything.

I equate the need for an operation as an indictment for something I've done wrong. It's the epilogue in the story of my life. Every day I wake up thinking about it. Most nights, about two or three, I wake with an anxiety attack. I walk around our dark, still house and try to figure out why I am so uptight about an operation hundreds of thousands have had, including a couple of my buddies back in hometown Cincinnati. After ten minutes of walking and deep breathing, I get on my knees and offer up some prayers.

I guess you could call a wild beseeching for help a prayer, the typical 'gimme, gimme' type that I say so often.

Then I walk some more, thinking back on my life, which prophetically has passed the biblical three score and ten. Why am I so obsessed with controlling my environment and any force that acts on me? Was I born with this compulsion? Did conception's genetic roulette wheel give me a double zero? Marty doesn't have this problem. She's borne our three sons, had an ovary removed, and a hysterectomy. She never expresses fear or anxiety, only concern about being away from the boys and me for a few days. She always says, "What has to be done, has to be done." I admire her courage, or is it her woman's innate practicality that allows her to just surrender?

Sitting back in the large easy chair, next to the hearth in my bedroom, I put my bare feet on the ottoman and look at the wall. The Mexican metal cross glistens faintly in a thin shaft of moonlight beaming into the room from a gap in the drapes. I wonder if the light from that same moon glinted off another cross hung with a twisted, broken body two thousand years earlier. Compared to that one, does my ordeal permit me such self-pity?

I stare, trancelike. When did the cross come into my life? When did I become aware of all it stood for? My mind seeks refuge in the haven of the past. As the cobwebs of several decades blow away, I recall the first encounter. I was five or six when my dad's mother placed the cross around my neck. It was ebony and silver on a black band. She told me to kneel down by my little steel cot. We started with, "Now I lay me down to sleep...." Even though she was seventy years old, she knelt right next to me. Since I'm whining about this operation like a child, maybe I should pray like a child. Grandmother really was good to me. I remember when I acted up and she corrected me, or made me stay indoors, or made me face up to something. She sure made me face up to our priest when she found out I lied to him about why I skipped choir practice. That Sunday, after church, I had to go to him and tell him. He stood over six feet in his vestments, as I waited below him and looked up. I thought I was apologizing to God. Whenever Grandmother made me see my little sins, she always said, "Bobby, someday you'll understand why I want you to be responsible for what you do." She was right, but I never knew that when she was alive.

I was in my twenties before I really understood why I lived with her and my dad until their deaths. One day I came across some yellowed newspaper clippings interred in a family Bible that had been hidden away in my aunt's basement. My parents' divorce was written up in *National Enquirer*esque-supermarket-checkout rack jargon. I knew as a little kid they were divorced, but I never knew the details. When I asked why I didn't have a mother and a father at home, they said, "Sometimes people just figure it is best if they don't live together. When you're older you'll understand." Every September when school started, I'd get that darn card to fill out my parents' names. I never knew what to put. The teacher taught me the word *guardian*. I learned to hate that word. It was like the mark of Cain to me. None of the other kids wrote it on their cards.

I also found the clipping about their wedding in Cincinnati, which I realized, after a slow take and some quick arithmetic, occurred two months after I was conceived. I could see it, a handsome, intellectual Princeton graduate and a pretty, petite, artistic girl, five years his junior, being captivated by his charm. That provincial Cincinnati suburb where both families lived sure hadn't seen any Princeton graduates, especially one from a family who couldn't afford such a prestigious school. I still don't know why my dad won custody of me. From the time I was about five I lived with him and his mother, who I now know was one of the greatest influences in my life.

Looking at my rumpled, empty bed, I feel the endorphin effect of remembering my childhood. It calms me down. I lapse back to the time when I had to leave my mother and move to my dad's house, which was owned by his mother, Laurie Bryant Christopher. Those first few days confused me. I had just spent a year living with my mother in a single room at her parents' house. I guess the divorce and custody battle were going on then. I remember the lavender-walled room that mother and I shared. It had a double bed, a nightstand, one dresser, and one chair. Every night when I went to sleep, I was alone. Mother worked a six-hour NRA established shift from eight until two in the morning at a distillery that my dad's brother, Edwin, managed. It was only after a lot of pleading that he gave my mother and her sister a job. He wasn't much on nepotism. Today, whenever I smell Lilies of the Valley I am back in that room snuggled up to her breast as we awake in the morning. She always smelled sweet like those delicate white flowers.

Grandmother Laurie's house was made of wood clapboard that was stark, old, and gray. Nothing fancy, just a wood house. It was taller than it was wide. Usually the poorer people were, the narrower their house. Only the houses in the rich neighborhoods were wide, with big verandas and sprawling rooms. They were painted white with shutters in colors of *good taste*. My grandmother's house was built in 1890, the year that two major railroads started to service the forming suburb of Hartwell.

Access to the rails brought settlers from the inner city, or basin, as it was known to the Mill Creek Valley suburbs and towns – St. Bernard, Elmwood Place, Carthage, Hartwell, Wyoming, Lockland, Reading, Woodlawn, and Glendale. The railroads also brought back smoke, rail-riding hobos, and their nemesis, the bellicose railroad bull, those men in suits and felt hats that carried guns and the license to shoot anyone deemed to be trespassing on railroad property. During the Depression, close to five hundred rail riders were shot by railroad bulls. Others were beaten with clubs and put in jails. One morning I was in the bathroom getting ready for school, when I heard a car pull up across the street with a screech of brakes. I looked out and saw a railroad bull jump out of his car, run up the bank and fire his pistol at a young boy, shouting, "Drop that coal, you damn nigger." I saw his target, a twelve-year-old boy from our school running down the tracks. He had been picking up some loose pieces of coal that had fallen from a passing train. The boy lived in the segregated "colored section" known locally as Dixie. Dixie was a street on the edge of town with a couple dozen shacks and ramshackle houses. The loose coal he picked up was the only source of heat for his family.

The exterior of all the houses near the tracks darkened a little each year as soot spewed from the coal-burning Baltimore and Ohio trains passing just fifty yards away. Folks had little money to hire a house painter. Putting food on the table took most of it. The street we lived on had eleven wood houses on one side. The other side was a thirty-yard-wide embankment that rose to the

B & O tracks. The north end of the street ended at a small mar-
shaling yard the railroad used for making up trains. The switch
engine pushed cars from the yard back and forth past the house
twelve hours a day.

Near the yard some hobos had set up a camp of cardboard
lean-tos. There was always a fire with a half dozen guys sitting
around smoking "butts" picked up from anywhere they could be
found or begged. I was told never to go near this camp. On occa-
sion one of them would knock on the door and ask to do some
work in return for a meal. Grandmother sometimes would let them
beat a carpet or cut the grass. She always fixed them a good meal,
usually leftover hash, peas, white bread, or some fried eggs. Once
I saw her slip a man, who, despite his ragged clothes, sounded different than the rest, a couple of worn shirts that belonged to my
dad. She said as he left, "There's an intelligent and educated man
who lost his business, but only after he mortgaged everything he
owned trying to save his business and the jobs of all those that
worked for him. Now he's just riding the rails hoping to find a job
somewhere."

I learned, with some shame and embarrassment, that
there was a "right" and a "wrong" side of the tracks. My side was
the wrong side in the eyes of some of my peers. I remember the
wider houses a few blocks away on the other side. The kids who

lived in those white, wide houses, or even bigger ones up on the hill, let me know that I was poor. Some of the taunts I heard were, "You live pretty close to Dixie." "That old gray shack you live in going to fall down?" There were remarks about my wearing the same sweater three or four days a week. No matter how tough you think things are, however, there are always those in a worse fix. One day a certain girl in my second-grade class was absent from school. When she returned, the teacher innocently said, "Peggy, we missed you yesterday. Were you ill?"

"No ma'am. I had to stay in bed all day so my momma could wash my dress."

But the tracks, wrong or right side, were part of my growing up. Trains were in our family, in our ears, our noses, and our eyes. Two uncles and a grandfather worked for the railroad. The sound of those steel machines huffing and puffing up the two-percent grade that paralleled our street is still in my memory. The chuch-chuch-chuch of the steam engines, and the acrid, sulfurous, nose-tingling smell of smoke were part of my childhood just like the sparse and worn furnishings of my grandmother's house. At night as I tried to fall asleep, I'd hear the mournful whistle of a passing train. That haunting, trailing peal always made me sad. As the whistle sound faded, I felt something or someone fading from me; a permanent home, my mother, my dad, who had to work out of town because he couldn't find a job in Cincinnati during the Great Depression.

I was born in 1929; my first ten years matched the span of the Depression. I remember one day when I was seven, being sent to the butcher's for two kinds of meat. The Christophers were addicted to meat, potatoes, and a vegetable, with meat the priority. I loved to go there because Mr. Oeh would give me a wiener to eat. Standing on the sawdust-covered floor behind the meat case in his fedora hat, brim turned up, and his blood-spattered white apron, he'd reach into the case for a red-colored frank and hand it to me. It sure tasted good. When I told him what Grandmother wanted, he looked at the dog-eared, greasy order pad that listed what she owed him inscribed in indelible pencil. "Sorry, Bobby, I can't let you have the meat today until Grandma pays some of this down. You tell her I'm sorry, but I have to live too. Tell her twenty dollars will let me give you meat again. Here, take this weenie, it's something new. Skinless they call it."

When I got home and told her this she sat down and put her head in her hands. I heard her whisper, "Good Father in heaven, what can I do, what can I do?" I'd never seen her cry before. I didn't know what to do. Finally I moved to her and put my arm on her shoulder. She patted my hand. "Bobby, things are hard right now in our country. A lot of men are out of work. Uncle Stanley isn't working, and your dad has to work out of town. That's the only job he could get, after he was out of work for so many months. I don't want you to worry. God will take care of us, but we can't always have what we want. That's why I had to say no when you asked for that toy fire engine. That's why Mr. Oeh said we have to pay him some money before we can get more meat."

I guess that's when I started to learn that things and people could mess up your life if you let them. Asking for or just wanting something didn't make it happen. I can remember the tight faces on the adults around me as we existed through the thirties. But, tough as things were, my folks usually made me feel good. They made me laugh, and even scraped up toys for me at Christmas and birthdays. Today, I know they shielded me from a lot of the agony of those Depression years.

When her quiet sobbing stopped, I just kept looking at her. I didn't know what to say. Then my grandmother told me how I could help. "Bobby, just be good and try not to waste anything...food, electricity, water, and never leave windows or doors open if the furnace is on. Oh, and try not to tear any of your clothes." Sometimes I would hear her talking to either my dad or Uncle Stanley about money. They were always saying they had to get some money for the HOLC, the mortgage holder on the house. The Home Owner's Loan Corporation was a New Deal organization set up in the Roosevelt administration to help people keep their homes. My folks never had to go on relief, but knowing what I do now, I'll bet it was close. I'd also bet that they would have done anything short of stealing to prevent it. Long before Archie and Edith Bunker sang, "...We don't need no welfare state," they felt this in their souls.

They did all they could to survive those hard years. My Uncle Edwin, Daddy's brother, and his wife, Jane, Mother's sister, teamed up with one of Jane's sisters, Duff, and her husband in a one-bedroom apartment. They split the thirty-dollar-a-month rent, taking turns in the one bed, for sleeping and whatever. Luckily Duff's husband, Craig, had a part-time job at night. A couple of times my dad took me to the apartment to visit. They were always nice to me and seemed to have the ability to pull a nickel out of my ear.

Uncle Craig was a little on the wild side, but a real charmer. He loved to read dime novels; those seven-by-ten pulp fictions that had a slick cover displaying World War I aircraft dogfights between Von Richthofen in his red Fokker tri-plane and some British Sopwith Camels. Or, the cover might show some Zane Gray cowboys, maybe some detectives in snap brim hats, and lots of guns. He had forty or more of these stashed in the clothes closet, to his wife's chagrin. One day a hobo came to the door in a tattered suit, minus the lapels, and a rope for a belt. My aunt answered and was about to get some food for him when he said, "Madam, forgive me for intruding, I'm not here to beg funds or food." Arrested by his diction and vocabulary, Aunt Duff paused.

"Yes, what can I do for you?"

"Despite my appearance, I'm an educated man whose mind is starved for something to read."

My aunt thought, ha, now I can get rid of Craig's library. She went to the closet and returned with an armload of pulp novels. Seeing these, the hobo drew in his breath and said, "Madam, I don't read trash." My uncle never lived that one down.

Like my parents, I was born in Cincinnati, a comfortable place to grow up. It weathered the Depression far better than the Dust Bowl states or the sharecropper-ridden South. Dorothea Lang didn't seek any subjects for her graphic black-and-white testimonies to the American blight in conservative Cincinnati. Nevertheless, there were plenty of soup kitchens with long lines of desperate men seeking food for their families. We also had our fair share of monuments to the cutting depth of the Depression –"Going Out Of Business" signs in store windows, hundreds of signs that read, "Not Hiring – Don't Apply," and dozens of idled factories with cold smoke stacks and broken windows, smashed by disillusioned and scared men.

In happier times Longfellow had christened Cincinnati, with poetic flair, "The Queen City." Winston Churchill said it was the most delightful of America's inland cities. Its origin was late eighteenth century. A city on the banks of the meandering Ohio River, it proudly boasted seven hills, resembling Rome on the Tiber. Rome's famous defender, Lucius Quinctius Cincinnatus, posthumously, and unknowingly, lent his name to the burgeoning American settlement. Settled by Germans and Irish mostly, the city grew because of its navigable river and its geographic location, a gateway to both the West and the South. River traffic grew as people migrated westward in search of new opportunity.

I think I still carry with me many strands of the conservative fibers that bound our city into an industrious metropolis. Is it conservative roots that make me a compulsive controller? Or is this a characteristic of not only me, but of my generation: all of us who grew up in the Great Depression? Why do I work overtime scheduling, if not controlling, as many of the events and directions of my life as I can? Why don't I know how to surrender to the inevitable? I grew up believing that *good* people were Episcopalians and Republicans, didn't belong to unions, and became doctors, ministers, or professors. If, like my Grandmother Laurie, they had a New England ancestry, that was a plus.

Grandmother would tell me how she came to Cincinnati in 1870 from Vermont at age five with her two brothers and her widowed, schoolteacher mother, Cynthia Bryant. The hardiness that most early New Englanders had ingrained in their souls was evident in both Cynthia and Laurie. That sinewy toughness sustained these early settlers who crossed an angry ocean in tiny wooden ships so they could carve out a home in rock-filled fields, and face Indians, British Redcoats, and cold winters. And while these hardy folk did this, they thanked a God above for all that they had.

After I had lived with Daddy and Laurie for a year she would take me to Vermont for the summer. The train ride from Cincinnati to McIndoe Falls, Vermont, took two days in Pullman berths and dining cars with white-coated stewards and finger bowls. We had to use the single bathroom at the end of each car, which always elicited the conductor's, "Passengers will please refrain while the train is in the station." Toilet flushing was accomplished by a direct dumping of the bowl's contents onto the tracks. I loved to flush the toilet and see the cross ties whiz past under the brass dump valve while I held it open. Needless to say, there was no EPA in 1936.

Grandmother and I stayed with her elderly cousins on their seven-hundred-acre farm. Cousin Fred and his brother Henry were archetypical Vermonters. They were a little reticent and flinty on the surface, but kind, and generous underneath. I learned that they paid for our rail fare, and all of our meals were free, otherwise we would not have been able to go. In their early seventies, they worked every day managing the three hired hands, fifty dairy cows, a maple sugar harvesting operation, and raising table fare of vegetables, pork and chickens, as well as food for the livestock.

They started with morning milking at six o'clock and didn't finish work until the evening milking after supper. They knew how to relax, though. Relaxation was reading National Geographic before an eight-thirty turn-in, or listening in on the calls of neighbors on the four-party phone line. Mary, Fred's five-foot-tall wife, stood on a footstool holding the ear piece of the wooden, crank-on-the-side telephone, smiling or sighing as the events, foibles and actions of her country neighbors came over the wire. And it was always a big day at the farmhouse when the new Montgomery Ward catalogue arrived. Hours were spent poring over its colorful pages, and lists of needed things were made before the book went to the three-hole privy used by the hired hands.

*   *   *

Clunk goes the air conditioner as it cycles on, bringing me out of my reverie and back to the reality of my pre-operation jitters. Still not calm or sleepy, I turn the lamp on and pick up *Generations* by Strauss and Howe. I've read a lot of the book. It's a fascinating depiction of the eighteen-year spans of human life that the authors believe can be classified into distinct "generations." They go into great detail, based on vast research, about the characteristics, mores, folkways, accomplishments, strengths, weaknesses and representative figures of each generation.

I have learned I am a member of the Silent Generation, those born between 1925 and 1943. Looking back to find the formula of my evolution and that of my generation, I realize that I will only know who I am by knowing who I have been.

I must have dozed off over the book, for the next thing I knew my wife was saying, "Chris, it's seven o'clock. Have you been in that chair all night?"

"I guess the better part of it. Thinking about that damn operation is working me overtime."

"Don't worry, Honey, you're healthy and have an experienced doctor. Try to think of other things."

"I did, my childhood. Is that normal, or is that a retreat?"

"Normal, I'd say. Why don't you share some of those childhood memories with me? I'd love to hear them."

~

C H A P T E R

2

"When I was child, I spake as a child, I understood as a child,
I thought as a child: but when I became a man,
I put away childish things."
I Corinthians 13:11

When I was a kid all of the grown-ups seemed to be four times bigger than me. I remember my dad picking me up and holding me above his head like a Raggedy Andy doll. He was six-foot-two and two-hundred pounds, so I was a pretty light load. Those big yards I played in, and that long porch I ran on end-to-end have all become diminutive. It's as if a magician waved a wand and shrank the places where I lived as a child. Trips back to my childhood homes make me feel like Gulliver in Lilliputia.

I remember when Grandmother Laurie used to take me on the train to spend the weekend with my dad. I loved the trip to Indiana because we rode an inter-urban street car. Indiana had a network of these sixty-mile-an-hour trains that linked many of the major towns. The red cars were plush with soft red upholstered seats and small light sconces between the windows. The floor was covered with a durable, dark red carpet that muffled the sounds of the wheels as they clicked over the track joints. We didn't hear the conductor when he came up behind us and asked for our tickets. You could flip the back of the seat in front of you so your companion could face you. There weren't many people in the car on our first trip so Grandmother flipped ours and let me ride backwards. I loved every minute of the hour-long ride from Indianapolis to Muncie. Between towns we rode on high steel rails just like the steam trains. In town we had to transfer to a regular streetcar or bus. These wonderful electric cars disappeared after World War II with the resurgence of auto and bus production and the end of gas rationing.

Daddy worked in different towns because he couldn't find a job in Cincinnati between 1934 and 1936. On one trip, when I was nearly seven, Grandmother said, "Bobby, you should be proud of your dad. He's not afraid to take a job wherever he can to support you. He's sad that he can't be home with us, but he's doing what's best for you and me."

"But, he did work here," I protested. "He worked at an oil station when Alice Rose and I took him his supper." We'd cut through the Phillip Carey field across from the main plant so it only took twenty minutes to Dad's station. She always made us stay far away from the hobos' camp by the switch yard.

Alice Rose, my second cousin, was the foster daughter of Grandmother's brother, Jack Bryant. Both of her parents were dead, so she would split summers with us and Grandmother's other brother, Maurice, who lived next door. She was twelve years older than me, and went to boarding school in the mountains of North Carolina on a trust fund set up by her parents. She was like a summertime older sister to me. We'd play games and go to the store together. Sometimes she'd put me to bed at night if Grandmother had to go to a meeting at church.

We took turns carrying Daddy's supper, which was either some cold chicken, leftover meatloaf, or a couple of sandwiches, plus some Mallow-Mar cookies, packed in a wicker basket with a red and white checkered napkin covering the food. Daddy always got all three of us a bottle of Coca-Cola from his station's pop machine. We'd sit on the stacks of black tires, with that rubbery smell that tickled my nose, and drink our Cokes while we ate. Often Daddy would have to jump up to wait on a customer. Sometimes he came back to us with a smile, and sometimes he'd be mumbling, "What do people think? Gasoline isn't water. We can't give it away."

The second shift at the Gulf Oil station was all my father could get in 1933. It must have been sad for my grandmother to see her son, a *cum laude* graduate of Princeton, with a snap-on black fake leather bow tie, asking customers if he could fill it up.

She told me the job only lasted four months because there wasn't enough business to keep the station open on the second shift. Most of the customers worked across the street at the Phillip Carey plant, which was forced to go to a three-day week due to the very low construction activity nationwide. Phillip Carey was a huge building materials producer, making asphalt roofing shingles, asbestos siding, paving joint, floor coverings, pipe and thermal insulations, and asphalt paints and paving materials.

The memories of that filling station and the Phillip Carey plant are such a part of me. In 1950, when I was twenty-one, I started my industrial career there as a graveyard shift foreman in the asphalt shingle mill. At my interview, I stood in front of the plant and looked across Anthony Wayne Avenue at the station. For just a moment I thought I saw my father, who was by then deceased, bound out of the station office in his khaki suit and khaki hat with the black visor and orange Gulf emblem, and start hand pumping gasoline up into the graduated, glass, gravity-feed dispenser. I felt a lump as big as a baseball in my throat. I knew then, as I was starting to support myself and a new wife of a several months, how far he had gone to support me in that awful decade of the thirties.

My dad laughed a lot when I was with him for a weekend in Muncie. He'd make faces for me by pulling his mouth from both sides so it was very wide. Then he'd put his thumbs in his ears and wave his fingers. When I laughed, he'd tickle me under my arms; then he'd hug me and say I was a good boy. Sometimes when we were in his room at the boarding house, we'd sit side by side, real close, with a lined, yellow pad, and he'd draw all the things I'd ask for, like planes, ships, guns, and trucks. He'd draw and ask me to draw the same thing. While I was drawing, he'd leave for a few minutes and come back with two greenish, six-ounce Coca-Cola bottles and a Milky Way, or a Clark Bar, my favorite.

At about three on Sunday afternoon, the three of us would walk back to the hotel where Grandmother and I stayed to get our bags. Daddy drove us to the bus terminal to catch the four o'clock Greyhound for Cincinnati. On the trip home I always felt funny. I was too young to know words like withdrawal, rejection, confusion or insecurity. I can still feel the hollowness that I felt after we'd said good-bye and were rolling down the highway in that high-up bus. I guess I wandered through most of those early years with a never-ceasing feeling of missing something.

Almost every week my mother would drive out to Laurie's house in her new husband's LaSalle and pick me up for a short visit. Mother was remarried to a man named Charles Biscay, whom I'd met a few times when she took me to their home in Avondale. I called him Uncle Charles. He wasn't as good-looking as my dad, but he was always pretty nice to me. He had been a catcher on the baseball team at Columbia University. A couple of times he tossed a ball with me. I knew my mother always called before she came, because Grandmother always told me when Mother would be at our house. And she always asked me if I wanted to go, to which I always answered with a joyful, "Yes!" When my mother arrived, she would visit with Grandmother for a few minutes. I'm pretty sure their talk was about me.

Once, my daddy was home from Indiana when Mother wanted to see me, and I had to decide whether to go with her or stay with him. I went with Mother. Before we left she and my dad talked in another room for what seemed a long time. I don't know what they talked about, but I heard my name mentioned a lot. In later years, I thought about the dynamics of the relationship between Mother, Daddy and Grandmother Laurie. I sensed that Grandmother liked my mother, but couldn't totally forgive her for the divorce. But my dad always said good things to me about my mother. When she and he were together, they seemed like friends. I'll never know their deep feelings, because they acted in a manner they thought was best. I never heard a slur or criticism from any of them about the other. Whatever hurts they may have had, were sublimated in deference to me.

It is times of peril and challenge that bring the best out in most of us, I believe. My parents, in the unhappiness of their divorce, thought about me. Everyday folk in the peril of the Depression thought about sharing, and in the life-threatening era of World War II, all Americans thought about how to give to their country...many with their lives. This quality of coming to the fore in a time of crisis is what I felt my family, and the families of my peers, exhibited and tried to instill in their Silent Generation kids.

As our nation, my town, and our family struggled through the Great Depression, there was constant evidence of people helping others. People did not turn hungry hobos away from their doors. They shared food, lodging, clothes, and meager funds with the more needy. There was no prevalent "me first" ethos, even though many of the donors themselves were looking for the next paycheck or meal. This same spirit of thinking about what was best for the common good, or the good of others, carried into World War II.

When Mother and I went out, we'd go to a moving picture show, like the time we saw the dashing Errol Flynn in *Robin Hood*, my first Technicolor film. Or we'd go to a department store where Mother would buy me a sweater or a shirt. One of my favorite things was when we'd go to the zoo. She'd explain things about the elephants, snakes, and the wonderful veldt that was unique to the Cincinnati zoo. These outdoor arenas were the first in America to allow zebras, lions, gazelles, and hyenas to roam in an environment like their native Africa. After we'd seen most of the animals, including going through the smelly, chattering, swinging monkey house and the quiet, glass-boxed, slithering snake house, we'd eat the bologna sandwich lunch mother had packed.

Then the high point of a happy morning, the carnival rides. We rode the merry-go-round, roller coaster, crack-the-whip, and finished up with a trip to the fish pond where I caught a number ten, earning me the grand prize of a paddle with a ball on a rubber band. If we didn't go to the zoo or a movie, we'd go to a place to get ice cream or a grilled cheese sandwich. I loved biting into the creamy, buttery, cheesy, toasted delights, whose taste lingered in my mouth until I drank some of my ten, two, and four Dr. Pepper.

In the fall of 1936, I was seven-and-a-half and mother was just over twenty-eight. She was only five-foot-one, with dainty hands and feet, and an eye-crinkling smile that personified her first two names of Joy Sunshine. She had soft, silken brown hair that framed her cameo-like face. Her deep brown eyes were the model for my own. She always smelled like Lilies of the Valley. That sweet fragrance was like her, delicate and charming.

On one visit, we were sitting in Eden Park looking at the first forsythias of spring. I asked her why she and Daddy didn't live together with me. She looked off toward the Ohio River for a while, then turned to me, taking my hand in hers and said, "Chrissie, it has nothing to do with you. Believe me, your dad and I both love you very much. Your dad is a fine man, it's just that he and I found out we like different things. But we both want what's best for you. Right now it's probably best for you to be with your dad. Okay?"

I wasn't sure what this "best" stuff was, but when I was with her, I felt her love and a tenderness that covered me like a warm, secure blanket.

*   *   *

Many times when my dad was away, Grandmother Laurie showed me pictures taken with the family's Brownie box camera. We'd be sitting on the couch in the tiny living room (four long steps would cover either direction) with pictures spread all around us. The mohair couch and matching chair may have been a good buy for folks with low incomes, but it sure did itch and tickle my legs when I had on short pants. I picked up a picture, and there was my dad holding me; I was three and dressed in a round Buster Brown collar and little short pants suit. Daddy was standing near the hackberry tree in the front yard and had a big grin as he looked at me. Another picture showed him in his R.O.T.C. uniform when he was at Princeton.

Grandmother had a box of medals that he had won in track meets and when the Princeton crew beat Harvard in a race. She told me what a crew race was, about the eight men with oars, and the coxswain. Her brother, Jack Bryant, had made a model of a nine-man shell, which enabled me to picture my dad as a crewman. At school, I told my friend Dick George all about my dad's sports. I felt so much pride at Dick's reaction.

One afternoon, when we were looking at all these pictures, Grandmother told me that before my dad went to Princeton, he had gone to Kent, an Episcopal-based prep school in Connecticut. She said, "Bobby, I hope that someday you can go to these schools." Her voice sounded funny. She turned away, looking out of the front window. I saw a tear at the corner of her eye. Just then I heard a car outside. It was Uncle Stanley. His secondhand, partially rusted Packard coupe made a funny sound when he turned off the engine.

"Hi, Mom, hi, Bobby."

"Hello, Son. Here, Bobby, see this one of your Uncle

Stanley in his army uniform? It was taken in 1919, right out in front of the house, when he came home from France.

Stanley said, "Here's a toy tank, Bobby. I got it from Sinclair Oil for buying a hundred gallons of gas over the last year, from that station down on Vine Street, you know the one where you saw their sign with the big dinosaur? They ran a promotion to get people to buy from them. When you wind it up it moves on its rubber caterpillar treads. See, like this."

"How about taking it into the dining room and getting it to run all over while Grandma and I talk."

I went out of the room with my foot-long model of a World War I British tank, but I overheard their conversation.

"Mom, the ink and paint company lost three of the five accounts they had. The magazines just went under. My boss said that they had to cut back on jobs, and since I am the youngest person in the traffic department I have to leave. He said he'd pay me to finish out this week."

"Oh, Stan… how awful. You just went there three months ago. Will things ever turn up? Do you think business will get better so there will be more jobs? It seems so long since everybody was working."

"I'll start making the rounds of some companies tomorrow."

"Want to stay for dinner, Son?"

"Sure. I hate to ask this, but...."

"You want to stay with us for a while? I'm glad to have you. I always need help of some kind, and we could go a few places in your car. You can use the front bedroom; your brother's only home two weekends a month."

I heard my Uncle Stan whisper, "Mom, you always know what we need. I love you. How about I take Bobby with me to pack my things?"

So Uncle Stan and I went to his rented rooms and packed two suitcases with his clothes, toiletries, three detective magazines that Grandmother made him keep out of sight under the sofa cushions, and a bottle of Old Overholt rye whiskey, that he also kept out of sight. Uncle Stan never put empty whiskey bottles in the trash barrel because Grandmother said, "What would the neighbors think?" The empties were discarded out in the "country" by Uncle Stan throwing them past my seven-year-old nose out of the moving car's window. "Roll the window down, Bobby, and sit back." Swish went one of National Distiller's finest, pitched with a perfect backhand flip onto some farmer's field that the neighbors would never know about. On the way home from a bottle run, Uncle Stan would stop at a store and give me two or three pennies, which were exchanged for a pair of red and black jawbreakers and a white coconut "moth ball." Uncle Stan said, "Don't try to bite the jawbreakers, just suck on them."

I asked Uncle Stan if he had played with my dad when they were little. "Not too much. Your dad is thirteen years younger than me. I used to watch him for Mom before I went into the Army. Mom was thirty-eight when he was born, and she hoped he would be a girl. She kept him in dresses till he was four. But even though he was younger, he and I always got along. When he went away to Kent School in 1918, I was in the Army overseas. He wrote me every week. Sometimes the letters would bunch up and I'd get a dozen at once if we were back from the lines in bivouac. After he graduated from Princeton in 1926, he and I became good friends. We shared a lot of laughs."

"How come he and my mother don't live at the same place?" I'll never forget the change in Uncle Stan's face. It became a blank mask with tinges of red. He told me my dad was a fine man, and that I'd understand this when I was older. Then he said, "Remember, your dad has custody of you." Custody must mean that my dad was the good guy. That night alone in bed, I cried into my pillow. I liked being with my mother. She made me feel good, and I was always proud when other kids would see me with her. I wished that she and my dad both lived with me.

Now that Uncle Stanley was with us, trips with him became more frequent. He became my second dad and I learned a lot. He was very kind and loyal to his mother. When the three of us were together, he would always ask Grandmother what she needed, or what she wanted to do, or where she wanted to go. He never said a cross word to her. If he was out looking for a job or seeing a couple of his army buddies, he always brought something home for her, like some white peppermint drops that looked like miniature hockey pucks, or some dark brown, sugar-coated horehound drops. These were her favorites, so I soon learned to like them too. In looking back at our survival of the Depression, I think the reason Uncle Stan never married was he felt his mother needed him.

He was very good to me as well. I know he didn't have much money, but many times I'd find a nickel or a couple of pennies in one of my pockets. He always asked me if I wanted to go with him to the store, or to see a friend. He tossed a ball with me in the front yard, and helped me light firecrackers on the Fourth of July. He always gave me a goodnight kiss, and would drive me to school if it was raining hard.

I knew Uncle Stan drank whiskey, but his occasional snorts of rye were not very apparent. I had seen men with too much to drink stagger out of McKee's saloon on Hartwell's commercial street, but I never saw Uncle Stan like that. He'd point out the town drunk, a man called Punk, and tell me how too much whiskey had ruined Punk's life. It seemed that the man had been a star athlete in high school, the fastest runner the school had ever known. Because of his speed, he went to New York to run in an Olympic trial, and somehow was tempted into taking some drinks. Maybe the big city was too much for a small-town guy. He never recovered. I guess the whiskey that my Uncle Stan drank helped him blot out the horrors he experienced in France. He almost died in the battle of the Meuse-Argonne from phosgene gas. He was just putting on his glass-eyed, corrugated rubber air hose mask when a German gas shell exploded nearby. Fortunately he caught only a minuscule trace of the deadly gas. A few days away from the lines allowed him to recover, but he retained a hoarseness. He never talked about his war experiences, but Grandmother told me about all the battles that he was in as a supply sergeant in General MacArthur's 42nd Rainbow Division.

Uncle Stanley contributed a large share of his earnings after the war to paying for my dad's education at Kent School and Princeton. After his death in 1960, I reflected on his lack of self-ishness. I realized I had a long way to go to live by the standard of care he unknowingly set. He never talked about it. He was devoted to his family, truly placing our needs before his. When he was out of work for a few months in the middle thirties, and learned of the family being cut off at the butcher's, he swallowed any pride he might have had and begged his older brother, Edwin, for a job.

27

Edwin was the plant manger of National Distiller's new Carthage, Ohio, distillery. Having just been hired after two years of unemployment, and not wanting to be accused of nepotism, Edwin was reluctant to hire relatives. But he relented and helped Stan get the night watchman's job at twenty-five dollars a week. Stanley gave fifteen dollars of his pay to his mother.

School started for me near the middle of the Depression. The years 1934 to 1936 saw me pass through kindergarten and the first and second grades; also through diphtheria, mumps, chicken pox and measles. Kindergarten is a hazy memory of finger painting, coloring, Farmer-In-The-Dell, new kids' faces, and having to change shoes everyday from street to gym and back to street. My guardians put an L and an R in my shoes. Only problem, they didn't put L's and R's on me. The first half of the year I walked to school in the afternoon from the house where Mother and I lived. In the second half of the year, I walked from Grandmother Laurie's house where I lived with Dad. Both were about a mile from the school. I never had to wear cardboard in my shoes, as I tramped over deep snow drifts, but it was a trek for eighteen-inch legs.

My first and second grades were combined classes, as the Depression dictated the combining of classes to reduce costs. I was in fourth grade before I had a "single" class. My first-grade teacher taught me something I never forgot. On the first day of school she said, "Children, as we start this year, and as you start your lifelong education, there is one rule we will live by in this class, and hopefully you will live by all of your lives." With that she turned to the blackboard and wrote **DO RIGHT**. This was never erased. Ever since that September day in 1935 I have thought of those two words when confronted with decisions that involved people, particularly when I thought I had a right to get even. A good teacher is second only to a good parent in helping a child to develop. I was blessed to have so many inspirational and effective teachers, who not only taught their subject, but also taught values. In my youth, rules and ethics were to be adhered to. Responsibility was each person's duty.

Good teachers were and should still be the guiding lights for any community's future. They are the guardians of any nation's survival and purpose. They ignite the beacons that throw light into the dark corners of ignorance and waste. Many tenets of my evolving creed of morals and values I can attribute to certain teachers— the way they caused me to see something that made it clear and lasting. One in particular, Miss Elberg, my eleventh-grade zoology teacher, told us that man was put on earth to work. At sixteen this didn't sound like the promise of a Garden of Eden, or a heaven, but in maturity I see the meaning.

To me, work is trying to help everyone and everything with which I come in contact, leaving whatever I touch a little better than I found it. I believe we are blessed with life, free will, and the brains and energy to improve, bring meaning to, and enjoy this earthly life. Another teacher said that happiness should never be a goal. Happiness accrues as a byproduct of meaningful works, rarely when it is our sole aim. I have been able to temper, in part— it's a work in progress—my inborn desire for survival, and some innate selfishness by reflecting on, and applying the precepts I learned from a host of dedicated teachers. I thank them.

In elementary school I met a kid who would become a life-long friend. Dick George and I played together, shot marbles as we walked to and from school, and related to each other in every way. We built snow forts together, worked on paper drives, joined the scouts together, and organized two Knothole baseball teams. He and I still see each other more than sixty years after our first-grade meeting. He became a teacher, and helped thousands of kids to a better life and value system.

In those early grades I also noticed the opposite sex. Once, when I was six, I was sitting at the soda fountain in Igler's drugstore with my Uncles Stan and Edwin, when a girl from my first-grade class, Patricia Drexel, came in. She was dressed in a white fur coat, white high top shoes and a white Russian-type fur hat. I spun around on the fountain stool, looked at her, and dropped my ice cream cone, all in a split second. I couldn't have reacted more if she had been America's and my idol, Shirley Temple. My Uncle Edwin, who was usually stiff and business-like, smiled, "What's the matter Bobby, that your girlfriend?" I guess if first-graders have girlfriends, she was. Patricia was smart, friendly and very cute. She lived in a big white house on the other side of the tracks, but never ever said anything to me about my side, or asked me who that old lady was with the funny hats and shoes.

Dick and Patty are both my good friends. Their spontaneous friendship was a positive influence when I was confused by the changes in my home life. They were peer models. They both had a mother and father at home, who watched with whom they played. They never avoided me, so I guess I merited their parents' approval. Patty's dad had a solid contract with Sears and Roebuck's to deliver things for them, and Dick's dad was a personnel manager for Formica. The two dads were never out of work in the thirties, which helped Patty and Dick have stable homes. I was sorry I left them after sixth grade when I was accepted by Walnut Hills High School, a select six-year college preparatory school across town. They could have gone, but elected to stay in the small-town atmosphere of Hartwell.

Every so often my mother would pick me up at school for one of our visits, but only after she had received permission from

Grandmother. My classmates oohed and ahhed at the beautiful lady who looked younger than any of their mothers, driving up in the green LaSalle coupe to whisk me off. They wanted to know if she was a movie star. Maybe the LaSalle and Mother's appearance erased some of my "wrong side of the tracks" stigma. I began to understand the value people put on material things and outward appearances. From this first realization of what motivates people, although it was mostly subliminal at seven, I started to build a library of knowledge about man's needs.

Food and shelter are man's primary needs, and his higher needs are security and recognition. If I wanted to be flip and glib, I would say, "Give a person a good meal, put a roof over their head, tell them not to worry, pat them on the back and they might do your bidding." In a positive manner, I applied this principle to meeting the needs of my employees, to the best of my capabilities, in the companies I managed or owned. I have always been amazed at how the planting of tiny seeds of knowledge, even in my early years, often produced a harvest of meaningful tools and techniques. Again, I thank parents, relatives, teachers, and friends for helping me to learn the lessons of life, and for planting the seeds of knowledge in the sometimes-receptive soil of my mind.

*   *   *

The blustery winds and spitting snow of December 1936 came to Cincinnati and I was surprised one Wednesday to come home from school and see my dad's car in front of the house. It was a gray Plymouth, covered with mud picked up on his drive from Muncie, Indiana. He had driven the narrow roads through heavy rain and sleet. I raced up the front steps and rang the bell. He opened the door, smiled and picked me up, and carried me into the living room where Grandmother and Uncle Stanley were sitting. "Are you going to stay home now?" I asked.

His grin faded. "Yes, Son, Daddy's going to be home with you from now on."

"Are you going to live here all the time?"

"Yes, we'll be living together here in Mom's house. I...I hope to be working here too."

"Bobby, remember when I told you that things were hard, and that we had to try and save everything we could?" Grandmother asked.

"Yes. That's why I couldn't have that fire truck, and we had to keep the windows shut when the furnace was running."

"Good boy, you remembered. Well, we have to still do all of those things. Your dad just lost his job in Indiana. The trucking company he worked for had to go out of business."

"Where will you work, Daddy?"

"I don't know yet, but I'll find something. I'm going to stay here with you, no matter what I have to do."

"I'll fix supper a little early tonight. There's an Evening Prayer Service at church. It might be best if we all went.

Daddy and Stan carried his two suitcases up to the room they would share, while I carried Daddy's brown and gray felt hats. Stan put one of them on my head, and called me a little gentleman. Supper was fried eggs, bacon, and some white toast with Cross and Blackwell's orange marmalade on it. Orange marmalade was more of a staple in the Christopher house than potatoes in a Dublin cottage.

We walked the quarter mile to the little stone and slate Episcopal Church on the other side of the tracks. The Christophers and the Bryants had been Anglicans or Episcopalians since fifty years this side of Henry the VIII. I knew that God and church were very important to my Grandmother.

She did a lot of work on church hangings and clergy vestments and saw that I went to Sunday School every week. She always helped me say my prayers at night, and would read Bible stories to me. She would refer to God and Jesus often when we'd be talking about almost anything. She taught me that everything that we had came from God. During the service I could see my grandmother's lips moving in prayer as she touched the shoulders of both of her sons. As I stood in the pew at Holy Trinity with Daddy, Stanley, and Grandma, I felt I had a family, just like the other kids.

We walked home with snow hitting us in the face. Daddy held my hand and told me about all the things that we would do together. After my prayers, I went to sleep quickly as visions of fun times to come filled my mind.

On the Saturday following the church service, my dad said he'd like me to go with him to visit a friend, a schoolmate from Princeton. Mr. Clopper had helped dad get acquainted with the school after they arrived together at the Pennsylvania Railroad station at Princeton Junction in 1922. Now he lived in a big white mansion on a hill high above the east side of Spring Grove Avenue. I had never seen a house this big. It had a tennis court in the side yard and a garage that had four double doors. There was a knight's armor in the front hall. Having never seen a suit of armor, except in pictures, I tentatively touched the handle of the sword that was in the suit's hand. "Don't worry, Bobby, there's no one in there," Mr. Clopper said.

We sat in a room that had a chess board and two huge wingback chairs, gathering the warmth from a roaring fire. The walls were lined with leather-bound books, and the floor was carpeted with an oriental rug that felt like I was walking in deep grass. A butler appeared and served us tea, which I had only drank once before. It tasted like lemon and orange. Mr. Clopper told me he had known my dad for more than ten years. They were at Princeton together, he said.

"Now let me get out some tin soldiers that I had when I was your age. These are the British that fought in the Crimean War. They were fighting the Russians. You can set them up, if you like, while Dad and I talk."

There must have been a hundred English grenadiers, with plumed hats, and mounted cavalry with sabers, Scottish soldiers in kilts, and some even had bag pipes. These were not like the soldiers at Woolworth's Five and Dime. I spent at least an hour setting them up in what I thought was battle formation. Too soon, Daddy called, "Hey, Bobby, put the soldiers away. It's time to go home."

As we were leaving, Mr. Clopper handed him an envelope. "Bob, give this to Bill Harris on Monday. I'll call him and tell him to expect you about nine. He's the general manager at Liquid Carbonic, which our family is invested in. He should be able to put you on."

"Thank you, Jansen. Thank you very much. I'm sorry I came to you about this, but I need to be home with young Bob."

"Sure you do, he's a fine looking boy, and he's lucky to have a dad like you. I believe the Liquid Carbonic thing should work out. Call me after you meet with Bill Harris."

And so, my dad came home, we went to church as a family, and my dad got a job as a salesman selling bottled gases like acetylene, carbon dioxide, and oxygen. If I could just get my mother to come live with us, everything would be okay. It was a new feeling, a mixture of joy at having my dad home, with the sadness I felt whenever I thought about my mother living ten miles away. I loved them both. During the day I was happy, knowing my dad was coming home that night; but in bed after prayers and kisses from

Dad, Grandmother and Uncle Stan, I'd think about my mother and feel that hollowness I had had for as long as I could remember.

I know now it was ambivalence that I felt before and after every visit with my mother. I wanted to be with her and enjoyed every minute I spent with her, but afterwards I'd have this deep, confusing longing, the feeling I couldn't describe. I'd fantasize about both of them coming to parents' night at school, or the three of us going to a movie, or sitting at the kitchen table for supper.

Even at seven I think we possess an innate practicality. The reunion of my dad and mother wasn't ever going to happen, and so I found other forms of security. Hostamoge was my twelve-inch-high Native American doll, and my every night sleeping companion. He had been given to me by Mrs. Richardson, a wealthy friend of Grandmother Laurie's. She summered on Torch Lake, Michigan where the Objibway people made these dolls. Hostamoge had long black hair, a reddish complexion, and an open face that carried a faraway look of sadness, subliminally sewn in by his makers. My Hostamoge was someone to talk to, to hold, and to love.

I remember how I grabbed him when, in bed in my dark bedroom, I'd see the small ray of light from a door, slightly ajar, playing reflective tricks with dresser drawer handles, turning them into the eyes of monsters. Or, when the faint glimmer of the gas street lamps would slip around the edges of the drawn green roller shades into the room and create demons of the walls, the mirror, and the dresser. Hostamoge and I would pull the covers over our heads and hope they'd go away.

Hostamoge was an important companion in the first year that I lived with Grandmother, but I relied less and less on him when my dad came home. After some of months, Hostamoge moved from my bed to a place atop the dresser. I'd still cast him a glance or a word, but my thoughts were now full of things I had done that day with my dad. Many evenings Daddy was home for a few hours around supper time, but sometimes he would go out to make a business call, or see some friends. Before he went out, or on weekends, we played with toys that he'd had as a child. They were heavy, cast iron, horse-drawn fire engines. Or, we'd try to unhook Chinese ring puzzles. He could do these, even with his eyes closed.

Sometimes, Daddy and Uncle Stan would sit at the kitchen table and talk about their jobs. They always let me sit there too. They said words like CCC, WPA, TVA, Roosevelt, New Deal, and sit-down strikes, and they always looked very serious. Even though I didn't understand what they were talking about, I felt pretty good throwing the terms I heard around to my schoolmates. And I was so happy to have these two grownup men nearby; I felt like I belonged. Little did we know of the devastation of the Great Depression and of the far-reaching effects the programs they talked about would have on our country, then, and for decades to come. Years later when I studied history, I realized how brave and determined my family was to support themselves, including me, and how determined they were not to be a burden on others.

These values, I now read in *Generations* by Strauss and Howe, were a cornerstone of the Silent Generation. While the Silents were described, by Strauss and Howe, as adaptive, quiet, and followers, and were as another author said, "born twenty years too late or twenty years too soon," we nevertheless became the caretakers who advanced civil rights and thought of what was best for others. The connotations of silent and adaptive suggest a group that is dormant, or that easily acquiesces to the themes of the day. The label silent implies that the group didn't speak out. I can't buy that as I think of Martin Luther King, a Silent Generation civil rights champion, and of all those of my generation who were the freedom marchers in Selma, Alabama, and other towns.

I like to think of my generation as one which adapted to the challenges of the times, but that adaptation was to the needs of others, and as a conscious decision. Not everyone can be a revolutionist. Time has proven that lasting changes are usually evolutionary more than revolutionary. I also believe we drove the engine of American economic expansion into the second half of the twentieth century. The often drug-related social cries of the Boomers in the sixties did little to raise the standards of our nation. Many of these folks protested, smoked grass, indulged in promiscuous sex, and lowered the standards of morality, but the ever-plodding Silent Generation kept the wheels of the nation turning. To negatively label all people in the Boomer Generation is unfair, and profiling of the worst kind, but so is it just as wrong to label, pigeonhole, and stereotype my generation as ambivalent, too quiet, and overly adaptive.

The values of the Silent Generation were in part inherited from our parents, but following these values allowed us to evolve into adults with deep humanity and tender social conscience. It has also been said that the Silent Generation possessed the lowest rate of any generation for almost every social pathology of youth: crime, suicide, illegitimate births, and teen unemployment. I believe our roots in the rugged soil of the Great Depression yielded the flower of compassion that is the hallmark of our contribution to the turbulent shifting of mores and values marking the second half of the twentieth century.

Of course to a seven-year-old in 1936, such broad-scene ideas were nonexistent. I was just happy with my dad home. However, the memory of those days, coupled with what I have learned through study and reflection, are the planks of my heritage. Who I was then has made me who I am now. My memories are a resource containing a wealth of values to be tapped again and again.

The images from those struggling days in a small wooden house on the wrong side of the tracks never leave me. Whenever I meet someone who needs help, I still see the long lines in front of soup kitchens and the poor hobos who came to our door.

~

C H A P T E R

3

"Many waters cannot quench love, neither can the floods drown it."
Song of Solomon 8:7

December of 1936 was the beginning of a new chapter in my life; my dad was home for good. We played together with his Mechano set, the forerunner of A.C. Gilbert's erector sets in the blue or red metal boxes. We built bascule bridges, radio mast battle ships, Mack truck replicas, and an elevator tower. Daddy said that when things got better he'd get me a new erector set that had an electric motor. When we made something I had a hard time deciding whether to keep it or take it apart. I usually elected, with some misgivings, to take it apart so Daddy would make a new one. Our working together gave me many happy hours. It made me feel good to be able to tell my second-grade pal, Dick George, about what we had built. I felt *normal.* The dull confusion and hollowness I had carried for as long as I could remember was fading fast. I had opened a chapter that had a real-life, stay-at-home dad. A dad who went to parent's night at school and talked with my teacher.

It was only a couple of weeks till Christmas, and Daddy and I were coming home from a business call. We had been to see a man down on Coleraine Avenue who distributed ice cream bars. He bought some kind of gas from Daddy for his refrigeration. He gave me a chocolate covered *Eskimo Pie,* and I saved the chocolate-stained stick, because if you saved twenty-five you could get a free one. While we were driving in my dad's three-year-old, standard model Plymouth, maneuvering between streetcar loading platforms and the curb, Daddy asked me to read the signs. He said it was good practice. When we stopped for a red light at Township and Vine Streets in Elmwood Place, I saw a sign over a one-story building with peeling gray paint. The gravel parking lot had a dozen old cars in it. I read the pale blue neon tubes over the door, "Walk-A-Show."

"What's a Walk-A-Show?" I asked.

"It's a place where people who really need money or a meal dance continuously until they drop, sometimes two or three days, with only a couple minutes rest each hour. The person who lasts longest gets the money, but they all get a meal."

"Did you ever do it?"

"No. Your mother and I went one time to one to see if we could. After we saw the exhausted couples who could hardly stand, we left. I thank God that we never had to do this, never had to go that far."

"Why would those people do it?"

"Because, Bobby, right now in our country, business is bad and a lot of people don't have a job. It's the only way they know how to earn some money and some food."

I absorbed what Dad said, but it wasn't until many years later when I saw the motion picture *They Shoot Horses, Don't They*, that I realized how brutal and punishing the marathon dances of the thirties were.

"Do we have money?"

"We'll have enough to live on. Daddy has a job, so don't you worry, Son. We're getting by and things will get better soon."

That was all it took for me. "Could we go see Santa Claus? The one at Pogue's?"

"Sure," Daddy said. But I saw the tightening in his face. "Maybe we can go this weekend. Yes, maybe this weekend." I didn't know that new salesmen didn't receive any commission checks until they built up some business, which usually took a few months. The starting draw was far less than commissions, Grandmother explained a few days later when I started mentioning what I wanted for Christmas. I'm not sure at seven I fully understood this, but I knew that I might not get a lot for Christmas because "things were hard" and Daddy was "new at his job."

That day when Daddy and I arrived home there was a tall handsome man standing on the stairs to the second floor. Grandmother was sitting on the first step putting pins into the bottom of his long, black robe, just like Mr. Attridge, our priest wore. The man was six-feet-four, had penetrating blue eyes and silvery hair. There was a purple, sleeveless garment over the robe. Grandmother, with a few pins sticking out of her mouth, looked up. "This is Bishop Hobson. Bishop, this is my son, Robert and his boy, Bobby."

"How are you? It's nice to see you. Laurie has told me about you both. I don't know what I'd do for my vestments if it weren't for her. Our diocese is very grateful to her for teaching all of the ladies she has taught to do the fine embroidery and sewing that our hangings and vestments require."

My dad stepped up to the Bishop and shook his hand. "I'm pleased to meet you, Bishop. Mom speaks of you often."

"Come Bobby, let's you and I go into the kitchen so the Bishop and Mom can continue the work."

That night at supper Grandmother told us about Henry Wise Hobson, the Bishop of the Episcopal Diocese of Southern Ohio. She said he was a combat Major in World War I, and one of the most recognized bishops in the entire country. He came to our little Holy Trinity church once a year for confirmation. A few years later I learned that he paid my Grandmother seventy dollars a month for teaching Cincinnati area ladies how to do the "good work" of embroidering altar, lectern, and pulpit hangings. Most of the women who came to our house for lessons came from Hyde Park, Wyoming or Glendale, and always in cars that were a lot newer and fancier than Daddy's standard model Plymouth or Uncle Stan's rusted Packard coupe.

One lady, Mrs. Richardson, was from Glendale, Ohio, a town north of Cincinnati, with tree-lined streets, large homes and pre-turn-of-the-century gas street lights. Glendale was home to many of the Procters of Procter and Gamble and their derivatives. Mrs. Richardson came in a car that was driven by a man in a gray uniform and a matching hat; the visor was black like his gloves and the long sleek car. While she was in our house, the driver would get out of the car and wipe off some cinders that a couple of passing trains spewed onto the hood. Of all the ladies that came to our house, Mrs. Richardson was Grandmother's favorite; she was also the most gracious. If I was there when she came, she always took time to ask me about myself. Usually she gave me a half dollar, and once a silver dollar.

After a sewing lesson and some cooperative work on the floor-to-ceiling altar wall hanging for the Cathedral, she and Grandmother would share lunch at our small dining room table. When Mrs. Richardson came, the table was set with a white linen table cloth and the good violet dishes. This setting I only saw on holidays. She and Grandmother would sit there over tea and talk for a long time. Mrs. Richardson was the lady who invited Grandmother and me to her summer home on Torch Lake in Michigan, where she gave me my Indian doll, Hostamoge.

The Saturday morning before Christmas, my dad woke me up. "Hey, Bobby, remember when you asked me to go see Santa at Pogue's? How about we go today? I only have two calls to make, and if you'll go with me, we can go downtown after." I was ecstatic; of course I would go.

Every Christmas, I remember and savor that one Christmas in 1936. We went to some welding shops where Daddy sold acetylene and oxygen. At the second shop, I saw men in leather aprons with dark goggles, hats, and big leather gloves. They bent over their work, making sparks fly everywhere as the white hot flame cut the metal like a hot knife in butter. Two men came over pushing their black monster-eyed goggles up on their heads revealing red, grease-streaked faces. They also took off their heavy protective gloves and shook my Dad's hand.

"Hey, Bob," one of them named Russ said, "How 'bout leavin' the boy here. We'll teach him how to use that gas you sell us!" My dad had told me that Russ was his first customer, and had given him a good order, which helped my dad make a good start on his new job. He liked Russ because he was open and honest, and dedicated to running his shop in a professional way. There was a good chemistry between my dad and Russ. My dad had been educated in the finest of Eastern schools; Russ had gone to vocational school, but not college. Despite the gap in their educational back-grounds, they shared the common bonds of being responsible men trying to provide for their families and a basic love of their fellow man.

"Maybe next time, Russ. Right now we're going to see Santa."

"You been a good boy, Bobby?" Russ asked as he squatted down.

I looked up at Daddy. "Yes, Bobby's been real good. He helps me, and he's doing well in school. Thanks for the offer and the order. Call me if you ever need anything."

"Stop back right after the first. We may, I mean may, get a big order from the shoe factory for a lot of forms. All cut and braze. Keep your fingers crossed, Bob. If we get it, we'll need a dozen extra tanks of each."

"I'm with you, Russ. Hope the shoe company opens their Norwood Plant. Let me give you a couple of calendars; sorry it isn't more. Maybe next year I'll have something more for good customers like you. Merry Christmas, and Happy New Year."

"Same to you, Bob. Hey, Bobby, tell Santa Russ said to bring you what you ask for."

We left the welding shop and drove down Spring Grove Avenue to downtown. We passed a large white building that had a high fence around it, topped with barbed wire. I asked what the building was. Daddy said, "That's the workhouse."

"What's a workhouse?"

"That's where men who have committed crimes...done some bad things, have to go. They are being punished by doing hard work for as long as they are there."

"It's like a jail?" I asked, as a chilling image of men in striped suits behind bars, that I had seen in movies or sneaked peeks at in Uncles Stan's detective magazines, popped into my head.

"It is a jail, but not as bad as a prison. The men in there haven't murdered anyone or stolen anything big. Usually they are there less than a year. Right now it's full because a lot of men are out of work and have stolen small things to live on. If they are caught, but haven't hurt anyone, they have to spend a few months there."

"Why did they steal?"

"Because they didn't have a job, or didn't know how to get welfare help. But, the law says to steal is a crime, and it's punishable. I know you would never think of stealing anything, Bobby, right?"

"No," I said, as the images of the men behind bars appeared again, making me afraid as I looked at the workhouse. I was glad when we passed it.

Soon we were taking the elevator up in Pogue's department store. A black lady in a yellow and brown uniform with brass buttons, and topped off with yellow pillbox hat, opened the door and said, "Sixth floor: toys, Santa Claus and household goods." As I walked out of the elevator, she patted my head, "Tell Santa what you want, Sonny. You been a good boy, I'll bet." She smiled at Daddy with a big grin, flashing a row of snow white teeth that glistened against her smooth mahogany skin. I liked her.

Dad said, "That's a nice colored lady."

"That's a neighbor lady."

"Why is she a neighbor?"

"Grandmother said I should always call colored people neighbors, and that I must never say nigger." In reflection, I admire my grandmother's admonishments, which were forward-thinking in Cincinnati of the thirties and forties, a city of segregated residential areas, bathrooms, depot waiting rooms, and swimming classes in the high schools.

"Mom is right, Son."

I didn't know where to look first. There were rows laden with everything I had ever dreamed of. There was a Lionel electric train layout with at least four trains all running at the same time; some whistled, others disappeared into mountain tunnels or activated crossing gates in the realistic scene. There were freight trains with red cabooses, and sleek passenger trains, some silver and streamlined. I pushed my nose against the glass partition that kept people from touching them and watched, fantasizing about owning the trains. After a time, Daddy said, "Hey, Bobby, want to see some of the other toys?" "Okay." I reluctantly pulled away from Lionel City and walked past kits for molding lead soldiers, erector sets, chemistry and microscope sets, and many little cars, trucks, and fire engines. I stopped to see the erector sets, and Daddy said, "Bobby, wait here a minute. I have to see a man back there about something." I watched the turning Ferris wheel constructed from the A.C. Gilbert number eight-and-a-half erector set in the big red metal box. Once I looked back toward the elevators and thought I saw my dad hand a man behind the train display some money, but I wasn't sure.

Daddy came back for me and we looked at the rest of the display, except for the dolls. We went to a small restaurant in the arcade that adjoined Pogues. I ordered my favorite, grilled cheese sandwich and chocolate milk. Daddy just had a cup of coffee. When he paid the bill, I noticed he had to empty his pocket of all its change. The waitress said, "Sir, you need two more pennies." My dad blushed and looked away. She said, "That's okay. I understand. Don't worry, I found a couple of loose pennies under a table this morning."

46

"Thank you, uh, Thelma. Thank you."

On the way home I fell asleep as we drove out Vine Street, following the tracks that carried the old orange and black number 78 streetcars we sometimes rode. When we got home I ran into the house and told grandmother all about the trains and the other toys. "Did you see Santa Claus?"

"Yes, but I didn't get to talk to him, because there were too many kids in line. Daddy said I could write to him and tell him what I would like." The next day we mailed my letter to the North Pole.

I know Santa received my letter, because when I came downstairs on Christmas morning I found a Lionel passenger train running around a ten-foot oval track. My eyes must have opened to double their normal size, because Daddy, Uncle Stan, and Grandmother all laughed. "Here, Bobby," my dad said, "Let me show you how to run your train." He knelt down with me, and put his hand on mine, then placed it on the control knob of the black transformer. He turned my fingers clockwise and counterclockwise to speed up and slow down the train. "Now you can be the engineer," he said as he took his hand away.

I handed my dad a box with the orange and black regimental striped Princeton School tie. Grandmother helped me buy it with money my mother had given me and a dollar Uncle Stan gave me for going to the store three times to buy him Lucky Strike cigarettes. I gave Grandmother a white linen handkerchief with a lace border and her initials on one corner, which my mother helped me to buy. I gave Uncle Stan three cotton handkerchiefs.

During that week when I was off from school for Christmas break, I heard my folks talking about the big flood. Every day there were pictures in the three newspapers of houses sticking up out of muddy water. My dad told us some of his customers were closed because their businesses were under water. In the fall and early winter of 1936 the Midwest suffered torrential rains and numerous snow melts. This combination produced hundreds of millions of gallons of excess runoff. The normally placid Ohio River at Cincinnati rose from its usual twenty-three feet to almost eighty. Every day my dad would tell me about this as we shared supper with Grandmother and Uncle Stanley. His work took him near the edge of the muddy water that had risen three blocks up into downtown Cincinnati. Thousands of families had to evacuate their homes because of the inundation along the Ohio River banks. Many areas along the creeks and small rivers that fed into the Ohio were also overrun by the turbulent, muddy, often waste-contaminated water.

My dad took me to old Doctor McGowan to get typhoid shots, as the flood greatly increased the danger of contracting this disease. The waterworks, sewage treatment plants, and finally the main electric generating station were all shut down when they became inoperable, submerged by the merciless flood. Daddy and I went to the hardware store and bought Mason jars, a wick and glass chimney assembly, and some kerosene. I helped him put together several kerosene lamps. We lived by this homemade lamp light for almost three weeks. I remember sitting at the kitchen table with my dad, seeing the yellow flame light from the lamp reflect off his steel-rimmed glasses, as he told me about what he had seen that day.

Schools were closed for over two weeks. I was happy the entire duration of the flood. This sounds terrible, as there was nothing but suffering, millions of dollars of loss, and the ruination of many lives, but I was in the cocoon of childhood innocence. I was helping my dad make lamps, and going to a brewery for five gallons of water every day with Uncle Stan. Against the background of the flood, I was absorbing the love that my dad now poured on me. Having him home every night and on weekends was a new and reassuring experience. Today, as I look back to that winter, I feel a tinge of guilt that I was happy, while hundreds of thousands of people suffered. Yet was it wrong for a seven-year-old boy, with no mother at home, to revel in the reawakened love of a returning father? I felt warm and secure in the knowledge that I had at least half of the normal parent quota. Now I was almost like all of the other kids.

One Sunday in January of 1937, Daddy, Uncle Stanley and I took a ride to downtown Cincinnati to see the flood. We drove as close as we could to the high water line, until a policeman told us to turn around. We saw the suspension bridge with the rushing, muddy water just a few feet below its span. Built by John Roebling, it was the first major suspension bridge built in America. After Roebling completed it in 1868, he started construction of the Brooklyn Bridge, which ultimately cost him his life after he suffered the bends from being in a deep caisson. Our bridge connected Covington, Kentucky, and Cincinnati. Its completion changed many lives by allowing the two states more and faster interchanges. In fact if the bridge hadn't been built, I would not be who I am.

When Grandmother was a young nineteen-year-old, she worked as a telephone operator in downtown Cincinnati. She lived with her mother, Cynthia Bryant, and her brothers, Jack and Maurice, on East Pearl Street. Cynthia was a school teacher at an elementary, one-room schoolhouse on Mount Adams. Some minor female troubles caused Laurie to see a doctor, and on the recommendation of a friend, she selected a Dr. Walter S. Christopher, whose office was in Covington at the Kentucky end of the Suspension Bridge. Grandmother would walk over the new bridge to his office. Her diary, which I found after her death, revealed that she was smitten with this handsome, bearded practitioner. His professional touch was more like caresses to her. She wrote many adoring notes about the doctor in her leather-bound journal. While she carried and timidly emanated her feelings for him, the doctor did not respond. In time grandmother and her mother became friends of the Christopher family.

Walter had two brothers and a sister. The two families would visit and share meals. Walter's younger brother, Robert, was

as smitten with Laurie as she had been with Walter. He soon started to ask her if he could call. At first, Laurie demurred, but in time
she said yes. After a year of courting, which included many hand-
in-hand walks across the bridge that Roebling built, Robert
proposed. Laurie became Mrs. Robert M. Christopher. Doctor
Walter moved to Chicago, took up pediatrics, and founded the
Walter S. Christopher School for Crippled Children on Chicago's
South Side. It still stands and bears his name today. Robert and
Laurie had three sons: Edwin, born a little over a year after the
marriage in1887; Stanley born in1890; and Robert, my dad, born in
1903. So, I say thanks to John Roebling.

Finally in late February the waters receded, leaving in
their wake thousands of mud-caked, debris-littered houses. Slowly
people returned to their homes and started the painful task of
salvaging their water-soaked assets. It was not enough that these
people suffered the deep pinch of the Depression; they now faced
the loss of furniture, clothes, and their hard-earned possessions
that were buried in the silt of the Mississippi delta. Like the victims
of the Dust Bowl, the flood victims suffered the double jeopardy of
both natural and economic cruelty. Thanks to work in later years
by the Corps of Army Engineers, who built dams and locks up-
river, the Ohio never again reached those devastating heights.

*　　　　　*　　　　　*

The year of 1937 was a happy one for me. Daddy and I did
more and more together. He would take a friend and me into the
woods on a Saturday, where we cooked bacon and beans on an
open fire. He showed us different trees and told us how to know
them by their leaves. I passed out of the second grade, survived
the measles, tossed ball with Dad and Uncle Stan, and listened to

the radio. Everyday there were several fifteen-minute serials. Jack Armstrong, Orphan Annie, and Don Winslow of the Navy. These were formula-based. Each day's episode ended with an unsolved mystery or impending disaster that was solved or averted at the beginning of the next day's program, only to end in another predicament. My psychologist friends of today tell me that those radio programs were not all bad, as we had to do a lot of creative imagining in order to be alongside our radio heroes. The instant gratification of television does not require this use of cognitive or imaging skills.

I also started listening to the "Lucky Strike Hit Parade" on Saturday nights. Top tunes such as *Pennies from Heaven, With Plenty of Money and You*, and *When My Dreamboat Comes Home* all echoed the hopes and wishes of a Depression-burdened people. I'd hear my dad humming these songs while he was shaving in the morning. Even though the Depression was still gripping America, we were able to laugh at simple things. One bright spot was my dad making sales manager at Liquid Carbonic. He tried to explain to me what that meant, but I missed the nuances. I only knew it was something better for him.

Another bright spot was the entry into Dad's life of a fine lady from Saint Louis named Claire Sprintz. I called her Aunt Claire when she visited us. I don't know where Daddy met her, but she was tall, with red-brown hair, blue eyes, and a soft voice, and she always brought me a gift. The three of us would go downtown, have lunch, and then Aunt Claire and I would go to a movie while Dad made a business call. At night they would go somewhere without me. When Aunt Claire went home to Saint Louis, we would take her to the train station on Sunday evening. She would give me a hug and a kiss on the cheek, and Daddy would say, "Bobby, why don't you go in the station and see if there is any candy you want."

Once I looked back and saw Daddy hugging Aunt Claire, and kissing her in a different way than she had kissed me. On the way home Daddy told me funny stories and whistled. Once in a while he would reach over and lightly rub my head and tell me what a good boy I was. Aunt Claire thought so too. Then he'd start whistling again. Whenever I mentioned her to my mother, she would ask me how often she and my dad saw each other and where did Aunt Claire stay when she came to Cincinnati.

One weekend in June, Daddy went to Saint Louis to see Aunt Claire. While he was gone, Uncle Stan took me to see a "donkey" baseball game. Don't laugh, it's true. The game was played with women sitting on donkeys. A woman on an ass (no double entendre intended, or implied) was stationed at all nine defensive positions, as was the batter. The game was really slow, because the pitcher had a difficult time in getting the ball over the plate. Maybe it was because the plate was covered with donkey droppings, which the umpire would clear with a shovel, not the usual pocket-sized whisk brush. When a player would finally get a hit, the stubborn mule wouldn't "run" to first base! We went home after three innings. I don't think this sport lasted very long; it went the way of wing walking and flagpole sitting.

What else did we do for fun? I was excited for weeks ahead of Fourth of July. I'd been saving my pennies, nickels and dimes. Daddy and I went to the fireworks store, where there were hundreds of brightly colored packages of firecrackers, everything from ladyfingers to six-inch cannon crackers that would lift a cast-iron manhole cover if one was dropped down the sewer. We saw Roman candles, skyrockets, flowerpots and a firework that shot a parachute into the air when it exploded. Uncle Stan gave me a penny if I caught the parachute when it came to earth. Daddy, Grandmother, Uncle Stan and I would sit on the front steps with a piece of smoldering punk and light firecrackers all day. At night, we'd light the sparkling, showering flowerpots, Roman candles and handheld wire sparklers. It was the best day of the year for me. But the next day, Grandmother would read to me from the Cincinnati Enquirer about all of the children who had suffered burns, lost an eye, or lost a finger from firework accidents. By the time I was in high school there were laws prohibiting the sale of firecrackers and other pyrotechnics to nonprofessionals. Anything larger or more explosive than a wire sparkler was prohibited, and could only be set off by licensed fireworks operators.

*   *   *

My third-grade year began in September, as the leaves started to turn from summer's vibrant green to the first blushes of gold and rust. The deciduous trees of the Mill Creek Valley turned the surrounding, rolling hills to a splash of warm color. My class shared a wood colony classroom with the fourth grade, as funds were still short in the public school system.

My friends, Patty and Dick, and I were in the A class. The other third- and fourth-grade classes were in the B, or slower learner's class. In the thirties, the Cincinnati Public School System classified students as A or B. This classification was a stigma for the B classes, and was not helpful to the student's self esteem or confidence. If the B student wasn't tougher than an A, the A might refer to him or her as a 'dummy.' Many times the B students carried chips on their shoulders. In later years this system was revised. A good teacher can balance the needs and learning speeds of an intellectually diverse class. But democracy and compassion aside, I think the gifted students of the Silent Generation benefited from being placed with other fast learners.

It was also the policy of the Cincinnati Public School System to never pass a child until he or she met the requirements of each grade. I remember in my first-grade class there was a twelve-year-old boy who must have had a learning disability. His knees were a foot higher than the low tables we six-year-olds occupied. Again, this practice stigmatized the boy. Today, we have special education classes for those who are not as gifted as others. This is some progress. The teaching of our youth is the most important thing we can do to strengthen our nation, even the entire human race. I do not think we in America devote enough money, offer incentives that attract the highest quality of teacher, or prioritize education properly. Crass commercialism and preoccupation with being entertained dilute our educational efforts and standards.

One rainy November day I looked up from my desk when the colony door opened. There, for the first time, was my dad standing in the doorway and entering my classroom. I felt proud as I saw a lot of the kids look at him with respect in their eyes. He was wearing his belted, natural-colored raincoat and a felt hat. He removed his hat with a slight flourish, and smiled at our tall, attractive teacher, Miss Shellinger. As a touch of color rose over her high cheek bones, she walked toward him. "Excuse me, I'm Bobby Christopher's dad. I brought his *Weekly Reader* money which I forgot to give him this morning. I like him to have the paper." When he said this, the kids all looked at me with approval. I felt warm and fuzzy as I knew I was accepted as a normal kid.

Miss Shellinger extended her hand and said, "Please come in, ah...Mr. Christopher," she said as she turned even redder. She then introduced him to the class, and I saw more admiring glances directed toward both him and me. I smiled as my dad left with a wave of his hat to me and a slight bow to Miss Shellinger. I felt even better when my "girl," Patty said, "Your dad is nice looking." After class, Miss Shellinger told me that she thought I had a very nice dad, and asked about my mother. I told her I didn't have a mother at home, and that she lived with Uncle Charles in Avondale. As I said this, I again felt a flush on my face, but it wasn't like the nice feelings I had earlier. I looked at my feet, feeling ashamed, for what reason I don't know. Miss Shellinger sensed my discomfort and said, "I see. Well, Bobby, you tell your dad that he can visit our class anytime. Is his first name the same as yours?"

"Yes," I stammered and left for home. In later years I realized Miss Shellinger was attracted to my dad. Knowing this makes me admire him a little more.

*   *   *

As the days grew short and gray, December brought snow and cold and many brightly colored Christmas catalogues. I spent hours with the catalogues, just wishing. The Daisy B-B gun was at the top of my list. I liked to play guns and war, but just saying "bang-bang" wasn't enough. I showed this picture to my dad, who said, "We'll see, Son, we'll see."

A week before Christmas, I spent the afternoon with my mother, who took me through a couple of toy departments. She asked me what I wanted. At one store, there were toy soldiers, copies of World War I doughboys painted khaki and wearing the basin-shaped helmets of the 1914-18 BEF and AEF, just like Uncle Stanley wore.

"Well, Son, I hope you can come and spend some time with me. You haven't been there at Christmas yet, and if you're a good boy, Santa might leave some of these at our house."

"I hope I can come. I want to be with you." Whenever the subject of me going to Mother's house on Christmas came up, Grandmother always said it was better for me to be home with my dad and her. I sensed that she didn't totally approve of Uncle Charles, or my being around him. I was always sad that I didn't get to go. As an adult, I figured that Grandmother saw my mother's second marriage as a reminder of the divorce between her son and Mother. Grandmother was tenacious in her love for the family.

"Yes, yes," Mother said as she hugged me, and kissed me on the forehead. "Come on, I'll drive you home." When we arrived at my home we sat in the car and talked about my school. Whenever I turned and looked at her, I saw a face that was a blend of love, sadness, and soft sweetness. My mother was a beautiful woman. One of the greatest regrets of my life is that I never knew her enough. I never had the chance to share so many things with her. This deprivation was one more stone in the foundation of my development. One more force that made me want to control all that I touched.

*　　　　*　　　　*

When I jumped down the stairs in my bathrobe on Christmas morning, I was thrilled to reach under the tree and pick up a fifty-shot Daisy air rifle. I looked from Daddy's smiling face to Grandmother's and then Uncle Stanley's, and then back to my new gun. "Can we go outside and shoot it?"

"Sure, but why don't you look at your other presents first."

I picked up a box that said, "Merry Christmas, Son. I love you, Mother." Inside were forty lead soldiers just like the ones my Mother and I had seen at the department store. I started to set them up when Daddy said, "Get dressed, and we'll go out and shoot your gun before breakfast."

In the backyard he set up some cans and a target. I shot and shot, knocking some of them over. "Good shooting, Son. Now tell me, what are our rules about the gun?"

"Never point it at anyone, and never leave it loaded and cocked." My dad had talked to me a lot about being safe and careful with the gun. I had overheard Grandmother and him talking about me being too young for a B-B gun. A lot of my classmate's parents wouldn't let them have one. Everyone thought that eyes would be shot out. I felt proud that my dad trusted me with a gun.

"That's good. Let's go in for breakfast, and maybe set up the soldiers Joy gave you."

During the holidays I spent a couple of days with my mother. As always, she was very attentive to me, asking about school, my Christmas presents and what my dad and I were doing. She said one day when we were parting, "Bobby, I love you so much. I'm happy that your dad is home now, but I want to see you as much as I can." I sensed that my mother felt that with my dad home all of the time, there would be a competition for me. I know she was glad that I had a parent at home, but I also know she wished that it was her. She never said a bad word about my father, but I know she was sad about the custody matter. I think she carried the hurt of not being awarded me for her entire life. This was confirmed to me by my Aunt Jane, her sister, and Uncle Edwin's wife.

We celebrated the ringing in of 1938 in traditional Christopher fashion. We ate a small piece of saved Christmas fruit cake, had a sip of red wine from a family glass that dated back to the 1700s, and beat some aluminum pans with a big wooden spoon at the stroke of twelve. Aunt Claire was with us from Saint Louis. She and my dad went out after twelve. As the neighborhood noise subsided, Grandmother said to Uncle Stanley with a wistful tone, "Stan, I sure hope this year brings us some better times."

"Me too, Mom. I'm working now, so maybe that's a start."

"Come, Bobby, it's late. Let's say our prayers and jump into bed.

"Aw, I'm tired. Can't I just go to bed?"

"God never gets tired of watching over us. I guess we can stay up long enough to thank him and ask his guidance for this coming year. Come on, kneel down here with me."

The first week back in school all of us told about our presents. I asked one girl named Peggy what she got. She didn't answer, and looked sad as she turned her head away, but not before I saw the tear in the corner of her eye. I guess this was an early lesson to me about sensitivity. Sixty some years later, I can still see this little girl, with the big glasses and anklets that usually had holes in them, as she turned from me. Back in the second grade, this was the Peggy who had to stay home from school when her mother washed her one dress. She lived in Arlington Heights in a three-room tarpaper hut with her sister, father, and mother. She lived on the "wrong side of the tracks." She always brought her lunch in wrapped newspaper. It usually consisted of a mustard sandwich...two pieces of thrift store bread with mustard smeared in between. I thought about my struggling family, but by comparison we were wealthy. I'll always remember her for teaching me about being sensitive, and that people can rise above their conditions. She got good grades and was liked by all of the girls, most of whom were comfortable by Depression standards.

Knowing Peggy also helped me realize how well off I was. I had clothes with no holes, a dad at home who did a lot with me, and a pretty mother who loved me. I also had a lot of love from Grandmother and Uncle Stan. In fact all of my family was wonderful to their only grandson and nephew. I was pretty happy as 1938 rang in; a B-B gun, some smiles and even a flirtatious giggle from Patty, lots of play with my dad, and some fun visits to movies and stores with my mother. The kids in my class all liked me. True, we were poor by economic standards, but we were rich in love.

*   *   *

In mid January I came home from school one day to see my dad's car in front of the house. He never got home before six during the week. I ran up the front steps and burst into the house, thinking he and I could play with my new Christmas things. "Daddy, daddy, I'm home. Can we play?"

Grandmother came out of the kitchen, wiping her hands on her apron and said, "Shh, Bobby, Daddy is sleeping. He doesn't feel well. We must be quiet."

"Why, what's the matter with Daddy?"

"He's just not feeling good. Let's be quiet so he can rest."

I played as quietly as I could with my soldiers until supper, but the entire time I felt funny. I felt a tinge of that hollow mixture of anxiety and loneliness that I had known so many times before. It didn't seem normal for him to be in the house and not be with me. He didn't come down. Grandmother took him some soup and tea on a tray. I got to go up to see him when he was awake. He smiled at me, patted my hand, and asked me how was school. Then he coughed and turned over. "I love you, Son. Help Mom for a few days 'til I get better." That night old Dr. McGowan came and examined Daddy. He talked to Grandmother in the hall, but I didn't understand what they were saying. He came back again two days later.

A week after Daddy first became sick, on a very gray, cloudy Wednesday, when I came home from school, Daddy was in the front hall dressed in a suit and wearing the orange and black Princeton tie that I had given him. I said, "Are you well now?"

In a soft, hoarse voice he said, "Not quite yet, Son. I'm going to the hospital where I can really get well." Grandmother handed him a duffel bag and Uncle Stanley said, "All set, Bob?"

I watched my daddy and Uncle Stanley get in the new black and gray Plymouth. Uncle Stanley got behind the wheel. Daddy waved at me and blew a kiss. As they started down the street he kept waving out the open window. I watched the car until I couldn't see it anymore. Just then a black steam engine came huffing down the tracks, pulling a train load of gray-black coal cars. Suddenly everything became gray as I watched my dad ride away.

C H A P T E R

4

Naught broken save this body, lost but breath;
Nothing to shake the laughing heart's long peace there
But only agony, and that has ending:
And the worst friend and enemy is but Death.
Rupert Brooke, 1887-1915

I am reflecting on a lifelong amazement about how we human beings handle grief. At seventy-two, I have, like so many others, experienced the loss of beloved relatives and friends. And I, like so many others, do not doubt the reality of death, or the inevitable pain of losing a loved one. As the cryptic axiom says, 'the only sure things in life are death and taxes.'

Since mankind's beginning, death has been met with an entire spectrum of human behavior ranging from solemn, self-flagellation by the bereaved to the hilarious toasting of the corpse in wakes. The lesson and lasting impact of death came early to me; at least, age eight seems early. My response was denial. I pushed this event onto the ROM of my subconscious. For many decades, I did not retrieve the material stored on that disk.

It wasn't until I became a septuagenarian that I processed the disassociated repression of the death that had emotionally shaped my life. I was taking a class at a community college called *Tales from Memory* and was asked to write an account of a trau-matic or character-shaping event. It took several days of thinking to come up with the subject. Both the thinking and the assignment were therapeutic. I wrote about the four-week period that had been buried in my subconscious for more than sixty years; January 20, 1938 – February 19, 1938.

My father had been confined to bed for a week with a respiratory ailment. At the end he was advised that he would probably not recover at home. I said a confused goodbye to him and watched my Uncle Stan drive him away from our home to Christ Hospital. That gray January day began a four-week experience that shaped the rest of my life. I stood on the curb and waved good-bye to my ailing, thirty-four year-old father until his Plymouth was out of sight.

When I was sure my dad and Uncle Stanley were gone, I went into the house, where Grandmother asked me to sit with her. "Bobby, you know your dad is very sick, which is why he will be in the hospital for a while."

"Where is the hospital?" I uttered, as a wave of fear washed over me. I was again sensing the dread of being deserted by the person I loved and had grown to trust, just like when I was younger and my parents divorced, and my dad went to Indiana. I looked in panic at Grandmother, who understood what I was feeling.

"It's in Mt. Auburn. You can go see your dad in a few days. Let me go first to be sure everything is all right," she said as she put her arms around me.

Grandmother went to the hospital every day. As soon as I was off to school she would take two streetcars to Christ Hospital, and wouldn't get home until eight o'clock at night, always exhausted. She would collapse into the chair nearest the door. I had never seen Grandmother look like she did on those nights in mid-January of 1938. Gone were the smiles and soft words I had seen and heard at Christmas and New Year's. She looked drawn, and the two creases over her nose had deepened. "Robert said to tell you he loves you, Bobby. He didn't eat all of his dinner tonight, but he did ask all about you. Perhaps you should visit him tomorrow, since it's Saturday."

"And when you say your prayers, ask God to help your dad heal. I may not be with you every night, Bobby, but please pray for him. He needs your prayers, so be a good boy and say them without me."

"Why? Where will you be?"

"I may be staying with Daddy for awhile to help him. I'll find out tomorrow if the hospital will let me stay with him. If I do, will you be a brave boy and mind Uncle Stan?"

"When you come home from school, you can go next door to Uncle Maurice's for supper. Margaret Jean will put you to bed and stay with you until Uncle Stan comes home at eleven. Can you eat lunch at school every day if I'm at the hospital?"

"Can I have a penny for a cookie?"

"Yes. I'll leave sixteen cents for each day. Miss Shellinger said it's ten cents for the plate lunch, a nickel for milk, and there's penny for your cookie. Your teacher is very concerned about your dad. If you need anything while we're at the hospital, just tell her."

"Will I see my mother?" I haltingly asked, as I again felt the loneliness I had felt so many times rise up in me. I was needing someone to hold onto.

"Your mother said she will come and be with you on Saturdays. Uncle Stan will bring you to see Daddy and me after Sunday school. I know this is hard, but I know you will be brave and help by being good."

My grandmother spent three weeks at the hospital, sleeping on a cot in my father's room. I went to see him once each week. He looked very tired. He hadn't been shaved because he was in an oxygen tent. The irony is that the oxygen cylinder was from Daddy's company; he had probably sold it to the hospital.

While Grandmother and Daddy were at the hospital and Uncle Stanley was working I was forced to do more things for myself. I picked out my clothes in the morning, took sixteen cents lunch money from the box of change set up for me, made my breakfast, and went to third grade. The red-faced, heavy ladies in the lunchroom got to know me, and always said hi as they peered through the misty vapors that floated up from the steam tables. They smiled when they served my plate lunch. I would go to Dick's house for several hours after school, using my Mickey Mouse watch to tell me when to leave. I went to Grandmother's brother's house for supper. Grandmother would call me on the phone at eight-thirty every night to see how I was and tell me about Daddy. My cousin, Margaret Jean Bryant, who was five years older than I, would bring me home and stay for a while. I liked her because she always did things with me like play Parcheesi or toss ball in the warm weather. She was so good to me, even seeing that I washed before bed and said my prayers. Uncle Stanley came home between eleven and twelve while I was asleep.

But I felt the hollowness again, the one I had known all during the custody battle and when Daddy was in Indiana. I did have moments of good feeling as I became more my own master, but most of the time I was confused, and felt that same emptiness I had known before. Not seeing Grandmother or Daddy every day made me feel alone again, cut off. At eight there was no way I could qualify, or begin to articulate, what I was experiencing. But it was like walking in fog, a mental and spiritual fog.

My mother's mother, Ruth Patience Allan, would ask me to come to her house for dinner on Thursdays. Mother's brother, Tom and sister Jewel, still lived there with Ruth and Grandfather

Joe. They gave me lots of hugs, took me places, and would slip me a dime or a quarter. True, I couldn't live with my mother and had a father in the hospital, but I did not lack for love. I learned from this that love is the greatest resource we have. If things are not "normal," I believe a person can still thrive if he or she has sincere love. Will not a flower bloom, no matter who waters and cares for it?

As I think about it, the giving of love and care might have been instilled in my generation because of our lack of affluence during The Great Depression. Without TV, we were a generation who took guidance mostly from our parents or guardians. Our base was the home or schools, where the pledge of allegiance was said, and churches where *America* was often sung. Our paramount influence was helping each other to survive the Depression. In most neighborhoods and schools, gangs were nonexistent. Our Silent Generation, labeled "adaptive followers," in all reality probably grew into an adult generation of caregivers. We may also be the keepers of certain values that, as a nation entering the twenty-first century, we are now re-seeking.

I lived most of each day alone, and January merged into February. My dad was still in the hospital, and Grandmother was with him twenty-four hours a day. She did come home, however, for one night to get fresh clothes and pay some bills. I went back with her on the three streetcars required to reach the hospital to see my dad, but he was asleep the entire time. My mother came and picked me up. She went up to the room to see my dad, but he did not wake up. When we left, my mother was crying. She said, "What a waste. He was always so big and strong, and full of life. Bobby, pray hard for his recovery."

"What's wrong with Daddy?"

"The doctors told your grandmother he has double pneumonia and strep throat, an infection in his throat. I think he had a case of pneumonia as a young boy that left his lungs weakened." Seeing my face, she quickly added, "But I'm sure he'll get well. All of the doctors and nurses are helping him. What would you like for supper?"

"Waffles."

"Want to go to the Toddle House? You remember the place where we sit at the counter, and pay by dropping the check and the money in the collection box that's like the ones on buses?"

I loved the Toddle House. It was a small brick building, painted white, with glass windows in front and small white hexagonal floor tiles. There were twelve circular stools at the Formica-topped counter. Two uniformed cooks, complete with white chef's hats, stood behind the counter and manned four large waffle irons. With deft moves, they would pull a large aluminum pot of batter from the icebox and ladle a generous glob of off-white batter onto the heated iron. With the other hand the cook would close the lid, and the aroma would waft into the room from the edges of the iron. Soon a steaming, golden brown waffle was on a plate in front of me with a large dollop of butter in the center. The butter quickly melted and ran into the little squares, just ahead of the maple syrup I poured from the thumb-operated glass and metal cruet. As I gustily ate my favorite dish, I saw my mother smile.

*   *   *

A few days before Valentine's Day, Mother picked me up at school and brought me to my house. She helped me make valentines to distribute from a post office we had made as a class project. She was very artistic and good with any craft. She showed me how to assemble little lace paper hearts on red paper, and paste Cupids with bows and love arrows on card stock. In all, we made twenty valentines. I loved it when we did things together. She cooked scrambled eggs for us, and we sat and ate together. She stayed till my bedtime, and when she left, she said, "I love you, Son. You're a brave boy to stay here. Uncle Stanley will be home soon."

"Why can't you stay with me?"

"I wish I could, but you know I don't live here…maybe someday."

When I heard the front door close, that hollow feeling I'd had so many times crept back over me. I looked around my dimly lit room and saw my old Indian doll, Hostamoge, on my dresser. I picked him up, hugging him as a fast passenger train, with its mournful whistle, rushed past the house. As the sound of the whistle faded, so did the glow of that evening with my mother. I held Hostamoge even tighter, and wiped my eyes on the sheet.

Monday, Valentine's Day, Patty and I got to be the postmen. She sorted the valentines in our little orange-crate and poster paper post office, and I delivered them to the kids at their desks. We had cupcakes and milk, which some of the mothers provided. I got a very pretty valentine that said, "I love you," but it was signed, "Guess who?" Rats!

On Wednesday I came home from Dick's house and saw Uncle Stanley's old Packard coupe in front of the house. This was strange, because he usually worked until eleven. I went up the steps, and he opened the door before I could get my key out. "Come on in, Bobby. Mom thinks it would be good for us to see your dad tonight. I fixed you a sandwich. We'll go after you eat."

I washed my hands, ate a peanut butter and jelly sandwich, and got into Uncle Stan's car. It was dark when we left home, and as we drove, it started to snow. There wasn't a lot of snow, just big white, fluffy flakes that melted as soon as they lit. The windshield wiper kept squeaking as it traveled across the partially wet windshield.

When we got to the hospital we went up in the elevator to number three. We entered the marble-floored hall, smelling the sickly-sweet odor of disinfectant. As we walked to Dad's room, nurses in starched, white uniforms, with their white, crepe-soled flat shoes that made no sound, scurried by us on their errands of care. There was an occasional bong-bong sound echoing in the hall from the coded intercom system. Those sights, sounds and smells have lingered with me to this day.

We entered room 314. It was different than it was on earlier visits. It seemed darker. When my eyes became accustomed to the dimness, I saw a man dressed in black with a small square of white showing at the collar of his black blouse. He wore a six-inch wide red scarf with gold crosses on each end, around his neck. It reached to his knees. The overhead light was off, so I easily saw two little candles on either side of a small gold cross on the dresser. As the candles flickered, they cast their tiny shadows on the drab, gray walls. Grandmother was there, and took my hand and said, "Bobby, Daddy is still very sick. Please go to the bed and pat his hand." I could sort of see my dad behind the transparent plastic-glass curtain of the oxygen tent. Next to the bed there was a round, green, steel cylinder, lettered **OXYG** with gauges and a hose running into the tent. I hardly recognized him; he was so thin and heavily bearded. There was a blank look in his eyes, which were barely open. I touched his hand under the sheet. He turned toward me, and his eyes flicked a tiny spark, as his brows tensed. His hand rose to meet mine, then it fell to the side.

The man in black brought us a small round silver plate covered with thin, white, round things that looked like Necco Wafers. He also had a stemmed silver cup. He dipped one of the wafers into the cup. "Jesus said, 'Verily, verily, I say unto you, He that believeth in me hath everlasting life. I am the bread of life'...." The wafer, now half white and half red, was passed under the curtain and placed on my dad's lips. My dad tried to chew it, and some of the crumbs stuck to his beard. Next the man gave Grandmother and Uncle Stanley a wafer and a sip from the cup. He came to me, placed his hands on my head, and made a cross with his thumb on my forehead. While he was blessing me, I heard a faint, hoarse whisper from the bed, "I...I love you, Son."

> "Almighty God, look on this your servant,
> lying in great weakness, and comfort him
> with the promise of life everlasting, given
> the resurrection of your son Jesus Christ
> our Lord. *Amen.*"

"Bobby, Uncle Stan will take you home now. I'll stay with your daddy, but be sure to say your prayers. We're proud of the way you have helped by being so good."

When Uncle Stan and I left Christ Hospital on that snowy, February night, he put his arm around my shoulders, and we walked across the snow-covered parking lot in total silence. I helped him brush the snow from the windshield. Still nothing was said. Finally, as we were driving home, he cleared his throat and asked, "Would you like to get some hot chocolate?"

"Can I get a cookie too?"

"We'll see."

In the ice cream parlor the waitress set down two heavy white china mugs with two thin green lines around the top, filled with steamy hot chocolate. She also set a little white china plate with the same two green lines, in front of me. On it were two vanilla wafers. I stared at these and suddenly saw the silver paten in my dad's room with the white wafers. "Will Daddy get well?"

"We sure all hope and pray he will," Uncle Stan said, as he looked away from me.

"Why was that man there?"

"He's a priest from the Episcopal Cathedral. He was giving your father communion to help...to, ah help him get well." Uncle Stan started to have tears in his eyes, which he quickly wiped with his napkin. "It was a service to pray for your dad."

"I pray for him too."

The next day I came home from school and saw a car in front of the house. Grandmother was home, sitting on the couch with a man I didn't know. I was glad to see her, but I halted at the entrance to the living room because I didn't know this man. I just stood there not knowing what to do; feeling that something was different, because she hadn't been home in the afternoon for weeks. She said "excuse me" to the man, and came out into the hall. "Bobby, come into the kitchen with me."

Grandmother seemed strange, wooden-like and detached. I couldn't tell what she was thinking, or what she was going to do. She looked like I always knew her, but she just didn't sound or act normal, which made me feel funny. I felt like I was being led to an unknown place, even though it was the same kitchen I was in every day.

She turned and with her back to the sink, looked at me for a moment before she said, "Bobby, your dad passed away early this morning."

I knew this was bad, wrong. I didn't say anything. How could I? I didn't know what to say. I just looked at her trying to grasp what I'd heard.

"Your dad suffered so much, these last two weeks. He's at peace now. I'm sure he's with God." She reached out to me, as I went closer and into her arms. "His last words were about you. He loves you very much."

I can't remember exactly how I felt, except it was like something shut down inside me. Like an electric motor that has been turned off, but takes time to stop. It was like I was slowly coasting to a stoppage of feeling. This was one more event, another tragedy that hit me. My defense was denial. My eight-year-old brain didn't want to, or maybe couldn't, process another major trauma. I just stood there in Grandmother's arms, until I finally backed off and said, "He won't be here anymore?"

Upon reflection, I realize her firm New England resolve kept her from breaking down in front of me. I remember seeing the small lump in her throat, just above the neckline of her dress, pulsating at a rapid rate. This happened whenever she was under stress. I'd seen this only a few times before. She just nodded, and said she had to go back to the man in the living room to finish the arrangements for my dad's funeral. As she left, "Bobby, why don't you change your clothes? If you want to go out for a short time in the snow, it'll be all right."

I went upstairs to change. I may never know what I actually felt. My mind must have rejected or shut out what it heard. I just changed to play clothes. How deeply did I repress what I'd heard?

On Friday, I was asked to go to Grandmother Allan's after school, as "arrangements" had to be made. When I got home at supper time I saw the arrangements in the living room. My father was there in an open casket. At each end of the casket were two floor lamps pointing upward. The top half of the casket was open. My dad looked like I always knew him, except he was very still, and his eyes were closed. He was dressed in an oxford-gray suit, a white shirt, and there was the orange and black, striped Princeton tie I had given him.

The bottom half of the casket was covered with a large shock of flowers. For a moment the smell made me light-headed. I stood by the casket looking at my dad, the man who played with me, took me on his business calls, and made me laugh. He was also the man who had been away for so much of my life, but who had come back to me and made me feel I was like all the other kids. I felt Grandmother's arm around me. "Bobby, he was a wonderful man, but he was very sick. He's not in pain now, he's with God." She trembled as she held me close. "I know you will be brave and help me. You can be a fine man just like he was."

Soon, many people arrived at the house. They would walk in with quiet, sad faces, pass by my dad, and pat me. Some of them knelt down by the casket, others crossed themselves. My mother didn't come, but Grandmother told me she had spent the day there cleaning the house and helping. Grandmother Allan, Uncle Craig, and a few others gave me money. Most of the guests were crying. Some of the men stayed on the porch and smoked, while a few of my aunts and uncles were in the kitchen with Uncle Stan, who fixed them a drink. When I went in there, I heard my aunts and uncles talking about my father. Mother's sister, Duff, was telling about one day when she and some high school friends walked by our house. She said that my dad opened the window and bellowed at them as he beat his chest. She cried, "Robert, what are you doing?" The reply came back, "It's just a bull anthropoid in mating season," to which the young girls all tittered. Duff added, "Robert was always the life of the party, but he was also so intellectual."

"Yeah," Uncle Craig chimed. "He was the life, but when he took on young Robert, here, he really buckled down. I'll bet he was the smartest guy that Gulf station on Anthony Wayne ever had. What a damn shame; he was just getting on with the sales manager's job at Liquid Carbonic."

Sensing me, they turned and said, "Bobby, your dad was a great man. We're here for you, but we know you'll do all right, you've got your dad's looks and brains."

I can only describe my feelings that night as bewildered. It was like walking in a dream. I didn't know what to do. I knew things were sad, but I liked the way my aunts and uncles said good things about my dad and me. Over sixty years later I still feel the love and warmth they extended that night.

Saturday morning broke with heavy gray clouds, and a warming temperature. The snow that had covered the ground the last night I saw my father alive was gone; only its dirty, gray residue was left. Grandmother got me up and told me that today we were going to lay my dad to rest. The smell of flowers floated up the stairs. I walked into the living room and looked again into the casket, half expecting my dad to say something. His open face, with the steel-rimmed glasses, the strong chin and closed eyes which I remembered as always ready to light up in a smile – it was all there before me, but in a place I just didn't understand. I only knew the man who picked me up, made me laugh, or took me places. I had never seen him lie so still. I never knew him when he wasn't moving, twirling his key chain, or hugging me. This dad who now didn't talk or touch me made me retreat into myself. I was too young to know what numbness meant, but I know now that's what I felt.

About eleven o'clock some men came in a long black car that looked like a closed truck. They closed my dad's casket and carried it out. The flowers went into another car. As they slid the gray felt-covered casket into the back of the car, it started to rain. The skies grew black, and the rain came down heavily, making the flowers droop. Grandmother called me into her sitting room. "Bobby, we're going to church now, where we will ask God to take your dad into his arms. Will you be a brave boy, and stay close to me?" I nodded, kissed her on the cheek, and wondered what was going to happen at church. I saw that she had been crying.

Grandmother, Uncle Stanley, Aunt Claire from Saint Louis, and I rode to church in the undertaker's black car with two fold-out seats in the back. I sat and faced the others. When we went into the church, I saw my dad's closed casket on a wheeled wagon sitting in the center aisle of the church, just a few feet in front of the sanctuary rail. When we entered our pew, Uncle Edwin, dad's older brother, and Aunt Jane joined us. It seemed that everyone in the church looked at me with a sad face. Many were crying. Then Mr. Attridge, the minister (it was a low Episcopal church, and the term father or priest was not used in the thirties), came into the chancellery and asked all of us to pray. He talked about what a good man my dad was, and how God must need him to call him at such a young age. He said my dad was a good son, a good father, and a brave man who had worked through the trials of the depressed times and had provided for his family. I grasped most of what he said, and I knew all of what I heard was good. I kept look-ing at the gray coffin, trying to picture my dad in his gray suit and orange and black tie, but it seemed scary with the lid closed. I looked up at Grandmother, whose face was very still, expression-less, and red-eyed. She put her hand on my shoulder and pulled me to her. I can still remember the trancelike state I was in. I expe-rienced many other deaths over time, but this was one where I had no conscious thoughts, just an existence through something that

I knew was bad, but couldn't process, except through childlike repression or disassociation. It was a huge lump that I didn't digest until I was in my mid-sixties.

We prayed more, and then we were dismissed with this prayer:

> Unto God's gracious mercy and protection we
> commit you. The Lord bless you and keep you.
> The Lord make his face to shine upon you,
> and be gracious unto you. The Lord lift up his
> countenance upon you, and give you peace,
> both now and evermore. *Amen.*

Everyone filed out of the church in a cloak of silence, faintly punctuated by the soft sounds of weeping. Many were wiping their eyes with white handkerchiefs. We got into the long black car for the ride to the cemetery.

Every step from the car to the gravesite made water squish up from the sodden ground. I was wearing my yellow oilcloth rain slicker and hat, which made squeaking noises every time I swung my arms. Grandmother took Uncle Stanley's arm, and also took my hand in hers as we walked to the blue and white striped dripping canopy, with its scalloped edges flapping in the wet breeze. It covered the open grave, the suspended casket, and piles of raw, wet, brown clay-laced dirt piled on both sides. There were mud-splattered artificial grass mats stretched around the open, seven-by-five-foot below-grade vault, whose inviting, silent presence exuded a finality that I took in on that rainy day, but did not process until more than sixty years later.

We gathered around the grave, getting as close to one another as the open umbrellas would permit. Mr. Attridge stood in the rain and intoned the burial service from the 1928 *Book of*

Common Prayer. At one point, Uncle Stanley and Uncle Edwin cast clods of dirt on the casket which had been lowered halfway into the grave. As the clods hit the casket, they echoed like knocks on the hollow door of an empty house. As the last clod hit, we heard, "Unto Almighty God we commend the soul of our brother departed, and we commit his body to the ground; earth to earth, ashes to ashes, dust to dust; in sure and certain hope unto the Resurrection unto eternal life, through our Lord Jesus Christ...."

I latched onto the phrase "eternal life." I had this mental image of a place in the sky where everyone I knew would be someday. I had seen the movie *Green Pastures*, and had heard many stories about heaven. These abstract concepts to an eight-year-old have to be converted to real time images, so I created this airy, cloudy place where I would be someday with my dad.

After the last prayer, the undertaker asked us all to leave. As we turned, my grandmother trembled and started to sink. I felt a sudden flash of fear. What if something happened to her? Uncle Stanley lifted her up on his arm. She said, "I'm all right." I squeezed her arm tighter. On the ride to our house, Grandmother kept looking at me with a sad look, yet beneath it I somehow sensed that New England resolve. Aunt Claire looked out of the window, but I could see the tiny, pearl-shaped, opalescent woman's tears inch down her smooth, pink-tinged cheeks. I guess she and my dad would have gotten married, if he had lived. I later was able to articulate what I assimilated that day when I saw how many people came to the viewing and the funeral. There were the family, many friends, business associates, people who came out of respect for Grandmother or Uncles Stan and Ed, plus flowers or notes from Princeton and Kent School classmates. I realized that my father's death touched many lives beyond mine and Grandmother's, and that no one's death is a singular thing. When someone dies, a part of those he or she leaves behind dies a little. Each of our deaths touches many lives, and as John Donne said, "No man is an island."

Back at the house, the family and a few friends came in. Uncle Stan fixed drinks for them, and Aunt Jane served small sandwiches. The people kept telling me that I was going to be "the man of the house." I wasn't sure what that meant, except that my dad wouldn't be there anymore. I am still not sure what my feelings were, as I did not fully comprehend my father's death. I must have, in self defense, pushed the reality of it below consciousness. I never thought about the funeral or the burial until twenty-six years later when my wife and I and our three sons saw *Dr. Zhivago*. The opening scene, showing the burial of the boy Zhivago's mother, brought back my father's burial. In the movie, after the funeral, the boy is alone in his bed and the wind rattles the windows of his room, making him realize his loneliness and his fear. When I went to bed the night of my dad's burial, blowing sleet pelted the panes next to my bed. I hid my face in the pillow and knew I was alone.

Many years later, sitting in front of the cinema screen, I gasped as what I saw and heard forced up the experience that had been so long buried.

I have long felt I was different from my peers. As my birth mates of the Silent Generation were raised in the shadow of Depression-denied material, I was raised in the dearth of parental presence and guidance. Being raised against both the backdrop of no mother or father at home, plus the rigors of the Depression, makes me reflect on how these conditions formed my character and the ethos of my self. Without male discipline at home, I made mistakes earlier in life, but I also learned the consequences of my misdirected actions earlier. As my development was shaped by the pain of losing a father so young, and not having a mother at home, so was the compassionate character of the Silent Generation shaped by the pain of the Great Depression.

CHAPTER

5

*Life is the art of drawing sufficient conclusions
from insufficient premises.*
Samuel Butler, 1835-1902

The day after the funeral dawned as a gray Sunday, with the ground covered by a thin frozen layer. I looked out of the window and saw the yard around our house shrouded in cocoon of white. Even the bass exhaust rumbling and treble whistle shrieks of the passing trains were muted in the heavy air. It was quiet; everything in our house was soundless. Everyone was speechless. At breakfast Grandmother Uncle Stanley, and I were like players in a slow-motion, silent movie. Finally, Grandmother said, "Bobby, let's get ready for Sunday school."

It was my first interface with other kids since my dad's "viewing" in our living room and his burial. The teacher said she was sorry, and the kids looked at me in a peculiar way, which did make me feel that I was somebody, but also that I was different. This sensation was brief, however, as we were soon learning about Moses and his forty years in the desert. How quickly events, good or bad, are relegated to the past, and current activities push earlier ones, only hours old, further back in time. Memories can be warm and wonderful, but the moment is the thing. Perhaps this is a healthy condition; otherwise we'd wallow in a trough of inactivity. The stupor and numbness I had existed in since my dad had gotten ill was pushed aside by the activity in my Sunday school class.

Grandmother came into my classroom to get me for the regular service. As she approached us, I was startled. She was wearing a black, heavy veil over her face. It was draped from her hat brim and reached to the mid-point of her neck, like a bee keeper's garb. I could sense the other kids looking at her, then at me, in disbelief, and I felt a flush of embarrassment.

This was my introduction to self-consciousness. Those kids in my Sunday school class looked at me as if I were different. In their eyes I was associated with something outside of their norm, something they didn't understand. Therefore, I was not like them.

This small kernel of understanding of how quickly people react with derision, dislike, or malice toward what they don't understand or trust, blossomed into full fruit as I matured. And I believe this relatively simple example of being outside the herd is the beginning of what motivates people to snobbery, financial and social boycotting, and racial and religious prejudice and persecution. I realize I have projected a small case to a much larger scale; but doesn't the tall oak grow to a thousand times the size of its tiny acorn? Doesn't hatred grow from little slights, and violence from envy and overreaction? How many times have wars been fought, people socially shunned, harassed, abused, even killed, because they were perceived to be different?

Not only do individuals feel self-conscious, but whole bodies of people do as well. If my generation listened to or read all that has been said about our "silence," we would carry the weight of self-consciousness as a class stigma. My so-called Silent Generation grew up, first in The Great Depression and then on the fringe of World War II. We were in awe of the preceding generation, called the GI generation, as they were the heroes of our nation. They were the soldiers who landed on the shores of France on June 6th, 1944, or who, while encircled in Bastogne, told the Germans, "Nuts," when asked to surrender. They were the brave fighters who stormed ashore on the bullet-riddled beaches of so many islands in the South Pacific, or flew countless bombing missions in B-17s, 24s, 25s, 29s, or fighter protection for the bombers in P-38s, 40s, 47s, or 51s. Most of us were too young, by a year or two, to serve in the Armed Forces, so we existed on the fringe. We worked on scrap iron and paper drives, did menial chores in hospitals, and purchased Defense Stamps. Many of us had family and friends who fought, but we were not in the public eye, nor were we a part of the million casualties our armed services incurred. We were on the sidelines of the total effort; we were outside the herd. I think we have always carried a feeling of self-consciousness because we were not "heard" from in the war. Our silence was caused by a timing coincidence. Were we born too soon or too late?

I myself carried for many years a feeling of self-consciousness that started with my dad's death. The negative effect of my grandmother's "bee-keeper's veil," which sparked ridicule of me from the other kids, lasted for two months. It brought back all of the feelings I had right after my parent's divorce and during the time my dad was away. I was back to being the kid from the wrong side of the tracks with no mother or father at home.

On the bright side, my grandmother continued to raise me with love, good direction, and spirituality. On a daily basis, she and Uncle Stanley gave me affection, support, guidance, and an open ear to compensate for my dad not being there. On that gray, dismal Sunday after my dad's funeral, Grandmother had said, "Bobby, we will miss your dad forever. You will have to be strong, mind me, and do your best at school. This is what your dad would want. Will you help me by doing this?"

I looked into her kind, deep-set brown eyes and said yes. I guess I knew what I was saying, although there would be many times after that when I deviated from that pledge. In subsequent talks, she summed up how she wanted me to live by saying, "Believe in God, and get ahead." It took many failures, new beginnings, and scars before I was able to make her wise directive my credo.

Every other week we would drive out to the cemetery and visit his grave. There was no money for a headstone, but the fresh sod made it easy to identify. We would spend an hour there, with Grandmother saying a prayer pulling some weeds from the family plot that held her mother, husband, and now my dad. She told me who the remaining spots were for. I saw all of them filled by the time I was thirty. At age fifty I purchased headstones for my dad and grandmother; I had always felt that their graves needed to be marked. Exactly why I couldn't say. It was an internal thing…a closure of sorts. I think that is why we have funerals, and why we, as a nation, spend millions of dollars to recover bodies from the sea, foreign lands, or from decimated buildings. I guess our inborn, genetically encoded will to survive cannot accept death until it is proven to us. Our ability to carry on with hope in the face of any tragedy is a fire quenched only by stark, in-your-face reality.

Closure after my dad's death was not as finite as it would have been had I been older. I was left confused and not sure what it all meant. Having a dead father was an experience that I muddled through as if I were outside a dream looking in. But, humans are resilient and so was I. The self-directed needs of survival, gratification, and fulfillment pull us from the abyss of despondency. As the trite but true axiom says, …"Life goes on." So did mine, as apparently did those of the entire Silent Generation – quiet, self-conscious and, for the most part, adaptive. We humans bend with the forces of life, as does the sinewy tree in the force of a gale.

While Strauss and Howe, in *Generations*, use the word adaptive in an implied derisive tone, I rebel at the implication of my generation being labeled a group of "me too's," or people that do anything to survive. Every person and every generation faces the broad, society-oriented challenges: environmental, social, financial, political, spiritual, and moral. Additionally, as individuals we desire mental and physical well being and to know that our lives were lived with purpose. To deal with these tasks often calls for adaptability. Did not Charles Darwin expound upon the need for any species to adapt to its environment to survive? I adapted to my new home life situation thrust upon me by some death-dealing microscopic, pre-penicillin and pre-sulfa drug microorganisms. My generation adapted to the denials of The Great Depression, being on the fringe of World War II, and coming of age in post-war America with its far-reaching social changes. Yes, my Silent Generation and I were and are "adaptive," but with good results. We survived our challenges and led the civil rights movements, ameliorated the negative part of the sixties upheavals, and helped lead post-war America to an economic expansion that was one of the longest in duration in our country's history. Did we make mistakes? Did we leave things undone? Yes, but life is an imperfect process; we were a part of that process, not its conclusion. As an individual did I make mistakes, or leave things undone? You bet, but it was from the errors of commission and the tiny daily sins committed that I learned.

*　　　　*　　　　*

As life without my dad progressed, I was more on my own. Grandmother was seventy-three and taking some medication for heart irregularities. I was a well of boundless energy and determination to have my own way. What I couldn't achieve overtly I soon learned how to achieve covertly. I had learned, through embarrassing moments, about self-consciousness, and tried to avoid it by affecting the image of my peers. I put on the mask of normalcy by wanting to dress, sound, and act like my peers. I never talked about my home life, except for mentioning my mother as if she were with me all of the time.

After I turned nine, I articulated what was to be for me another of life's hurdles. One day after Sunday school, Grandmother asked me what we had covered that morning. I told her how we had talked about the Lord's Prayer. She asked me to recite it, which I did. She asked me if there was anything in it that I didn't understand. I asked, "What is temptation?"

"It is someone, or something that tries to get you to do something that you shouldn't do. Remember when the serpent in the Garden of Eden tempted…uh, tried to get Eve to eat the fruit that God had told Adam not to eat? The serpent was a tempter. Usually a temptation looks all right, like the fruit on the tree of knowledge, but is not. It's like a trap that's covered with something you care for, like candy, but underneath, its steel jaws are ready to snap shut on you if you succumb to the temptation. Do you understand?"

I said I did, but the trap simile wasn't grasped until years later. As I progressed through the fourth, fifth, and sixth grades, I was confronted with many temptations. No fruit from the tree of knowledge, but candy, stolen cookies, telling lies about being late or where I'd been, peeking at Uncle Stan's lurid detective magazines, and even picking up some loose change that I found in the cushions of the couch or easy chair. It seemed natural to satisfy my early sensual desires in whatever manner was easiest.

As I grew older, the temptations I faced became larger, more dangerous, and reached deeper into my soul. Temptation is not a temporary thing. It stays with us, at least with me, every day of our lives. As one wag said, "Age is a great reformer," but in my seventies I still see the tempting snares of things just outside the line of propriety, legality, and morality. Geriatric temptations can be things as simple as an extra piece of pie, cake, or fatty meat that can clog aging arteries, to slick business deals that appear legal but defraud or steal from others. The list is endless: extramarital sex, gambling, drinking, bad-mouthing others, income tax cheating, lying, padding expense accounts, misrepresenting ourselves or facts for our sole gain, and weaseling out of commitments and responsibilities. But temptation does have its soothing balm...rationalization.

I think the toughest temptations I faced were in my thirties and forties when, as a manager of cyclical businesses, I was confronted with recessions that threatened the life of the business and the jobs of loyal employees. The need to severely cut costs to avoid going under posed the temptation to shave product weights and quality for the duration of the recession. Luckily, after a few instances of succumbing to this short cut, I had a mentor who convinced me of the deleterious long term effect of this short term expediency. The adage I picked up from this that I tried to remember and employ from that time forward is, "There are no shortcuts in life."

*   *   *

With my dad gone I found myself becoming more dependent on my classmates. I sought the warmth and acceptance of the group. My headstrong will, unchecked by any male discipline at home, had to give ground as I fitted into my class. Dick George and Patty Drexel were a constant help to me. Dick and I would work together on paper drives, or building toys from orange crates and Kraft two-pound cheese boxes. In the sixth grade we joined the Boy Scouts together, and formed a Knothole baseball team (the forty's equivalent of Little League, without the over-aggressive and interfering parents). We signed up the guys, talked a haberdasher into sponsoring our team with hats and shirts that said, "Harry's Men's Wear," and motivated our team to a league championship.

One game in particular will always remain with me. As a social gesture we were scheduled by the league administrators to play Glenview Reform School. The day of the game finally arrived after all eleven of us had spent a week of anxiety and speculation. A bus pulled up to the Hartwell playground and out came a guard with a twelve gauge, double barreled shot-gun, followed by twelve tall, sixteen- to eighteen-year-old youths, some black and some white, and then another guard with a shotgun. We were twelve and thirteen years old. We all looked at each other in surprise and fear. Our clean red and white jerseys were in contrast to the dingy work shirts and jeans of the inmates. We all had spikes and good-look-ing leather ball gloves; they were shod in black, high top gym-shoes that had holes around the little toe and incomplete lacings. Their ball gloves were worn and small, like the ones Ty Cobb and Honus Wagner played with.

Dick George was on second base and I was the catcher. Our pitcher, Eugene Sears, had a severely deformed right foot, known as a club foot. Every time he followed through on a pitch, he came down with most of his weight on that foot. His family could not afford an operation, so Genie, as we called him, just toughed it out in both baseball and in our school lot football games. His courage and determination to overcome his handicap inspired all of us. I never forgot him or that game with the reform school guys. Our Class A team played seven innings, which theoretically puts up twenty-one batters. Genie struck out nineteen that day, grimacing on every pitch. I know; I caught him. We won five to nothing! After the game we gave them the customary cheer, but shied away from any handshaking.

We watched the twelve boys and their gun-toting guards re-enter their bus for the trip back to confinement. The picture of these boys, just a little older than we were, their armed guards, and their despair stuck with me for the rest of my life. What was the difference between those silent, drab-shirted inmates and our smiling, sparkling-shirted team? Was it home life, abuse, lack of healthy community, or lack of love? What a waste! I believe that my Silent Generation felt the pain of the exploited, the derided, the persecuted, and the poor; just as we pre-teens felt the pain of those boys who had just come to play some ball. This awareness led many in our generation to become the caretakers, and civil rights workers of society. In my lifetime I have seen many walls of prejudice come down, not all the way, but with a healthy start. While our fingers and tongues are the most sensitive feeling points we humans have, it's our hearts that sense and possess the most meaningful feelings. Yes, Cain, we are our brother's keeper.

*   *   *

Dick and I also talked about girls. I can't remember when I first started to see girls as more than someone to tease or say funny things about, but the girl I always wanted to think well of me was Patty Drexel. Ever since I had seen her at the drug store, I was aware of her. I guess at about that same time, the girls started to think about us boys as more than someone to deride. As fifth-graders we somehow began to explore the other sex in games; one was called "post office."

I was ten years old. My hero was the black-masked, rapier-wielding, Zorro, who would race across the sepia-toned celluloid movie screen to save a fair damsel from some villain and then receive her grateful kiss. I used to dream of saving my classmates, Joyce, Mary and especially Patty, just like Zorro did.

Confused about how to realize my girl-centered fantasies, I asked my buddy Dick, if he had ever kissed a girl. "Sure," her replied smugly with a worldly glow on his pre-pubescent face. "I did lots of times, like when we played post office at my cousin's."

"Can we play sometime?" I cautiously advanced.

"Yeah, maybe next week at Patty Drexel's birthday party," came back the reply, accentuated with a dreamy look.

After a week of Zorro-based fantasizing, the big day of Patty's party arrived. There we were, eight girls and eight boys wearing party hats and eating chocolate ice cream and devil's food cake. I was agog with anticipation!

"Hey guys, how about we play post office?" Dick asked, causing some male, "Aw gees" and female tittering.

We started! The names of all of us were put into two caps, girls in one and the boys in the other. The "postman" picked one from each hat and sent the girl with "mail" (soon to be "male") into another room. The boys were blindfolded, so they didn't know who was in the other room. The blindfold also protected the girls' modesty. The boy then entered the other room where a girl was awaiting, in most cases, her first kiss.

At last my turn! Feeling my way I sensed a fair damsel and grabbed he in true Zorro-like passion. Alas, my first parry landed my eager mouth on her nose...rats! Not to be discouraged, I ventured on. Aha! Lips found lips, but what an odd sensation: it was not in the libido, but olfactory! As a potpourri of food, gum and natural odors accompanied that first kiss, I quickly exclaimed, "Why you're Mary...I can tell by your breath!" Not understanding women yet, I was stunned when she ran from the room crying. Can you beat that? It wasn't like I squeezed her too hard or anything. And this is how my first kiss ended. To this day, I've always wondered if it was as good for her as it was for me.

Fifth-grade passion aside, as a class we formed a solid community. We shared birthday parties, games at recess and monthly trips to the Cincinnati Symphony. Maybe the propinquity of living through the Depression bonded us, or maybe the values that most of our parents or guardians instilled in us contributed. They were values that came from a mostly lower middle-class cut of conservative Cincinnati's social strats, espoused and taught to their children by relatively poor, but dignified, responsible people who had suffered through the sacrifices of World War I and the trying challenges of the Depression. Most went to church, knew where their children were and had something to share with the namdic rail-riding hobos who always worked for their food as they passed through Hartwell on their endless search for a job, their dignity, or maybe just the next meal.

*   *   *

Between fourth and fifth grade, Grandmother Laurie and I spent the summer in Vermont on her cousin's farm. When we arrived back in Cincinnati just before school started, we heard that

Germany, under Adolph Hitler, had invaded Poland. The British and French declared war on Germany a few days later. This event, to a ten-year-old, was remote. This European war was not in our daily lives, except I heard Grandmother say to Uncle Stanley, "It won't be long, Stan, until we'll be drawn in." It's only in hindsight that I see that as the chapter of the Great Depression was closing, another chapter with far-reaching effects was just opening. A chapter that would claim over fifty million lives world-wide. Our country was recovering from the Depression, thanks to many government programs that had been instituted over the last five to six years and the ramping up of the arms and defense industry to supply Britain, then Russia under the Lend-Lease-Program. Selective Service was instituted, which took some of the unemployed off the streets. But, a ten-year-old is insulated from these major happenings. I was playing and seeing more of my mother. It seemed that Grandmother was more lenient about the number and length of visits with her, I guess because of my dad being gone. I even stayed overnight with her and Uncle Charles Biscay in Avondale. I would also take trips to South Bend with Grandfather and Grandmother Allan. Their son, my mother's young brother Uncle Tom, who was ten years older than me, did a lot with me. He was my hero. He played football for Hartwell School, had to get married at eighteen, and would give me a nickel or dime whenever he saw me. Some people said he was a little wild, but he was my pal.

Under Grandmother's tutelage, church-related activities were a large part of my life throughout grades three to eight. I became an altar boy, went to church-sponsored youth retreats, and was active in a young people's group. Grandmother's deep faith emanated from her in almost everything she did, yet it was never self-righteous, pedantic, or oppressive. She never preached, just cited examples from the Bible or prayer book. If I did something wrong, she would ask me to kneel down and ask God for His forgiveness. I'm sure I soaked up a lot of what she believed in, plus what I assimilated at Sunday school and as an altar boy. I think back and realize that it was a slow osmosis, like that of the capillaries; but like those vital feeders of our life, my assimilated faith fed me many times as my life progressed. I also know that my faith would submerge to dormancy as I wrestled with secular and sensual desires, temptations, and self-indulgence. But I thank my grandmother for planting the roots of a sustaining core faith and direction in my inner consciousness when she said, "Believe in God, and get ahead."

*   *   *

I hope the metaphor of the stick floating in the stream of life is not too trite, but it always seems to fit when I reflect on how our lives, at least mine, take different turns. I picture the stick catching at a particular place, hanging there, then breaking loose, and going to another stopping place. Maybe a child playing in the stream picks up the stick and pitches it ahead, behind, or out of the water. I feel I have floated, like the stick, down life's stream, catching here and there, and being propelled in new directions by outward influences. If you don't like my stick and stream metaphor, how about a road of life with a never ending series of forks? One such catching place or fork that drastically changed the direction and outcome of my life presented itself near the end of my sixth-grade year.

One spring day, my entire class was given a test that was issued by the Cincinnati Board of Education. It was not like any test that we had taken that year. It was mostly English and math.

There was no explanation about it, just take it and turn it in. I forgot about it, until three weeks later when my grandmother told me that I had done well on the test and would be allowed to go to Walnut Hills High School for grades seven through twelve.

"What's Walnut Hills," I asked in shock. What was this? Not stay with my class at Hartwell School? Where was this Walnut Hills?

"Bobby, this is an opportunity for you. The school only takes student who are capable of doing A work, if their teachers approve them. You have been approved. Walnut Hills is in a class with only a handful of schools in the entire country. They teach Latin in the seventh and eighth grades and offer subjects that are not offered at Hartwell School. Also, you will meet a lot of bright children from all over the city."

"But, I want to stay with my friends."

"It's best that you go. It's a real opportunity. Once you start you'll see the wisdom of your going there."

I sulked for a couple of days, but since the start of my seventh-grade year was a few months off I forgot it as Dick George and I became very active in Scouts and baseball. I learned that no one in my class was going to this other school, even though several of them had been approved.

I slowly accepted the idea, as the firmness of Grandmother's resolve on doing what she thought was best for me permeated our relationship. I could cajole her into letting me stay up later some nights, or playing baseball, which she thought was a pastime of ruffians, but on some issues there was no give. She came from the granite state, Vermont, and her resolve could be like her native New England granite. As I thought about this large change in my life style, the thought of a new adventure helped me accept the inevitable. I guess I lived up to the quality of being "adaptive" as my Silent Generation has been described. In reflection, thank God! And, thanks to a caring, visionary, and resolute grandmother, who pushed a dubious, provincial pre-teen down the correct fork in his little road of life.

CHAPTER

6

"And then the whining schoolboy, with his satchel,
And shining morning face, creeping like a snail
Unwillingly to school."
Shakespeare, *As You Like It*

In his seven-year-old Oldsmobile coupe, Uncle Stan and I crept the ten miles from Hartwell to my new school. I didn't yet know that this school would turn out to be such a great influence on my life. As we pulled into the traffic circle of Walnut Hills High School on that September morning in 1941, we found ourselves in a line of cars, all a lot newer than ours. Kids were milling around on the stone steps of a domed brick building that resembled Monticello. Older boys were animatedly talking to older girls, all of whom were dressed differently than the kids back at my grade school. Almost everyone I saw exuded confidence; a comfort level with themselves and their place. I, on the other hand, was full of apprehension about fitting into this apparently sophisticated group. And, I wasn't too sure I had on my "shining morning face."

Unwillingly I got out of the car, new satchel in hand, and at a snail's pace made my way to a group of boys who appeared to be my age. I edged up to an open, smooth-faced boy and said, "Hi, I'm Bob."

He smiled and said, "I'm Paul Tobias. Are you an Effie?"

"Effie?"

"That's what they call seventh-graders."

Paul introduced me to two other boys, David Riechert and Clarence Heldman; they seemed to have known each other for a long time. Later I learned they were all Jewish and had shared elementary school and Temple. This was my first introduction to Jewish kids, several of whom remained my lifelong friends. I had heard the words Hebrew and Jew in my Sunday school classes, but I didn't know what they meant in everyday life. Somewhere in my memory was a nagging thought that they were supposed to be different. But, I knew Jesus was a Jew and I quickly learned that these kids were just like me. The thought that there should be any animosity between us was quickly dispelled. All of these kids seemed to do well in school; better than I did, anyway. I'll always be grateful to Paul for making my first moments in this new society pleasant. His gesture of warmth opened the door for me. It's amazing what just the extension of one's hand can do for another.

In a few weeks I became Clarence's friend. He was dark, squat and well-muscled, and possessed sparkling, black eyes. One day, in a newly formed familiarity and preteen candor, I said, "You look like an ape, I'll call you Ape."

In retaliation he said, "Well you're as tall as a moose, so I'll call you Moose." Both names have stuck for a lifetime. Occasionally he would say to me with tongue in cheek, "Damn you, Moose, what am I going to do when my kids come up to me and say, 'Hey, Ape, can I have a dime?'"

Each day brought new discoveries: a new subject, Latin *(amo, amas, amat)*, names of suburbs I had never known, the elegant casual dress of the upper-classmen, and the deep-seated school spirit felt and expressed by faculty and students alike. I admired the seniors who played football and basketball, acted in plays, sat on the student council, hummed Glen Miller tunes, and jumped into convertibles with good-looking girls after school. The juniors and seniors were members of the "GI generation," so named by Strauss and Howe. Little did any of us know in that September of 1941 how appropriate this name would become.

My schoolmates came to this elite public school from all over the greater Cincinnati area. No one could attend Walnut Hills without having scored above ninety on the entrance exam. Over the years many groups, motivated by I know not what, have tried to have the entrance exam eliminated; but sound-thinking, responsible, and visionary parents and administrators have resisted this and won out. The school has turned out national teachers of the year, Nobel Prize recipients, and leaders in every field; even protester Jerry Rubin, for instance. Founded in 1895, Walnut Hills High School was the first accredited college preparatory school west of the Allegany Mountains.

The diversity at the school was a major part of my education. In provincial Cincinnati, class, parochial, and ethnic lines were fairly well established, so I had had very limited contact with anyone except the mostly lower middle class WASPs with whom I grew up. Catholic kids went to parochial elementary and high schools. Most of the Jewish kids lived in Avondale, and the wealthier and socially elite lived in just four or five suburbs. The economically less fortunate lived in the inner city. But our school drew talented students from all areas of the city, bonding us together with the commonality of high IQs and a desire to excel. As we progressed through the year, the differences in our social, ethnic, religious, racial, and economic backgrounds softened, and we blended into a near harmonious coalition of loyal Walnut Hillers.

From these years I learned that if people are given a common task that requires the entire group for its achievement, differences melt into common bonds and a propinquity that destroys established prejudices. We did, however, have one flaw in our embracing of diversity: swimming classes were segregated into black and white. This practice was thought to be normal in pre-war Cincinnati, where factory locker rooms, bus and train depot restrooms, and many eating and drinking places were segregated. After the war the school eliminated segregated swimming. The citywide prejudices took longer, as evidenced by the race riots in the "long hot summers" of 1967-68, which paralleled those in Detroit, Newark, Plainfield, and Los Angeles.

On my first day as an Effie, I was assigned to a homeroom of other seventh-grade girls and boys. The term Effie was derived from F being the sixth letter of the alphabet. Effies were sixth formers (seventh or lowest grade). Eighth-graders were E's, or fifth formers, but since eighth-graders were sort of in no man's land emotionally, they were dubbed E-flats. Juniors were B's and the seniors were A's. The annual prom for just juniors and seniors was called the B. A. Prom.

On that first day of school, our homeroom teacher handed out the card I dreaded, the one that listed our personal facts, in particular, one's parents. I hid my card from the boy next to me as I wrote the stigmatized word "guardian" after my grandmother's name.

Most of the kids were friendly; we all shared the new adventure of being at a school away from our own neighborhoods. I felt at ease after just few days; even began noticing cute girls, especially Nancy Hattersley. I was excited by the older girls as we passed in the hall. They displayed feminine attributes; so different from the twelve-year-olds in my class. What an excursion into the beautiful state of being in love with womankind! The hairstyles, casual elegance of dress, and poise made me so aware I was male. This manifestation of girls into young women, coupled with the natural hormonal changes in my own body, marked the beginning of a lifelong quest for female companionship and the attendant quenching of desires: spiritual, mental, and physical. I can still see these girls dressed in cashmere sweaters, accented with white, round Peter Pan collars; pleated, plaid skirts; white, turned-over bobby socks; and saddle shoes. Most wore a single strand of pearls, and a black and gold high school sorority pin affixed on a very evident protrusion of the sweater…ah, ah, ah!

The 'hero' upper class males were both idols and mirrors of my self-consciousness at not dressing like them. I compared their saddle shoes and button-down, British-roll collars to my brown, Buster Brown, sharkskin-toed shoes (that provided longer wear), and my childlike round collars. No one in the neighbor-hood I lived in dressed like these high school "knights of the round table." I finally talked my grandmother into a pair of saddle shoes, but never convinced her that wearing white and brown shoes in the winter was appropriate. She was from the Missionary Generation, Strauss and Howe's label for those born between 1860-82, who believed that white shoes and summer dress came out on Memorial Day and were put away on Labor Day regardless of the temperature.

I did some neighborhood grass cutting and leaf raking for a few bucks so I could buy my first button-down shirt. The pull to be part of the herd is a strong one. Luckily, the herd I sought was made up of top students with solid homes. I believe the need I had to be part of that group is not much different than the compulsion that drives neglected kids in depressed neighborhoods to join a gang.

In time, my friends invited me home for a meal or to play after school. Most of them lived in houses like I had never seen before, except in the movies. A few families had maids and furnished their homes in very fine taste. My eyes were opened to what some people could own and enjoy. Several of my friends talked about what they did at "the country club," or where they went to camp in the summer. My "club" was the public playground in front of the Hamilton County Home for the aged, and my summer camp was three days at Scout camp for inter-troop contests.

Slowly I assimilated the various lifestyles and socio-eco levels of my peers, which made me realize that there were better things to be had. My awakening to the broader scope of status and money could be compared to our mythical ancestor Adam's awareness of his nakedness after eating the forbidden fruit. As I daily ate the fruit of knowledge in the classrooms and halls of Walnut Hills, I saw my nakedness in my social rank and lower economic level. There must have been potent seeds in that fruit, because in time they germinated and grew into the "drive toward over compensation tree," which I would eventually climb to drive and sustain my adult life.

I was an ardent worshiper of several seniors. When one of them would smile or even look my way I was elated, especially if the football players said something to me as I passed through the locker room. I would hang out on the steps after school and listen to them talking about girls, the upcoming football game, or just acting neat (the forties equivalent of cool). One senior was particularly nice to me; "Tots" Hinsch, a basketball and baseball player who smiled when we passed in the halls. Fifty-five years later I worked with him on fund-raising. I hadn't seen Tots since he graduated in 1942, but in 1996 we teamed up on the Alumni Foundation to help raise $12,500,000 to build the school's new Arts and Science Wing. Our Foundation was one of the first to raise private money for a public school. I believe this practice will continue to spread in our nation as public school systems are always short of funds. Why? Because school levies are not always passed by the voters, many of whom don't have kids in school anymore. The ever-rising costs of special education programs, as well as the cost of maintaining aging buildings, tap already stretched funds. I think my Silent Generation, as a whole, would build or retro-fit an entire school rather than duplicate a sports stadium with taxpayer money. I know I would.

Little did I think as a timid Effie, that someday I would be working nationwide with 16,000 alums to raise money to sustain and enhance this nurturing facility. I am grateful for the opportunity to put something back into a school whose established values and dedicated teachers steered my life down a rewarding road, even though it had deep holes, rough bumps, and shoulders of despair.

The first minor bump came in my Latin class when my grades started to falter, mainly because I wasn't studying. It seemed that I hadn't totally made the transition from little boy to college prep young man. Each day when I went home to small-town Hartwell, I still wanted to play drugstore-cowboy with my elementary school friends, but it wasn't the same. We didn't talk the same school language. I was moving in a larger and different circle, one of more diversity and wider influence. Eighteenth-century economist, Adam Smith, wrote, "The source of all wealth is sacrifice." I had to face up to it. To benefit from the wealth of Walnut Hills High, I would have to sacrifice my hometown ties and friends. Nothing is gained or taken without something else being surrendered. If we cut the tap root of our home tree, we have to adopt new sources of nourishment: physical, mental, and spiritual. I'm not claiming to be Abraham moving at God's direction "to a promised land," but ten miles from home was a far piece to a naive twelve-year-old. Seventh grade was a series of pendulum swings in ethos from blue-collar Hartwell to sophisticated, erudite Walnut Hills. I did pass Latin, thanks to Grandmother hiring a tutor. Everything has its price and payoff!

A highlight of that year was my first date! The juniors and seniors put on a variety show, complete with Rockette-like, leggy girls, kicking to the skies in their very short skirts and high heels. I asked Nancy to go with me and she accepted! My mother drove us, sat with us, took us out for a coke after the show, and drove Nancy home to her huge, white Colonial house in Amberley Village. That night I was big man on campus when I walked into the auditorium with my petite, pretty mother on one arm, and equally petite and cute Nancy on the other. All I lacked was the '41 Ford convertible like the one a senior hero took his girl home in.

First love may not have the depth or total fulfillment of adult love, but it certainly is beautiful in its innocence and new-found awareness.

On a December Sunday morning, I was getting ready to go to church to serve as crucifer and altar boy when Grandmother called out, "The Japanese have just bombed Pearl Harbor." As she said this I had a flashback to a newsreel showing Japanese bombers, with red circles on their wings, bombing the American gunboat USS Panay in China four years earlier. Grandmother's excited voice meant something big was happening, but I didn't even know where Pearl Harbor was. In church Mr. Attridge said a prayer asking God to guide our country in the days ahead. He directed me to hold up the American flag while the congregation sang *America*. I could see some of the ladies wiping their eyes with little white handkerchiefs.

The next day at school students gathered before class to talk about the sneak attack. A couple of seniors were talking about enlisting. In homeroom we sat quietly as the principal told us that we had indeed declared war on Japan and Germany. He allowed us to hear President Roosevelt's speech to Congress, playing the radio into our public address system. One of my teachers explained the seriousness of the attack. She said the dropping of Japanese bombs, in their well-planned attack, had wiped out a large part of our Pacific Fleet.

Pearl Harbor instantly transformed the sophomores, juniors, and seniors of our school into the GI generation. Many of them would lose their lives defending the freedom, values, and principles upon which our Nation and our school were founded. A bronze board was erected with the names of all the teachers and students who went into the service. In time, gold stars were placed in front of those who had made the ultimate sacrifice. I knew some of them, which brought the war into the halls of our school, yet the war was still abstract because it was so far away. No bombs or artillery shells fell on Cincinnati, nor on any part of America; so to a teen secure in a solid school, the war was "over there."

In 1941 there was no television, only radio and newspapers to inform us about the war. President Roosevelt, in one of his radio "fireside chats" asked all Americans to purchase defense stamps and war bonds to help buy munitions, planes, tanks, and ships. He also asked us to donate every pound we had of waste paper, rubber, and scrap metal. These materials were needed to make the tools of war; the tools we needed to keep America out of enemy hands. Once a week our homeroom teacher gave us a chance to buy defense stamps. They came in ten-and twenty-five-cent denominations. We pasted them in a book, and when we had $18.75 worth, they were converted into a bond that paid $25.00 after seven-and-a-half years. The homeroom that bought the most stamps had its name read by the principal.

My Boy Scout troop, like troops all over the country, was expected to work on scrap metal and paper drives. On Saturday mornings our troop held meetings at the Presbyterian Church in Hartwell. Soon Herschberg, the local waste material dealer, showed up with his open-stake truck. My patrol of six climbed aboard, and we started a house-to-house canvass for either paper or metal. On the metal drives we were often given a souvenir

World War I, German coal bucket helmet. One of us would put it on, making a contrasting picture; an American boy in full khaki scout uniform of knickers, high socks, emblem-decorated shirt, and colorful neckerchief standing at attention with the German helmet and saluting the rest of us. But, while we played and laughed we were hustling scrap. We all hoped the metal we brought in would end up in a cannon barrel that would help America win a battle. After the drive we were tired and dirty, but not too tired to stop at Dudley's drugstore for a fountain cherry coke and a Butterfinger bar.

While we scouts did our part, our country was taking a pasting in that winter of 1941-42. We were losing South Pacific islands, including the Philippines, and losing lives. Many of our soldiers were taken prisoner by the Japanese. German U-boats were sinking a lot of Merchant Marine supply ships in the Atlantic. Despite news censorship we knew our country faced a dark prospect, yet we early teens were insulated by age, distance, and lack of mature experience, and were shielded by a national ethic of "we will prevail." How many times has this creed been tested? How many times is it yet to be? Many enemies, from British Red Coats to subversive terrorists lurking in their murky shadows of deceit and cowardice, have tested us; but the American spirit arises when needed. Americans can cast aside their so-called "soft living" and muster up the courage and determination that carried our forebears across raging seas in tiny, wooden sailing ships.

Our scout troop was told to extinguish gas street lamps on assigned blocks of the neighborhood during blackout drills as a preparation for bombing attacks. I sawed off a wood broom handle to a four-foot length, and drove an eight-penny nail into the stick, bending it into a hook. When the alarm sounded I was to pull the lamp's gas valve lever down with the hook to extinguish the flame.

On the all-clear signal, I pushed the lever up. Fortunately, no Axis or Japanese bombers ever flew over our country. My scout assignments were minor in the big picture, but I felt good about doing them. Grandmother would pat me on the head when I came home from one of my jobs. She knew what war was. She had suffered through two years of worry while Uncle Stan was engaged in several bloody campaigns in France.

Almost everyone in the nation did something to help, from the minor act of saving cigarette-pack tinfoil to the ultimate act of dying on the sandy beach of an island no one had ever heard of. Before the war ended in 1945, more than 10,000,000 people were in the armed services. Their vacated places in civilian jobs, particularly in defense plants, were largely filled by women. These earnest and quickly proficient women did every kind of job: riveting, welding, delicate electronic wiring, lifting, truck driving, aircraft ferrying an unending list. The gals came from every walk of life; farmers, housewives, dancers, nurses, barmaids, and high-society ladies, to name a few. They melded into a work force that out-produced every other nation in the world and gave our men at the fronts the tools to carry out their job of beating the Germans and Japanese in battle.

Pictures of war plants being awarded the Government's "E For Efficiency" flag looked like sorority pictures. Yes, it was a sorority of women, bonded together by a common purpose of helping the cause, and at the same time giving solace and a warm heart to servicemen. Many of these dedicated women had given up a husband, lover, son, nephew, niece, daughter, or friend to the services, while they worked countless hours of tiring overtime to turn out the materials that enabled us to prevail. The movement of women from the home to the workplace changed the roles of both men and women forever. Defense plants became a showcase of the new contributions women could make. "Barefoot, pregnant, and in the kitchen" was gone forever.

Despite all of our helpful activities, my Silent Generation and I were never exposed directly to the grim reality of war casualties unless someone we knew was killed in battle. At the movies, we saw newsreel pictures showing the death camps of Hitler's "pure Aryan" regime and the calloused horror of his "final solution." In arrogance beyond comprehension, he had targeted all people of Jewish descent, as well as gypsies and homosexuals for annihilation throughout Europe. The horrid news of his "work" did not reach our teenage world until near the end of the war.

For the war years of '41 to '45 we pretty much carried on a normal student life. Many basic items became in short supply because the demand by the services and armament producers had top priority. We learned to live with the shortages, adapting because there was no choice. The war dictated the rationing of gasoline, meat, sugar, canned goods, shoes, and whiskey, coupled with a scarcity of cigarettes and silk stockings (nylon hadn't been perfected yet). America's never-ceasing search for beauty aids produced liquid, skin-hued leg make-up. Some girls even learned to paint a seam line on the backs of their shapely gams! Painted legs were ersatz, to be sure, but good enough to draw a desirous look and whistle from passing males.

A new entity formed in every community: the ration board, which took its seat alongside the draft board. These associations were ruled by Federal guidelines and rules, but were decentralized. If someone went for clarification about their allotment of ration stamps, or to verify their draft status, they might see their plumber, dentist, minister, neighbor, or schoolteacher as the administrator. Stamps and stickers were issued for rationed items; when we bought something, we surrendered the required number of stamps, which meant we had to budget our eating, clothing, and the most difficult item, gasoline. The A sticker, the lowest category of gas allotment, was for four gallons a week, about eighty miles. Defense workers, doctors, and clergy received B and C stickers, which entitled them to a higher allotment.

Through radio, newsreels, and papers, we followed the progress of the war. We heard and saw descriptions of invasions from LSTs, tank duels, naval battles, air strikes, and battles in African deserts, Italian mountains, and coral reefs in the Pacific, but these places were far removed from Cincinnati and the continental United States. When an alumni, friend, or family member was killed, however, it was not a remote event. Knowing who had been killed made me feel both sad and lucky. In time "lucky" would turn to twinges of guilt; I had been spared fighting in the war due to age, but should I have been a part of it? Had I missed out?

We members of the Silent Generation seemed to have had little voice at the time. We would be heard from later, in the aftermath of a war that took an estimated fifty million lives. We would speak silently, through actions, in the rebuilding of a devastated world, and in healing the raw wounds of racial prejudice exposed in the conflict of World War II. At the beginning, African Americans were relegated to menial jobs; cook's helpers, quartermaster truck loaders, and clean-up workers, but not allowed to "fight." At the end of the war, due to protests, African Americans were distinguishing themselves in every branch and type of combat. But, this change was not without resentment and white-race-placed obstacles. There were similar segregation practices in defense plants; for example, riots erupted in Detroit factories over the lack of equality. The war didn't do much for racial equality, but it did expose the tender quick of America's skin which the Silent

Generation inherited from its forebears. We couldn't fight the bullet war, but we could fight the war against prejudice.

*   *   *

My eighth-grade year didn't seem like much; I sometimes feel thirteen-year-olds are nondescript in-betweens. More Scouts, Knothole baseball, and another tough year in Latin are all I can remember, except for that other big date with Nancy. In the forties there were high school fraternities and sororities. We had plenty of parent chaperones and, on the whole, we kids conducted ourselves with proper decorum. As I approached the end of my eighth-grade year, many of my friends were two years older than I and belonged to BOA, one of the top fraternities. I was invited, as a potential freshman pledge, to attend their spring dance. My mother drove us this time also, but did not go into the Pavilion Caprice ballroom at the hotel. She came to pick us up after the dance. I was a stiff dancer and lacked the conversational skills of movie idol Cary Grant. Luckily Nancy didn't smoke, so I didn't have to perform the romantic and intimate lighting of two cigarettes like Paul Heindich in *Now Voyager*. I quickly inhaled a couple of cigarettes on trips to the rest room, because I didn't know her views on smoking. We survived the evening, with me rarely stepping on her toes. Twice we danced to *Moonlight Becomes You*, which tune I whistled all that next summer before my freshman year. Nancy was, and still is, sweet, considerate of others, and enthusiastic. As her husband Frank said to me one day, fifty-four years after that dance, as my wife and I were playing golf with them, "You know, if anyone can't get along with Nancy, they need to look in the mirror." I agreed.

As a freshman I was neither a little boy nor a man, but I saw myself as more mature than I really was. Suddenly I was a member of BOA, elated at being accepted and wondering why I was chosen. My humble home on the B & O railroad tracks was hundreds of social miles from those of my cotillion-set brothers. Maybe my acceptance paralleled the horse race practice of periodically breeding a sturdy plug into the highly developed but potentially fragile thoroughbred strain.

While I was trying to grasp, with a minimum of study, the three R's (algebra, English, Latin, and social studies), I was also learning about the three B's – not Bach, Beethoven, and Brahms as Grandmother would have preferred – but ball, beer, and broads (forgive the crude term for girls, but the alliteration demands it). Then there were the three S's: smoking, snoofing (our high school term for necking), and socializing.

My poor grades and late weekend hours started to take their toll on my seventy-eight-year-old grandmother. Her heart medicine had been increased, and I saw the deepening lines in her aging face. I was a self-centered fourteen-year-old, striving for identity and peer acceptance. I was not as aware of her condition as I should have been. Everything in my life at that moment was about trying to achieve acceptance and identity. Noted psychologist Abraham Maslow has written in his hierarchy of needs that when man has satisfied his three basic needs of food, shelter, and sex, he seeks the higher needs of acceptance/security of belonging, and recognition. The highest need, self-actualization, is usually not met until later in life. Being on the freshman football team helped a little with needs four and five, as did my fraternity membership.

We freshman football players often scrimmaged against the varsity team, mostly seniors who were heroes to me. One guy in particular, Jack Beyersdorfer, class of '44, was a three-sport star. He played fullback as I did, and had helped Walnut Hills win many games. One day in a practice scrimmage I was called to run the ball against the varsity when Jack was playing strong side line-backer. When I got the ball, I put my head down and headed for the line. Thanks to a good block by my friend, five-by-five Ape, I got through and headed for Jack. He made a dive at my ankles, but slipped. I brushed by him saying, for what reason I don't know, "Oh no you don't, big guy." On the next play he clobbered me! Afterward in the locker room I started to apologize for my brash yell, but he stopped me and said, "You got guts, kid." I couldn't have felt better if I had been anointed by the gods of football. I saw Jack at a reunion fifty-one years later, where he said, "Ya wanna try that run again?" I hugged him and said, "You're still my hero." He died in 1996, but his sports records still stand at our school. A champion is always a champion.

The next B was beer. The beer-drinking group drove convertibles, lived in wealthy sections of town, and dressed well. To a provincial from the Mill Creek Valley these guys, and a few girls, became something to emulate and join. Coupled with a host of movies showing suave couples smoking and drinking, it was a doorway to what I thought I desired.

The next course in my non-academic education was girls. I won't use the vulgar term broads, because I have never thought of women in that way. I truly revere them. I'm fairly certain my reverence for women originated with the love and nurturing given me by two grandmothers and a mother whom I deeply longed for and loved. I have never received anything but kindness and love from all of the women I have known.

There's a popular country western song titled *To All the Girls I've Loved Before.* When I hear Willie Nelson and Julio Iglesias sing it, I think back to my freshman year: Nancy, Sonny, Mary Lee, Patty, Woozy, Jean, Marilyn, and Terry. I thought my fraternity pin should be shared with every girl I took out, until I was called on the carpet by my fraternity and had to promise to be more discreet.

Feeding on the success I had with girls, regardless of age, I developed a conceit that was fast-food for my identity search. Like fast-food, it was not nourishing. I had no trouble being served beer in many cafes because of my mature looks; this also fed my shallow, but soon-to-crash, ego trip. By the end of my freshman year, I can attest to the validity of the cliché that says, "You can't get something for nothing." The price I paid for too much heavy dating and petting, plus my consumption of mind-deadening beer, was a six-week stint in summer school to make up Algebra I and Latin. When I told Grandmother this, she said a phrase I always disliked, "Those that dance must pay the piper."

C H A P T E R

7

"Example is the school of mankind, and they will learn at no other."
Edmund Burke, 1729-1797

On the first day of my sophomore year at Walnut Hills High School, I walked down the halls between the rows of dark green steel lockers, carrying both my books and the weight of my freshman year. The onus of failures in two school subjects, in my behavior, and in establishing an acceptable reputation melded into a burden very heavy for an undisciplined fifteen-year-old. I also knew I had heavily taxed the health of my seventy-eight-year-old grandmother by my wild and wasteful ways.

Stinging from the realization that I had not measured up, I started to muster a determination to redirect my life. When I reflected on my freshman year and laid it next to my grandmother's values and those of our school, embodied in its motto of *Sursum ad Summum* (rise to the highest), I knew I was wrong. I had no one to share this with and I wasn't mature enough to seek guidance, so as usual I looked inward and made my decision. I would try harder in school and be less of a worry to Grandmother.

Today I realize that my steps on the road of my freshman year were not made on the proscribed pavement, but in the tangle of roadside burrs and briars. As I tore my way along this self-chosen and thorny route, I stopped to eat both the fruit and tares of life's orchards. I thanked Adam for eating the fruit of the tree of knowledge, because by his act he imbued us with the knowledge of right and wrong. And like Adam, I learned some of life's lessons from my indiscretions: the tares of drinking, goofing off in my studies; and being consumed with my pursuit of girls. As twenties tennis star Bill Tilden once said, "Champions are born in the labor of defeat." Here's hoping!

I wasn't able to play football because my failure in two subjects made me, by a very sound school rule, ineligible for a semester; another price I paid for my wild year. With no football, no current flame, and a smarting urgency I spent hours every night on my homework; a new experience! On some nights my grandmother would call to me to see if I was all right as I was translating an account of Julius Caesar leading his mighty phalanxes on a foray into Gaul. I knew she was gratified to see me working this way. One Monday night, several weeks into my sophomore year, I had to prepare a report on Robert Koch for my physiology class. Koch, the nineteenth-century German bacteriologist and physician: had located the bacterium that produces anthrax. He also developed a vaccine to prevent it in cattle, and anthrax became a thing of the past, that is until the bio-terrorists of the twenty-first century began to emit it from their spores of hate.

When I thought I had a polished presentation I asked Grandmother to listen to my ten-minute report. She sat on a chair in the hall and I stood on the stair landing, the same landing that Bishop Hobson and many priests had stood on while Grandmother measured their albs, chasubles, and cassocks. I could not know on that night that in a few days the bishop would again stand there. I made my report and saw Grandmother's face relax into a soft and satisfied smile. "That's good, Bobby. I'm very tired tonight, so I'm going to bed. Don't work too late."

I beamed as I saw her faint smile when she looked at me. "Okay. I just need a few more minutes on my plane geometry."

"I'm proud of the way you are taking ahold of your studies. Goodnight," she said as she passed me on the stairs, pausing to kiss my cheek. As she turned, I noticed the lump in the hollow of her neck pulsating rapidly. She climbed the remaining steps in a halting manner. An hour later I went to bed, after listening to a half hour of Kay Kyser's "College of Musical Knowledge" on our table model Philco radio.

The next thing I knew Grandmother was standing over me as I awoke, with the morning light barely seeping around the drawn, green window shades. "Bobby, get up, quickly. I don't feel well, help me!" she gasped and started to fall toward me. I swung out of bed, grabbing her frail arm, propping her up while I led her to the big rocker in her sitting room. I eased her into the chair, where she sagged, her face an ashen gray-white.

"Can I get you anything?" I stammered.

Her eyes opened, but nothing came from her slack mouth. She just looked at me with a sad, forlorn, but yearning look. I ran to the telephone, got a number from the alphabetical desk pad, and called Dr. McGowan. I told him what was happening. He said he'd be over as soon as he could drive the eight miles from his home in Bond Hill. I went back to Grandmother, who pointed to a small bottle of pills on her table. I gave her a pill. The doorbell rang. I leapt down the stairway and let the doctor in. I pointed to the stairs, which he took two at a time.

When I joined him at Grandmother's side he was listening to her heart with his stethoscope and looking into her eyes, the lids of which he had pushed back. He turned to his black bag and extracted a hypodermic syringe and needle. "Put these in a pan of water and boil them. When the water boils, bring them to me—in the pan." He took the sterilized syringe and filled it with a fluid.

He pulled her nightshirt sleeve up and injected the fluid into her arm. She rolled her eyes and again fixed them on me. Her thin, blue-pink lips started to move as I put my face near hers to hear. I heard nothing, but her hand touched mine with a barely perceptible half squeeze, then it fell to her side, and her eyes glazed over while her tired, frail body sagged to the side of the chair.

Old Dr. McGowan, who had tended to my dad before he went to the hospital, had cared for Grandmother for thirty years, set my broken arm, and helped all of our family, patted my shoulder. "She's gone, Bob." I just stood there looking at Grandmother's now lifeless body. After a while he said, "Let's lift your grand-mother to the bed." I'd guess she weighed ninety-eight pounds.

Uncle Stan, just home from his graveyard shift at the distillery, came up the stairs. He knew Dr. McGowan's car when he saw it parked in front of the house at seven-thirty in the morn-ing. He knew it was the sign of something bad.

He met Dr. McGowan in the upstairs hall. "It's Mom?"

"Yes, a stroke and heart failure. I'm sorry, Stan, she's gone.

"Did she just go? Did she suffer?"

"No, she went quickly. Stan, for my records, how old is she?"

"Seventy-nine next month."

"She was a brave lady. Her spirit probably kept her alive longer than most doctors would have predicted."

"She was always that way."

"Can you make the funeral arrangements, or should I help?"

"I…I will. I'll call Vorhees in Lockland."

While Uncle Stan and Dr. McGowan were talking I just looked at Grandmother, thinking how during the last two years I'd been hard to handle; but I also remembered our working together on my Robert Koch assignment last night, and how pleased she had been.

I didn't know what to do. I stood there as a wave of all the feelings I had experienced so many times before flooded my mind and body. The same repression and numbness I felt when my dad died invaded me again.

Uncle Stan put his arm around me. "Bobby, what do you want to do?"

I thought about what Grandmother would have wanted me to do. "I guess I'll go to school."

"Okay. I'll be here when you get home."

I put on a light blue oxford cloth, button-down collar shirt and tied my navy blue knit tie. Next came the sharply creased gray flannels and the navy and white saddle shoes, all bought with forty-cent-an-hour drug store wages. I guess in my bewilderment and unprocessed grief, I concentrated on the first everyday task I could turn to. When I glanced in the mirror I felt I had done as Grandmother always advised and "put my best foot forward." I enjoy remembering what I wore that day as I walk today through twenty-first century high schools and colleges. The garb I see is a full-spectrum extremity from "the good old days." I often think of what Grandmother said about this, "Clothes do not make the man." Well, maybe not entirely.

I hitchhiked to school and explained my tardiness to the assistant principal, who was sympathetic. But he did ask me, "How shall we list your guardian now?" There it was: stark in-your-face reality. I fidgeted and indicated I didn't know. He told me not to worry and to stop back when it was resolved.

The day was a haze in which I floated through classes and skipped lunch in favor of two Lucky Strikes. After my smoke in the school's designated area, I called my mother. Uncle Stan had already called her. She said she'd pick me up after school and drive me home. A desire and fantasy began to evolve—would I be able to live with my mother? When she arrived, she was warm and consoling. I still didn't know exactly how she felt about Grandmother, but she said only good things about her as we sat in the parking lot at school. When we reached Hartwell, she told me she would be seeing a lot more of me. She said I should help Uncle Stan with the funeral and think about what I was going to do. We would talk the next day about the future. I kissed her goodbye and said I wanted to be with her. "I love you, Son. We'll talk tomorrow. I'll be there at supper time."

I went into the house where I found a note from Uncle Stan saying he was at the funeral home. I went up to Grandmother's sitting room where I had held her as she died. It was one day short of the demise of summer, and the western sun was beaming into the window making the room mellow with sunshine. But the sun always casts a shadow, and in the shadows of the room were so many memories of what Grandmother and I had shared. Images of her nursing me through chicken pox and measles, and of her helping me with knotty, fourth-grade, long-division problems. I could see her sitting at her desk writing to various bishops and priests about their vestments, always sealing the envelope with blue sealing wax, and an imprinted C in English script.

I touched the big rocker, thinking back to my early days when we sat together there and she read to me from Sheherazade's tales of *The Arabian Nights*. I sat down in the rocker and looked at the books on the side table: *The Book of Common Prayer, Anthony Adverse*, and Hemingway's *Death in the Afternoon*. How ironic: instead it had been death in the early morning.

I could see Grandmother in every corner and I started to cry. I was now old enough to know all that she had done for me and all that she stood for. Every memory was a recasting of her acts, always done for my benefit. She provided comfort, love, instruction, healing, and tireless efforts to guide me onto a path of right action. I heard a slow freight passing. Its steady chuck-chuck seemed to echo, "Bobby, believe in God and get ahead." The sun had set, the room was no longer warm with its glow, but the image of my extraordinary grandmother would never set below the horizon of time. Her example was the greatest schooling of my life.

*   *   *

That night, Uncle Stan and I talked about how we would live. The paltry sum he earned at the distillery didn't leave much for my support. I could go back to working part time at Abe's Drug Store, but when I did that in my freshman year, my grades had suffered. Grandmother's salary from the Episcopal Diocese was gone and Stan's estimate of her "estate" was low. The house carried an over fifty-percent mortgage with the government-backed Home Owners Loan Corporation. On the unresolved note of our future, we went to bed. I guess the catharsis of my afternoon crying made sleep easy.

The next day I began to realize how much Walnut Hills meant to me. Grandmother's death sharpened my focus on what still remained that I could cling to. Other than my daily relationship with her, my school was the main stabilizer, the rock of my life. It was a steady, always-there base of values, rules, guidance, and most importantly, community; a solid brick house in which to live. My classmates and my dedicated teachers were the mortar that held the bricks together. Walnut Hills, and all that it stood for, was a constant in a world mortally consumed in World War II and filled with my personal challenges. I remembered my sixth-grade protestations about going to this school so far from home, and my grandmother saying, "You must go, and someday you will thank me." She was right. Walnut Hills was my new home.

Fifty years later the school is still a solid base for me. I have been blessed more than once with the opportunity to work on the Alumni Foundation with its capable executive director, Debbie Heldman, and alums from a myriad of classes ranging from 1932 to the mid-nineties. We envision, fund raise, and support a continuum of projects that sustain and enhance this one-hun-dred-and-six-year-old bastion of values and academic excellence. Thank you, Grandmother Laurie, for making me go to Walnut Hills.

Not sure of how or where I would live, I reached out for solace. I saw former girlfriend Sonny Theiler in the lunch room, eating alone. I stopped by her table. "How are you, Sonny?"

She blushed, "Fine, Chris, how are you?"

I sat with her and told her about Grandmother's death.

She reached across the table and took my hand. "I'm sorry, Chris. Tell me about her, please."

I told her about my home life, which before that day I had always been reluctant to share. She listened as I talked, always looking into my eyes. I felt better after our talk, and asked her if I could walk her to her next class. She said I should call her that night. I was touched by her warmth, which she gave me so spontaneously. I was afraid that she would be afraid to be close to me since I had dropped her for another girl during the previous school year. There wasn't a hint of rancor or reticence in her attitude toward me. She truly carried out forgiveness and compassion. Every night for the next week we talked at least a half-hour on the phone. After Grandmother's funeral I started hitchhiking to her house in Hyde Park for a "parlor date." Her parents were always polite and left the downstairs to us, where we drank Coke, ate cookies, shuffled on the rug to *Dancing In The Dark*, and snuck in a little necking, always punctuated with some fake coughs for her parents' benefit. Sonny helped relieve some of my grief.

The day after her death, Grandmother was viewed at the funeral home. Uncle Stan had taken care of everything, even picking out Grandmother's favorite plum-colored dress and a single gold brooch. I steeled myself from crying as I looked at her peace-filled face in the ecru, sateen-lined coffin. My mother stayed at the funeral home with me for the two hours. I had to talk with many people, including a lot of clergy for whom Grandmother had made vestments. When the funeral home director indicated it was time to close, Mother asked Uncle Stanley and me if we could talk at our house.

Mother said that she had been working on how and where I should live. She said that now that I was fifteen I could choose. Any previous custody agreements were altered by my grandmother's death. I just sat there listening, alert for what I wanted to hear.

"Chrisee, everyone in the family loves you. You've got several choices. You can stay here with Uncle Stan, which might be hard for him. Or Grandmother Allan says you can live with her on Mystic Avenue. Then Uncle Edwin and Aunt Jane say that you can come to Long Island and live with them. And," she paused and touched my hand, "you can come live with me and Uncle Charles. Which...."

"I'll come live with you!"

With a smile, and some tears, she hugged me sighing, "Thank God."

Uncle Stan looked solemn, disappointed, and wistful. He put his hand on my shoulder, "Yeah, Bobby, I guess that's best. I'll miss you."

Mother said quickly, "He can come and visit, Stan, maybe stay overnight on a weekend."

We agreed I'd move to upper middle class North Avondale on Saturday, two days after Grandmother's funeral. I was excited about being with my mother, and in a neighborhood with no train tracks running through it. I would be more like the other kids at school and in my fraternity. The vision of a more conventional home, plus the rock-solid foundation of Walnut Hills High, made my spirits soar. One door closes and another door opens.

I stayed home from school on Thursday, the first day of fall and the day of Grandmother's funeral. It was clear, bright, and sunny. Fall was always my favorite season, although it has often been poetized as bittersweet. It offers the sweetness of harvest time and trees painted with Nature's warm colors of russet and gold, juxtaposed against the bitterness of dying flowers, the approach of winter, and the end of summer. Maxwell Anderson's words in *September Song* tell us how "...the days grow short when you reach September." For me, the fall of 1944 offered the sweetness of being able to live with my mother, laced with the bitterness of losing the woman who had nurtured me and given me so much love for ten years.

The church service at Holy Trinity was scheduled for one o'clock. At twelve, a long black car pulled up in front of our house. A tall, handsome man carrying a black valise came up the walk. I recognized him. It was Bishop Henry Wise Hobson, who had confirmed me three years earlier, and whom Grandmother and I had visited with so many times at the Cathedral or at our house for vestment fittings. He rang the bell and I let him in. He said he wanted to conduct Grandmother's funeral out of respect for all she had done for him and the diocese. We were surprised, as Bishops did not normally bury rank and file parishioners; of course Uncle Stan said Grandmother would be pleased and that we were honored. The bishop put his vestments on at our house and said he would give us a ride to the church. When he was vested he stood on the landing where he had so often before and asked, with a twinkle in his eye, "How's the hemline?"

Tongues in our parish wagged for months afterwards about the bishop coming out to Hartwell to bury old Laurie. There was a mixture of approval, respect, and twinges of envy. Grandmother was a doer, often unsung in her quiet, effective, and dedicated manner. She had served Holy Trinity for years on the altar guild, as a representative to conventions in the diocese, and as a Sunday school teacher. But every church seems to have a sprinkling of people who resent those who do things and are recognized for it. Organized religion is a great institution; sometimes the fallibility of human nature sours it.

My mother joined Uncle Stanley, Uncle Edwin, Aunt Jane, and me in our family pew. In the center aisle, Grandmother's gray felt coffin sat in the same place my father's had six years earlier. The bishop's eulogy was beautiful. He told of her deep faith and her many acts of service to God and the diocese. He also mentioned my saying I would be starting a new phase of my life, and that he was sure I would be carrying many of the values Grandmother had represented.

I rode to the graveyard with Mother, and we talked about my moving into her house. I was excited about the room I would have and the small study she would make for me in the loft. I couldn't believe I was going to awake every morning and go to bed every night with my mother in the same house. The sadness of losing Grandmother was with me, but I was so elated about my new life.

Grandmother was going to rest between her husband and my father, her beloved son, whom she had mourned so deeply. I was asked to drop a few clods of dirt on the half-lowered casket as the bishop read "dust to dust, and ashes to ashes." A breeze blew through the trees above, making some of the gold and red leaves slowly flutter onto the casket. Yes, the days had grown short in that bittersweet September.

CHAPTER

8

*"We hold the period of youth sacred to education,
and the period of maturity...."*
Edward Bellamy, 1850-1898

"Time to get up, Chrisee."

I fought my way out of the cobwebs of sleep trying to figure out where I was and who I was hearing. The strange sounds penetrating my foggy state were ones I couldn't remember having heard. Finally, the veil lifted. There was my smiling mother sitting on the edge of my bed. For the first time since age four, I experienced the pleasant and assuring realization that I was once again with my mother. I had just awakened from the first night at my new home in North Avondale. Here I would live with my mother and her second husband, Charles Biscay. We had agreed I would call him "Pop." My nineteen-month-old half-brother, "Buzz," was also there. I looked around the room, taking in the furnishings, then back to Mother's unlined, thirty-six-year-old face. I felt a swell of warmth; a new segment of my life was beginning. The years of living with Grandmother and Uncle Stan by the B & O tracks were replaced by a home with a mother, no railroad in front of the house, and even some of my Walnut Hills schoolmates down the street. Like a cicada, I was shedding my outer shell. Good-bye to "the boy from the wrong side of the tracks" with no mother or father at home. Little did I know on that happy morning that, like the cicada, I would go through this molting process several more times before I matured and gained partial mastery of my soul.

A couple of days later I met my neighbor, Bobby Stix, who was one year ahead of me at school. Like most of our neighbors, Bobby was Jewish. In fact, North Avondale was more than ninety percent Jewish. I saw no difference between us. Still, as I was assimilated into the neighborhood I picked up on the subtle, defensive demeanor many Jewish kids exhibited—a form of humorous self-deprecation. This defensive mantle was understandable in view of centuries of persecution by popes, Spanish royalty, Catholic and Protestant Christians, Hitler's "master Aryan race" ideology, Semite Arabs, and even Babbitt-like chairmen of country club membership committees—"and what was your mother's maiden name, Mr. Green?" Their reluctance to trust the goyim who surrounded them is understandable.

I'd heard the crucifixion story many times, but I also remember Grandmother telling me that the Hebrews had given the world the concept of a single god, and that God had given the commandments to Moses. I learned that we both prayed to "The God of Abraham, Isaac, and Jacob." Jews were not only a part, but actually the founders of my religion, and now they were a big part of my community. Walnut Hills High attracted diverse religions, nationalities, and races. The mixture of cultures and economic ranks taught me and thousands of my Silent Generation that the hateful, destructive walls of prejudice were wrong. In all honesty, I'd have to say I learned more about tolerance at school than I ever did in church.

I've already said that being born and raised in the abyss of the Depression ingrained deep compassion into the Silent Generation and made us a vanguard in the movement for civil rights and more tolerance in postwar America. World War II proved that the blood shed by Jews, Native Americans, Asians, and African Americans, as well as Anglo Christians in defense of our country, was all the same color; it contained the same red and white corpuscles. The mourning for those who died, regardless of race, nationality, or religion, connected those left behind with the common denominator of grief.

To my joy, Bob's dad Nathan drove us to school in his green Cadillac convertible. In time "Nate" became almost an adopted uncle and I became *mishpokhe* (extended family) to the Stixes. Bobby's older brother Charlie was a Marine in the South Pacific. My mother's brother Tom was also in the Marines, but I wasn't sure where. In that September of 1944, the war was still raging in both Europe and the South Pacific. My Uncle Craig, of dime-novel collecting fame, was stationed in the Marshall Islands. He sent me his navy peacoat, unnecessary in the 100-degree island heat. It had official navy anchors on the buttons, and wearing it made me the envy of my friends.

By the end of 1944 the Allies were winning the war, yet there was grim work ahead before it would be completely over. The Battle of the Bulge had just been successfully concluded after General McAuliffe's famous Christmas Day reply of "Nuts" to the Germans who asked for his surrender while the 101st Airborne was surrounded in Bastogne, Belgium. From that point on, the Germans were in steady retreat until their own surrender less than five months later. Many South Pacific islands, including the

Philippines, had been retaken, and much of the Japanese navy had been decimated. Regular bombings of the Japanese mainland and key German industrial cities were relentlessly carried out.

While the killing raged in Europe and the South Pacific, the home front was at peak production. Almost every American was contributing in some way; big jobs, little jobs, direct work and indirect work; but all melded together into a unified effort to supply and support our fighting forces. My Silent Generation mates were volunteering in hospitals, where we carried food trays into the patients. I did this with the "Ape," Dickie Weiland, and Paul Tobias. Military service had taken numerous hospital workers, either through volunteering or the selective service draft. Many girls, including my future wife Marty worked in the maternity wards, where they would hold and care for the newly born.

SOLDIERS *without guns*

The nation was adapting to the rationing of many things that were taken for granted before the war: gas, meat, sugar, canned goods, rubber, shoes, and liquor. The rationed item that was the toughest to cope with was gasoline. If you wanted to "double date," and the other guy had the car, you had to come up with a gas stamp. We learned we could buy benzene, which burns hotter and faster than gas, without a stamp, so we'd buy four gallons of gas and three of benzene. Not the best thing for the car, but it gave us a few extra miles.

My one questionably ethical act during the war concerned cigarettes. Cigarettes were not rationed, just very scarce, because tons of them were being sent to the soldiers. Acting on a tip I overheard on the streetcar, I went to a place on Peeble's Corner one day after school. A blank window and door faced me, and I entered an equally blank room, save for an empty counter. I stood there, rocking back and forth in my saddle shoes, and then called timidly, "Anybody here?" A swarthy, wispy man came through a single door in the wall-to-wall partition. He looked like his latest bath might have been last month. A burning cigarette dangled from his thin-lipped mouth. Through the door behind him, I could see hundreds of stacks of popular-brand cigarettes.

"Whatta ya want, kid?"

"I…uh, I uh want to buy some cigarettes."

"Ya old enough to smoke?'

"Uh, yes I am."

"Yeah, how'd ya find us?"

"Some old guy told me."

"Okay, whatta ya want?"

"Three cartons of Luckies."

"Nine dollars. Money on the counter first."

"Here," I said as I pushed nine singles (three weeks

allowance) across the counter, where his hairy hand with dirt-packed fingernails snatched it up. He disappeared into the back. The door opened again a couple of inches, and a blonde with frizzy hair peeked out. The man came back with the cigarettes. The legitimate retail price had been a dollar fifty per carton, so I was paying double, or thirty cents a pack. But at school, I sold them for forty-five cents a pack. I liked the fifty percent profit on the nine-dollar investment.

I guess I never felt much guilt after I saw all the cigarettes the monkeylike man and his blonde had siphoned out of the distribution system. Today I'd pass on this activity, but at fifteen, with a never-satisfied need for date money, cigarettes, and clothes, I thought I was quite industrious. On future trips to the cigarette store the man called me, "The Lucky Strike Kid." After six months the smokes shortage disappeared and my "business" fell apart; my first lesson in the irrefutable law of Supply and Demand.

*　　　　*　　　　*

I made a lot of references at school to having a mother and a pop at home. I was bursting to tell everyone that I was like them. Around my friends I'd always add comments such as, "my mother did this for me," or "we all went to the movie," or "my parents chaperoned a fraternity meeting at our house." Belonging is paramount to most of us, particularly teenagers swimming up the river of peer pressure and striving for identity. My new home life was helping me feel more like my schoolmates, yet, at times I would suddenly feel like a small child separated from his guardian in a large crowd. It was a sense of floating in a nether land, wondering where and who I was. Somehow I always returned from these moments of doubt to a renewed awareness of my mother's love.

My school was another rock to cling to. My resolve to do better, which I had adopted before Grandmother's death, was still with me. However, this determination was sorely tested almost every day. Geometric propositions, the chicanery of Macbeth, the excursions of Caesar and his centurions into Gaul, and the intricacies of the human endocrine system in physiology class were challenged by girls, making the baseball team, girls, holding a fraternity office, girls, scrounging up money, and girls. To this day, I have not yet told our three grown sons that my social skills and knowledge of human nature were acquired from intermixing with the entire spectrum of richest to poorest, and the breadth of religious and racial presences at my high school. This benefited me at least as much as the academic subjects. I stressed to my children that studies should always come first as in, "Do as I say...."

Of course, there is a cost to everything, and my social life was sometimes at the expense of studying. But, I was passing all my subjects and even boasted an A in physiology. Sciences were my best courses; I had a vague ambition of becoming a doctor. My skills in drawing, however, were a minus ten. So when I needed to make an illustration for physiology or zoology depicting a glandular system or specimens from the various phyla, such as protozoa, amoebas, and paramecia, Mother, who was very artistic, lent a hand to her older son. She was so often there to help me, while juggling the sometimes not-so-subtle tensions of a household with my stepfather, an infant son, and the very active life of her new "boarder."

Growing up with my grandmother, who balanced the rigors of the Depression, while caring for her adult sons and raising a headstrong grandson, and then moving in with my mother, who was doing an emotional tight wire act, imbued me with a great respect for women. I have always liked sports and going around with my male buddies, but girls—women—get my first place vote. I guess I was a '40s feminist for decades before Gloria Steinem, NOW, and the ERA. A few years after I married, I realized most of the girls I had ever pursued bore a slight resemblance to one of the influential women in my life.

Two weeks after I moved to Mother's, one of my fraternity brothers gave a party in his recreation room, where I met Patricia Pease. A quick glance reminded me of my grandmother. She said she had transferred to Walnut Hills from Hillsdale, a private girl's school, because she felt isolated. I interpreted her reason to mean: no boys. We danced to *I'll Walk Alone*, *Begin the Beguine*, and the poignant *I'll Be Seeing You*. I asked her for a date, and she said, "We'll see," which two phone calls later changed to "Okay." That first meeting ignited a tempestuous romance of nightly calls, weekend dates, and frequent warm kisses. This trysting lasted until the spring of 1945, when I met Betty Huttenbauer, a dark-haired Jewish girl, two years my senior.

If I had to come up with a single word to describe Betty, it would be gracious. She had the ability to make everyone in a group feel comfortable. She never made distinctions about religion, race, or economic level; she saw each person as someone to be accepted. I never saw her become ruffled; she was always in control. In later life she did volunteer counseling at Longview

mental health hospital, and then at a Roman Catholic girls school.
I liked the advice she gave to the young, uniformed girls, who had,
or thought they had, done something wrong. After listening (and
she was an excellent listener) she would say, "Think about what
you will do from this day forward." She felt what was past was
gone; what was important was living and doing right from that day
forward. Her advice combined the Jewish spirit of *Yom Kippur*
with the Christian tenet of redemption. Betty was exhibiting the
tolerance our Silent Generation worked to establish. What better
example than a devout Jewess working with Roman Catholic girls?

Betty and her husband John, a Walnut Hills grad and a
WW II combat naval officer, are still my good friends more than
fifty years later. Betty and I played tennis, went to dances, and took
trips to her farm in the six months before she went away to college. We shared V-J Day, when World War II ended with the
Japanese surrender after the second atom bomb was dropped.
Betty threw a party for our gang at which I was the only Gentile,
at her second home, a horse farm north of Cincinnati, whose barn
boasted a tack room nicer than my living room.

Celebration of the war's end brought people out of their
homes by the millions. In downtown Cincinnati, Fountain Square
(our equivalent of New York's Times Square) was black with
jostling, singing, happy people. Some, after a few drinks, were
climbing the thirty-foot fountain statue, while others freely kissed
the person next to them. Surprisingly, there was little destruction
to human limb or property.

In the spring of 1945, America was winning the war against Japan, but to actually conclude it, invasion of the Japanese home-land seemed inevitable. The build-up of men and material was in full swing. Men were being staged in Australia and other islands in the South Pacific. Casualties estimated from this invasion topped a million. But extraordinary science from Albert Einstein ($E=MC^2$) and Robert Oppenheimer among others, averted this particular tragedy by enabling the development of the atomic bomb. Its development at Los Alamos brought a sudden end to the conflict. Many still decry its use. But in pragmatic calculations, many more lives were spared, and the advent of the atomic and hydrogen bombs ushered in a new era for the earth and humankind. The previous ages of ice, stone, bronze, and iron—all of history's ages—pale in the blinding flash of nuclear fusion and its by product, the Atomic Age.

It has been said that the high carnage of World War I meant the "loss of innocence" for mankind. Now civilians, like combatants, were at risk from aerial bombs and long-distance shelling. Compared to World War II and its global civilian death toll (nearly twenty-five-million) the earlier war was minor. Repeated bombing of London and other English cities, dozens of German cities, Tokyo (not even counting Hiroshima and Nagasaki) killed millions. To all of these, add the six million lives extinguished in the Holocaust and the slaughter of so many more as the *Wehrmacht* cut its brutal swath across the plains and steppes of Russia. If World War I caused humanity to lose its inno-cence, World War II caused it to lose its soul.

Betty and I had just started going together when I made first-string catcher on the school baseball team. Stepfather "Pop" was happy; he had been a catcher at Columbia University as a col-lege teammate of "Iron Man" Lou Gehrig. I have since wondered why I was allowed to play baseball while so many Americans were dying in the war. This reflection has burned a deep gratitude into my mind and soul to all of those men and women who risked, and often gave, their lives so that I and others could go to school and play baseball. Near the end of the nineteenth century, Rudyard Kipling said, "Lest we forget." I pray we never do.

One afternoon, after we had lost a game to Withrow High, Mother announced that Uncle Tom was home from the Marines, and that he had almost lost his life in March on an aircraft carrier sixty miles off the coast of Japan. We saw him at a family party the next night. He didn't talk too much about what he had been through, but the Cincinnati papers carried his picture and reported a lot of what happened. Tom was on the *USS Franklin* – CV 13, an Essex class carrier. The *Franklin* was a part of Task Force 58, which included carriers, cruisers, and destroyers sent to disable, through carrier-launched bombers, all of the airfields in southern Japan. This tactic was to ensure no air defense of Japanese-held Okinawa, scheduled for invasion by American forces on April 1.

During the attacks on Kyushu, the Japanese threw all of their land-based aircraft at the American carriers. One slipped through the radar screen and dropped two five-hundred-pound bombs through the *Franklin's* wooden flight deck. They exploded in the hanger deck, touching off a series of internal explosions in already-fueled and bomb-laden aircraft ready for launch. One of the bombs hit near the Marines quarters killing twenty-two of the twenty-six Marines. My Uncle Tom happened to be atop, or he too would have been killed. Before the explosions stopped, almost half of the ship's entire force had died. The ship was dead in the water, with a nine-degree list to the starboard. Men were running every-where, trying to put out fires and hose down ammunition stores to keep them from exploding in the intense heat of the fires. Two cruisers came alongside and took survivors off the *Franklin*, and the *USS Pittsburg* pulled the powerless carrier out of the battle zone.

The *Franklin* was able to get up steam and limp in to Ulithi. "Big Ben," as the ship was affectionately named, never returned to service, but she was the most decorated ship in the Navy. Her chaplain, Commander Joseph T. O'Callahan, was the first chaplain ever to be awarded the Congressional Medal of Honor. "Papa Joe" helped Tom get through the trauma of his ship's bombing. He became a beacon of comfort and courage for the remaining crew, heading damage-control parties, administering final rites next to burning pyres of equipment and men, and leading sailors into gun magazines to hose down ammunition. Uncle Tom received a Presidential Citation for jumping into the gunner's seat of a twin Bofors 40 millimeter anti-aircraft gun when the gunner was killed. My Uncle Tom, whom the gossips of Hartwell Avenue referred to as, "that Allan boy, who you know had to get married at eighteen," was also "the Allan boy" who stayed married until his wife's death. He was also a football star, who taught me about playing, and he always had a few bucks, which he didn't really have, for me. He was my hero, and after his picture and the account of the *Franklin's* ordeal was publicized, he became the hero of all the

Hartwell Avenue gossips who now said, "I always liked Tom. I knew he'd do something great."

The summer after my sophomore year, I worked at U.S. Shoe Corporation's Norwood plant. Nate Stix, Vice President of Manufacturing, gave me the job. My friend, Ape Heldman, also worked there. Fortunately for the efficiency of the factory, we were in separate locations; he and I *always* indulged in a lot of horseplay and heavy kidding. Ape was a born practical joker. Our class had been the first one in high school to receive "sex education," taught by coach Whitey Davis. To liven things up, Ape once put a pair of girl's panties on the bulletin board with a note, "Found in Whitey's sex education class." On other occasions, Ape and I would stop at a red light in his father's car and blow the wolf whistle ("woo-woo") at crossing women. It always brought a response; either a smile, a glare, or even an "up yours" finger! He and I had installed the whistle without his dad knowing it, for a while anyway. One time Ape forged, illegibly, a doctor's signature on my swimming class excuse so I could catch an extra smoke. The excuse went into the Ohio State Board of Education files in Columbus, but I'm sure the statute of limitations has run out.

Every morning Nate would pick me up in the Cadillac convertible, top down, of course. We then stopped by for Abie Cohen, Chairman of U.S. Shoe, who was immaculately dressed in a light gray, double breasted, chalk-stripe suit; French-cuffed custom shirt; light gray Homburg hat; and black, imported leather shoes, polished to a mirror-like shine. The two executives rode in the front, and I, the rough, factory work-clothed kid sat in the back. As we drove into the plant parking lot, there were gaping eyes and whistles. It was even funnier after work, when I was almost black from moving dirty materials all day. It was a rich contrast; dirty me in the back, and the well-groomed chauffeur and liveryman in the front.

Factory men worked hard, but had a camaraderie that showed up at the annual "shoemaker's picnic," a company-sponsored event. There was a lot of beer drinking and horseshoe pitching, a constant throwing of good-natured barbs, and avid consumption of pounds of "shoemaker's chicken" (ham salad made with the butt ends). After a few beers, some of the guys shared stories of old times in the shoe industry.

They told about two rival saloons on opposite corners of Norwood, up the street from the plant. In the early days of the Depression, both had "free lunch counters," like many saloons nationwide in those days. The purchaser of a five-cent mug of beer could indulge himself at the counter in roast beef, potato salad, pickles, stale bread, and assorted green-tinged cold-cuts. Usually, before the eater picked up any food, he had to shoo away the circling flies. One of the owners, "Rump," had an innate gift for marketing, and desired to gain market share. So he installed screens on his windows and doors. He advertised that people should frequent his establishment and enjoy "fly-free" eating and drinking. This visionary soon doubled his business. His competitor not being as bright (ha, ha) took a more basic approach. He caught a hundred flies and put them in a Mason jar. Quietly, one gray afternoon before the plant let out, he slipped into Rump's saloon and released the flies in various corners of the room. There's nothing like good old American competition to even out the playing fields of commerce.

On the job I received raw materials from suppliers and delivered them to the different work stations throughout the plant. Gradually the workers got to know and trust me. They respected

Nate, who had a folksy, hands-on approach to management. If Nate liked me, they could too.

I started seeing the missing and smashed fingers from the presses, poor quality clothes, and glazed eyes from the monotony of repetitive operations. I heard talk of economic struggling, marital problems, and sick children whose treatment took hard-earned savings down to nothing. These were the days before health care programs. On the ride home, I saw the fine clothes of Nate and Mr. Cohen. I rode in a Cadillac and I saw the parking lot at the factory full of old Plymouths, Willys-Knights, Chevies, and Fords. Why the difference?

Observations and questions about factory life seeped into my subconscious daily, filling a mental reservoir with knowledge and concern from which I would one day drink in my management career. The social and economic strata at U.S. Shoe paralleled what I saw at school. There were big differences in what people had, just as there were big differences in what people could do. America did not have the caste system of the Hindus, but there were invisible, fairly rigid lines drawn around neighborhoods, groups, and areas of participation. My Silent Generation absorbed the presence of these lines, and in maturity worked to erase them through proactive efforts in the civil rights movement. As Strauss and Howe, commenting on the Silent Generation folks say, "[they]… had a keen sense of how and why humans fall short of grand civic plans or ideal moral standards. Silent appeals for change have seldom arisen from power or fury, but rather through self-conscious humanity and tender social conscience." It could be said that if my generation was silent, perhaps in silence one hears more clearly.

My youthful, but astute social observations were like taking in food that is not digested and converted until later. It does not become action until it is processed by the enzymes of maturity and reason. My comparison of the economic process of management and ownership with that of the hourly workers, planted a seed. However, I was to experience long periods of rough harrowing and tilling before it would spring forth into stalks of reality. As the *Rhinestone Cowboy* sings, "There'll be a load of compromisin' on the roads to my horizons." And there were.

*　　　　　*　　　　　*

Every so often, in my twilight years, I hear music from the '40s. One song in particular stirs up a memory, both sad and glad. "Workin' for the Yonkee Dollar," the chorus line of *"Rum and Coca-Cola,"* belted out by the Andrew Sisters, reminds me how the "smart set" and I used to drink rum and cokes. Drinking and smoking was our self-styled "rite of passage" to adulthood. It was never a problem to get served in a bar, as I looked several years older than my age. My appearance, coupled with a draft card sent to me from France by older friend and grad, Lou Gallop, assured a beer or rum and coke anytime. Experimenting with alcohol was the "in thing" to do.

Like many laboratory experiments, this one took time, some hard lumps, and a lot of wasted resources both mental and physical, before I learned the results. One night, a year after I was married, we had a small party for several friends and I had too many rum and cokes. The next day I couldn't remember anything I'd said or done the night before. It scared me; I am the kind of person who seeks control of his surroundings and actions. I talked to Marty for hours and prayed many times throughout that weekend, asking for God's help. On Monday, as I was going to work, like St. Paul on the road to Damascus, I was figuratively hit with a lightning bolt. But I wasn't struck blind; I was made clear-sighted, seeing the waste that came from drinking. I remember stopping at a red light and saying aloud, "That crap is poison. No more, ever, ever, ever!" And other than a sip of communion wine, I have never taken another drink. I thank my wife for her counseling and inspiration, and I thank God for His lightning bolt!

*   *   *

In my junior year, my zoology teacher, Miss Elberg (God rest her soul) opened my eyes to the beauty of nature, creation, all forms of life, and the never-ceasing quest for knowledge and truth. She taught us the wondrous quality of our universe and of ourselves without ever trudging in the ruts of dogma. I felt an instant chemistry with this well-educated and dedicated maiden lady, and I did many extra-credit projects for her without ever feeling overworked. I wanted to please her; I wanted her approval. One day, we asked her why we were on earth. She said, "Man was put on earth to work, and to leave it better than he found it." This was burned into my soul next to Grandmother's admonition of "Believe in God, and get ahead." Walnut Hills had many fine teachers, all non-union then, but Miss Elberg stood highest for me.

Although Miss Elberg was the pinnacle of my school's teachers to me, there were many other fine ones. Most of the women were unmarried, which my wife and I feel contributed to their excellence. It was almost as if the love they had was poured into their students. Their work was their life, and we lucky students were the blessed recipients, although we didn't realize it at the time. As an old saying goes, "Too late we become smart."

I was leaving Miss Elberg's classroom late one afternoon, after having dissected the nervous system of an earthworm for extra credit, when I bumped into former girlfriend, Patricia Pease. She smiled and said, "How are you, Chris." I stammered something back; I hadn't talked to her in more than six months. Not having a steady girl at the time, I called her that night. Soon we were an item in the school paper's gossip column, and wedded into a serious romance that lasted for several years. It became a relationship that taught me a lot about girls and about myself. She was a mirror for my voids (Dorian Gray, I know thee!) We were dating at least twice a week, plus spending time together after school. In movies and TV shows, "the names of the characters have been changed to protect the innocent." But here, "I'll change the activities of the characters, not the names, to "protect the innocent." Enough said!

One night while I was doing my homework, I picked up the book, *Fortitude*, by Hugh Walpole. Our English teacher had assigned the first hundred pages. The opening line caught my

attention: "Tisn't life that matters! 'Tis the courage you bring to it."
The story was easy to get into; I felt a kinship with the protagonist,
Peter Westcott. It seemed that he and I had dealt with many of the
same challenges. I came across a passage which opened my mind
to what I might expect as I strove to become an entity.

"But, concerning the Traveler who would enter the House
of Courage there are many lands that must be passed on the road
before he rest there. There is, First, The Land of Lacking All
Things — that is hard to cross. There is, Secondly, The Land of
Having All Things. There is the Traveler's Fortitude most hardly
tested. There is, Thirdly, The Land of Losing All Those Things
That One Hath Possessed. That is hard country indeed for the
memory of the pleasantness of those earlier days redoubleth the
agony of lacking them. But at the end there is a Land of ice and
snow that few travelers have compassed and that is the Land of
Knowing What One Hath Missed...The Bird was in the hand and
one let it go...that is the hardest agony of all the journey...but if
these lands be encountered and surpassed then doth the Traveler
at length possess his soul and is master of it...this is the Meaning
and Purpose of Life."

Reading the passage over three times helped my six-
teen-year-old mind get its first grasp on the premise that life would
have hurdles. But these hurdles were there for a purpose. Had I
been a seer, I might have known I would travel through the four
lands over my life's journey—through finding myself, truly finding
God, developing my career, meeting my life's mate, rearing my
children, serving society, learning of what love is made, seeing the
end and accepting it, testing whether I had mastered my soul, and
finally knowing the "meaning and purpose of life."

That night I equated my years with no mother and father
at home, living in a poor neighborhood, and the eventual loss of

my father and grandmother, with the "Land of Lacking All Things." I thought hopefully that living with my mother in a conventional household in a more affluent neighborhood was the "Land of Having All Things." I felt a quick punch of fear in my stomach as I looked at the third land: "The Land of Losing All Those Things That One Hath Possessed." Would my new home and my mother's love be taken away?

"Hey, Chrisee, how about taking a break? Cookies and milk?" My anxiety faded with that reassuring call. My mother was there!

*   *   *

"Hey, Moose (even the coaches used my nickname), stop in my office Monday," said Walnut Hills High football coach, Willie Bass. When I sat down in his tiny cubicle, he looked at me with penetrating black eyes that bored through steel-rimmed glasses as if they weren't there. Willie was a wiry man of just five-foot-eight and one-hundred-fifty pounds. He had worked our team hard in preseason practice and through a ten-game season where we barely won five games. I hadn't played much because Willie wasn't sure of what I could do, and he favored seniors over juniors.

I was waiting to hear why I had been called, but he just looked at me as if he were conducting judgment day. Finally he said, "Moose, I didn't play you much because I didn't think you had enough fire in you. But I liked the way you went into our last two games when I told you to. You never said, 'I can't play that position.' Just went in there and tried. I like that."

I couldn't believe what I was hearing, or that Coach Bass had noticed me that much. "I'd like to play more, if I can."

"That's what I want to talk to you about. The other day on the track you lost by only a half step to the fastest guy in the school. Running like that can be good for a running back."

"Really? I'd sure like to try."

"Good. I'm going to give you a ball, and you keep your cleats and pants. Over the winter, I want you to practice handling the ball and running with it as much as you can."

Most days when the ground wasn't covered with snow, I'd get a seventh-grader to center the ball to me, for a quarter. I'd move left and right, practicing cross steps, speed changes, and just running straight ahead with my head down and the ball tucked in my gut. Kids would pass the field and mumble something about some nut out there playing football by himself!

When I wasn't practicing or struggling with Algebra II, I was sailing through Zoology and passing okay in English and Latin III. Patricia and I dated steadily. At my fraternity's early spring dance I gave her my pin. The orchestra leader announced it, and played *Always and Together*. Patricia and I got along great, but I was never certain her parents thought I was the best choice for their only daughter. To her credit, she prevailed, and always defended me to them.

Summer came to close out a very happy junior year, and Patricia went away to a camp in Michigan. I worked out and did a lot of Saturday night babysitting with three-year-old, half-brother Buzz. No girls; just work, and hanging out with the guys.

About a week before preseason football practice, Grandmother Allan out in Hartwell asked if I would come and stay with her for a week or so to cut up a huge tree for firewood. The utility company had taken it down because it interfered with their power lines. I asked Mother, who agreed, I think, to ease growing tensions in the house. They were not severe, but I could never be sure my stepfather was totally comfortable with my living there. I saw the effects on my mother; it showed in her face and in her more guarded manner when we were all together.

Grandmother Allan, a cheerful lady, always made me feel good. And my social life was a lot freer because she laid down no restrictions. I worked hard sawing the tree into fireplace logs, cutting her huge lawn, and shoveling coal into the coal bin. She told me the work would help me get into shape for football; she had a way of getting people to help her out with heavy jobs. When the week was up, I asked if I could stay on to finish the tree. Mother thought about it and said yes. Then one week ran into another. I kept bringing more of my clothes to Grandmother's. When preseason practice started, I was still there. Finally the work on the tree, and the hard, hot, grueling preseason practice passed, and Coach Bass named me first-string fullback, and strong side linebacker on defense! I started school while staying with Grandmother Allan.

There I was again, like the cicada, shedding another outer shell; this time the security of living with my mother and stepfather. I have never been sure exactly why I left; I guess I was a headstrong boy who wanted the freedom to come and go as he pleased. Mother, when my move was definite, began what would remain an ever-present mien of ambivalence—the absence of tension, but the presence of a loss.

∽

C H A P T E R
9

*"When he had spent everything, a severe famine took place through-
out the country, and he began to be in need…But when he came to
himself he said, 'How many of my father's hired hands have bread
enough and to spare, but here I am dying of hunger! I will get up
and go to my father, and I will say to him, 'Father, I have sinned
against heaven and before you; I am no longer worthy to be called
your son; treat me like one of your hired hands.' So he set off and
went to his father. But while he was still far off, his father saw him
and was filled with compassion; he ran and put his arms around
him and kissed him. Then the son said to him, 'Father I have
sinned against heaven and before you; I am no longer worthy to be
called your son.' But the father said to his slaves, 'Quickly, bring
out a robe—the best one—and put it on him…for this son of mine
was dead and is alive again; he was lost and is found!' "*
Luke 15: 14-24

*   *   *

It was early afternoon on the Saturday of Labor Day weekend, and the sun was filtering through a large picture window
behind the bar in the Roselawn Tavern. My buddy, Rich Haller and
I had finished our last day of preseason football practice. Two half-
filled bottles of Royal Amber beer sat in front of us, with some of
the white-collared brew in frosted glasses. I reached for mine as I

heard the warm lilt of *To Each His Own* from the corner jukebox. The seventy-eight rpm record had captured the distinctive baritone of Eddie Howard singing about how "a rose must remain with the sun and the rain, or its lovely promise won't come true. To each his own and my own is you."   Looking past the end of a lighted Lucky Strike, I saw my girl, Patricia Pease, drive up in her parents' two-tone, brown Olds. I hadn't seen her since June. We arranged to meet that afternoon after football practice. That morning, she had arrived from the Michigan camp where she had spent the whole darn summer.

Suddenly, the warmth of the sun was everywhere in her smile, which glowed through the car's windshield; in the barroom, made light with the love song; and in my heart, knowing I'd made the team and that she was back. "Come on, Rich, I haven't seen her in ten weeks!" Draining my glass, I stubbed the Lucky out in an overflowing ashtray and made for the parking lot. When she got out of the car, I felt as if sunshine were pouring from me, not the sky. I pulled her into my arms and shamelessly hugged her right there on the edge of the highway as cars whizzed by, some with catcalls and appreciative honking.

I was happy to have a girl of my own again. It had been a long summer, and at seventeen, a steady girl was as important to me as anything could be. My mind raced thinking about every-thing I wanted to do with her. We decided to double that evening with Rich and his girl Joyce to see a movie, get something to eat, and spend a lot of quiet time in a secluded park. I had just read *This Side of Paradise* by F. Scott Fitzgerald, the "voice of the Lost Generation," who matter-of-factly described the "petting parties" of the twenties' girls, whom he dubbed with the sobriquet, "flap-per." My Silent Generation, myself included, didn't refer to our backseat explorations as petting, we were just silent about "being together."

*   *   *

Walking through the school lobby on the first day of my senior year wearing saddle shoes; gray flannel slacks; and a light blue, Oxford cloth, British roll, button-down shirt; made me recall how, five years earlier, I had walked there as a naïve seventh-grader looking at all the older guys wearing the uniform I now wore. I saw some seventh-graders looking at me in the same way. Yep, I had it all—football player; a steady girl; enough money for dates, ciga-rettes, and beer (thanks to weekly contributions from three of mother's sisters, who were happy I was living with their widowed mother); and vice-president of my fraternity. I was a real big-man-on-campus, I thought. I hadn't yet read the scripture about, "pride goeth before a fall." No, I hadn't read it; I later learned it, like so much of my acquired knowledge, the hard way.

On the football field, after a few action-filled games, a lot of seventh- and eighth-graders would try and say "hi" to me as we passed in the halls. Memories of early years, when I did the same thing, flashed back. I remember how thrilled I was when some of the football and basketball players would nod or smile. I did the same, which didn't hurt my image or my ego. As the season progressed we won only half of our games. Everybody in the school thought it would just be another season with no titles. Our academic school was fifty-years-old, and no one remembered our ever having won a championship.

Two games before the season ended, on a cloudy November afternoon, we were scheduled to play the mighty Hughes High School. They usually beat us, but Coach Bass told us we could win if we really got some fire, his favorite word. Coach Bass never used any two-bit psychology on us, he just said exactly what he thought and wanted. His praise was scarce, but meaningful. He wasn't a "rah, rah" type, or a "let's get one for the Gipper" speechmaker. He was a down-to-earth, no fancy stuff, knowledgeable coach. He got the best out of me, without many words, but with an occasional kick in the rump.

At last, game time came after a half-day of school that felt like a week. The referee's whistle blew and the ball arced end-over-end into my arms. I made about ten yards on the return. Our first play was a quick-opener by the halfback; three yards. Then our great quarterback, Jerry Kanter, called the fullback pitch out. He squatted under the center, "Hup one, Hup two," and the ball came into his sure hands. On the second hup, I started towards right end. Jerry made a perfect pitch right into my hands at waist height. Tucking the pointed end of the ball in my armpit, I cut up field and headed for the goal line fifty-five yards away. I straight-armed a linebacker cut back to mid-field, having crossed I didn't know how many limed yard markers, with only the safety and a cornerback between me and the goal. I feinted to my left, digging my cleats into the soft loam. Then I cut right, running for the corner. I got tackled on the ten-yard line by two guys after a fifty-yard run. On the next play, Jerry faked the pitch out and threw a perfect screen pass to the halfback—touchdown! Walnut Hills 6, Hughes 0.

And that's how the game ended. The rest of it, after those opening plays, was a fierce defensive battle, but we won! We had beaten the mighty Hughes. The last game of the season was to be against Western Hills, a powerhouse from the west side of town. Western Hills High continuously turned out professional, major league players. Despite the win over Hughes, everyone thought it would be just another season.

That final game was at our school on a sunny Friday in mid-November. Coach Bass's pre-game talk was surprisingly simple. "All you guys gotta do is what you know how to do. They're stronger against the run than the pass. So, Jerry, mix 'em up. And Moose don't let anybody lay a hand on Jerry."

Dressed in our blue and gold jerseys, we filed onto the field though parallel lines of cheering students. The band was playing the school fight song, and the cheerleaders were gyrating and shouting. "Two, four, six, eight; who do we appreciate? Walnut,

Walnut, Rah, Rah, Rah!" The big, bad, red-shirted boys from Western Hills were already on the field, glaring at us as we trotted out.

The first quarter was a see-saw with no score. Then in the second quarter, Jerry called a new formation we had practiced for a week. We lined up with an unbalanced line with Jerry still under the center. I was one of the two deep backs, the other was a flanker. When he got the ball, Jerry faked to the halfback, while I started for the right end. Jerry flipped it to me on the run, and I cut down field, straight-arming two defenders as I picked up speed and raced for the sidelines. The big, mean-looking linebacker had the advantage of the angle on me and finally caught me with a lip-splitting head tackle after I'd gained twenty-five yards. We were on their twenty, and just like in the Hughes game, Jerry threw a perfect pass for a touchdown, and nobody laid a hand on him.

We scored again in the second half. I must have made twenty pass blocks and as many tackles on defense when the gun went off. Walnut Hills had beaten the second powerhouse of our league 13-0. The fans went wild, but on the field we just stood there for a stunned moment until the realization of what we had done registered on our mud-streaked faces. My face was a mixture of dirt and blood, but I didn't feel a thing.

In the locker room twenty-five happy boys, in various stages of undress, laughed and snapped each other on the rear with wet towels. Coach Bass tersely said, "I'm proud of you guys, you did good today." He passed by me and put his hand on my shoulder, "Moose that was your best game of the year." Then with a twinkle in those penetrating black eyes, "You wanna keep the cleats and pants over the winter?"

"Thanks, Coach."

The hilarity finally subsided, and a quiet pervaded the locker room. Dirty uniforms had been cleaned out of lockers where they had resided for three months, along with overripe sweat socks and that medallion of masculinity, the athletic supporter. We all looked at one another, knowing we would not be playing together any more. A chapter closed on those wooden locker room benches as smelly tee shirts and strong memories disappeared into duffel bags.

Patty was waiting for me outside the locker room. We went to dinner, a party at Fred Texton's, and enjoyed some quiet time on a private girl's school playfield, with only the moonlight to silhouette our clinging bodies. About eleven, we headed for her house, but stopping at DeSale's corner to buy the next day's *Cincinnati Enquirer*. I tore through it to the sports section. In bold letters, read **"Eagles Win City Championship"**. We had done what no team (called Eagles) at our school had ever done. And under the caption was my picture running the ball on a twenty-five yard gain. Wow! Patty leaned over, kissed my cheek, and said she was proud of me.

On Monday, seventh and eighth graders wanted my autograph; another card, as in "the house of..." I was building with my ego. But self image, youthful adulation, and recognition aside, I was again experiencing a feeling of queasiness. In my new home on Mystic Avenue, I'd have periods of confusion about where I was, who I was, and what I was supposed to do. Grandmother Allan was uplifting and jolly, and cooked things I liked, but I thought about not being with my mother. And yet, it was I who slowly slid away from living with her and Pop. At seventeen, I couldn't articulate what I later processed. I deduced that there had never been a real maternal bonding. Our relationship was more intellectual than emotional or dependent. I'd lived too many years away from her. Our relationship was not built like a fine mosaic containing thousands of the tiny tiles of daily contact and shared experience.

At Grandmother Allan's I was "free" from serious discipline and master of my life but my freedom left me adrift in a sea of emotional searching. One morning at school, after a period of uncertainty the previous night, I met Patty on the front steps. She smiled warmly, and I said, "You're the one reality in a world of chattering ghosts." I'd read this in *Arrowsmith*, Sinclair Lewis's award-winning novel, which had been assigned. When I saw her, the phrase just popped out. She took my hand. "I'm glad," she whispered.

I was passing every subject, with A's in chemistry and a true interest in the pathos of Hamlet's struggle with his father's death and his mother's remarriage. Did I struggle with my own mother's remarriage? Did I, in teenage imagery, see myself as the soulful Dane? No, I reasoned, I wasn't too soulful; I was in total control of my life, making all of my own decisions and directing my actions, with accountability only to myself. At seventeen, I was an adult, but didn't know I lacked the maturity and experience of one. I was fast spending my small fortune of spiritual teachings, the discipline of my deceased grandmother, and the stability of an ordered home to seek a good time. However, the thread of survival that ran through my soul kept me trying to play by most of the rules. I passed my subjects, I honored my Grandmother Allan, and I showed up for the game of life everyday, but I did what I wanted to do with no restrictions. The values Grandmother Christopher had instilled in me were dormant during that winter of my discontent. I had achieved the recognition I never had as the poor boy on the wrong side of the tracks in Hartwell, but I wasn't emotionally ready to handle it. I blew my small treasure of acquired identity in a spree of self indulgence.

When spring arrived, heralded by the annual blooming of hosts of Cincinnati's forsythias, I made first-string catcher on the baseball team. I had the pleasure of going up against a future big league player, manager, and coach, Don Zimmer. The "Zim" had a great career, ending it as assistant to Yankee manager, Joe Torre. Zim's team, Western Hills, always beat us in baseball (just like they almost did in football). His school turned out greats like Herman Wehmeier, Jim Frey, and Pete Rose.

As graduation neared, a hollow feeling began to invade me. I saw the end of a period in which I had grown, found recognition, learned a lot, both academically and socially, and enjoyed a stable community. And graduation opened a scary new door.

When I learned that Patty was going away to college, my forebodings increased. Was I about to enter Walpole's "The Land of Losing All Those Things That One Hath Possessed?" I didn't dwell on it, but Patty's going away, no more adulation by seventh-graders, and no more Walnut Hills, made me anxious about what lay ahead. Most of my Silent Generation classmates were eager to get to college and were scheduled to leave Cincinnati. My four-year college fund of fifteen-hundred dollars, accrued from the sale of Grandmother's trackside house, couldn't cover Eastern school tuitions. I was enrolled at the University of Cincinnati, the "street-car college," in pre-med.

But before college, on a June night, dressed in a summer formal in the school auditorium, my three hundred classmates and I marched slowly to the stage as the orchestra played Elgar's *Pomp and Circumstance*. I saw Mother and Pop smiling at me. I'd made it! Diploma in hand, I bolted from the stage, kissed Mother, shook hands with Pop, and jumped into Dave Ellis's car with Patty for an all-night celebration.

The following week I started a summer job at Cambridge Tile Company as a lab assistant. I was entering a new phase of my life, the finishing school for adulthood, a career path, and mar-riage. No longer the football star in the cloistered halls of embrac-ing and nurturing Walnut Hills High, I was joining millions of my Silent Generation mates in a world no longer under the yoke of the Depression or the potential of a war. It was a world of opportuni-ties cast in the euphoric light of victory. It seemed my only chal-lenge was to go out and become the man I wanted to be. But, like the prodigal son, I would continue to waste my fortune of values and direction.

*   *   *

My chemistry class at UC had 140 students. I was in the back row and couldn't hear the instructor. This was culture shock number one; the next one came when I tried out for the football team. The team was almost all World War II veterans, most of whom had played in the service. An eighteen-year old boy wasn't up to the experience of these twenty-three-year-old near-professionals.

I pledged Beta Theta Pi, a leading fraternity, and to my amazement I was once again chosen to join the elite of the school. Our fraternity threw dances and parties attended by couples, many of whom were married; the veterans going through school on the GI Bill, and the wife working. Almost everyone at these affairs had a date. I went to the first few parties as a "stag," a new and unpleasant experience. Like an outcast I watched couples laughing and hugging each other. I'd think about Patty away at Sullins College in Virginia, and wish I had a girl with me. A lot of beer flowed at these parties, which I consumed in place of a date. It was a poor substitute; how do you kiss a mug of beer goodnight?

I was floundering in college. I knew I should be there because it was the "thing to do," but I couldn't focus on how to get to where I thought I should be. I let Patty's absence, the impersonal environment of college classes, and the intimidation of being surrounded by older, GI-Generation guys distract me. I had gotten by in high school because I could think on my feet and quickly absorbed what the dedicated teachers shared. College was different; any charm I might have had with my high school teachers didn't impress my Profs.

My schedule of inorganic chemistry class and lab, English, math, and medical German and its lab soon became an overloaded plate. I should have worked for awhile before starting college. It would have given me a taste of reality.

Often before starting my homework, I would write a three- or four-page letter to Patty pouring out my love, loneliness, and lust (repressed). I'd feel lousy and have a hard time getting back to my studies. There was no strong motivation in my life and no one needed me. I was just satisfying my basic needs of eating, keeping clothes on, and having a roof over my head, while spending Grandmother Christopher's small bequest. I couldn't identify any personal goals with Grandmother's "get ahead."

Many of my classmates were four to six years older than I and most of them veterans. I felt intimidated, like my Silent Generation mates, I stood in the shadow of these GI heroes. Whatever I had done that seemed meaningful paled in their aura. They were serious, while I was still fumbling for direction. At that time I wasn't aware of the void in my life created by the absence of God. I wasn't going to church because I was too tired from Saturday night partying. I wasn't saying prayers or doing anything for others. I studied less and less as I couldn't muster up the motivation to put college at a higher priority than sensual pleasures, which were nothing but an escape from the "Waste Land" in which I floundered. I had no real love in my life, and having been raised in a matriarchal environment, I drew my inner strength from women. Like T.S. Eliot, as he suffered from his marital problems and created his *The Waste Land*, I was creating mine, not with pen, but by obsessively chasing diversions from the challenges at hand. The result was predictable—by late spring I decided to drop out of college.

Patty had become history. College distances and immediate needs for both of us slowly diluted our high school romantic bonds, but not without the wrenching pains of withdrawal. And, while we struggled, suffered, and eventually parted, I'm sure her mother emitted a sigh of relief. I missed Patty's loyalty, warmth, and easy conversation. They hadn't written *Heartaches by the Numbers* yet, so I just poked along in a hollow, tuneless state. She had been an important part of my adolescent years; a rock in my turbulent teens. In later life, our paths crossed and she became a friend to my wife and me. When I told Grandmother Allan about the breakup, she said in her compassionate wisdom, "Chris, things usually happen for the best." She was right!

My egocentric, self-willed house of cards made of duces and treys had been blown apart in the swirling winds of wasteful living and lack of direction. My actions at this point were reactive, not cognitive. Some innate drive, the human's natural drive for survival, led me to seek a job. The Management, Administrative, and Research building of Procter and Gamble in Ivorydale was my first stop. Bingo, I was hired as a lab assistant in the photographic department. Luck, divine intervention, or coincidence—I'll never know—but I had a job at forty per week, about the cost of a good lunch for two today. I've heard that coincidence is God remaining anonymous—who can say?

Learning about photography was fun. I worked the darkroom and was eventually allowed to go along on photo shoots. As

160

time passed, I learned how to do my job easily I began to feel I was prostituting myself. It was honest work, but repetitious. I wasn't being utilized to the extent of my potential. I started to take on second jobs, such as selling coal, fans, and other items at night. I had this vague idea that I needed to do something that required more brain power. In my frustration, I drank more. I would occasionally run into a former schoolmate, home from an Eastern school, who would ask, "Hey, Moose, what are you doing?" I'd stammer something about a job at P & G to earn enough for another year at UC. He'd tell me all about "back East," ending with, "That's nice, Moose. Good luck." Then I'd go get a half-dozen beers.

After a year I took a full-time sales job, but kept on selling fans and coal at night. My mother and pop moved to Pleasant Ridge, and bought a floor fan from me. Her neighbors wanted one like just like it, so one Sunday I called on them. To my surprise their daughter was a Walnut Hills alum, class of 1944. Martha Surnbrock was blonde, attractive, and had graduated cum laude from Walnut Hills. She had just graduated from the Business Administration College at UC after five years of co-oping. She and her parents were very cordial to me and the date I had brought along.

Door-to-door selling didn't work for me. "No, we don't need storm windows" (not to mention doors closed in my face) was disheartening, and I had no steady girl. So when I wasn't wearing out shoe leather and getting calluses on my doorbell finger, I hung out in Hartwell cafes with old grade school friends. Like me, they were working, not going to college. After work, we'd play touch football, then go drink beer and bet on pin ball games. A real stimulating life! I hoped Grandmother Christopher wasn't looking down from heaven.

One day I was driving by Holy Trinity, the church of my youth, when I saw Art Hill, my sixth-grade Sunday school teacher. He was standing in the yard with a group of high school boys. I stopped my second-hand Jeep and approached him. We exchanged smiles, "I'll be darns," and some hugs. Art dismissed the boys with a, "See you guys Friday night." We sat on the Parish Hall steps and shared what each of us had been doing since our 1940 class. I learned he had been a tank commander in General Patton's Third Army and had been in several bloody battles. I tried to get him to tell me about Patton, a hero of mine, and his experiences. But, like most veterans who have seen combat, he was reticent about it. He just said he thanked God everyday for being alive.

He was a postulant for holy orders (wanted to become an Episcopal priest), probably motivated by his survival in combat. He was forming an interdenominational boys and girls club for teenagers living within a ten mile radius of the church. He wanted to get the boys to play football in the Fraternal Order of Police league, but wasn't sure he could coach. He asked me if I knew anything about football; a half-hour later I was the coach of the team.

At Art's urging, I returned to church at Holy Trinity. It brought back my early life with Grandmother Christopher. Mr. Attridge was still the rector and welcomed me home. Over the altar was a stained-glass window with Jesus looking heavenward as he prayed in the Garden of Gethsemane the night before his crucifixion. The sun beamed through the window, imparting a divine aura to the figure. As I sat and looked at this during Sunday service, and all the mistakes and wasteful things I had done over the last two years welled up in me. I got on the kneeler, and looked toward the image of Christ. I felt my grandmother next to me in the pew, and saw her face as I had in boyhood. Being back at Holy Trinity was coming home. It belied Thomas Wolfe's famous novel.

I started saying prayers again on my knees. On many nights these would last a half hour and were marked by tears as I told God of my shame and the sorrow of closing Him out of my life. I begged Him to help me find the way back to doing what I should. "Dear God, I know I cannot bargain with you, but in your Grace, please lead me to a place where I can use my skills and all of the talents you have blessed me with. Those precious talents I have foolishly buried! If I ever have children I will make sure that they know of you and your gracious mercy and I will try through example to reflect your love." After such a session, I would sleep well. To this day I'd swear that on one of these nights in a dream I heard, "for this son of mine was dead and is alive again; he was lost and is found."

*   *   *

Coaching the boy's football team was like a dream come true. I used the plays from Walnut Hills. Art conned a sporting goods store out of equipment and uniforms for our twenty boys. The girls were cheerleaders and helped prepare food for post-game parties. I loved working with these kids. They were enthusiastic, dedicated to learning, and relatively obedient to my directions. We started winning all of our games.

Soon, more and more folks from church came to see our boys play and excitedly cheered them on. We finished the season with the league championship. Yes, we had won the cup, but the real victory was in the spirit and open-mindedness instilled in those teen boys who were a mixture of Catholics, Seventh Day

Adventists, Presbyterians, a Holy Roller, Methodists, Baptists, some non church-goers, and even a couple of Episcopalians. Life had taken a turn for the better. I wasn't setting any sales records on my job—barely making ends meet—but I was drinking less, and feeling good about what I was doing. The void in my life was no girl.

I started to search my memory for possible dates, but the two or three that might be possibilities were away at private schools. I'd never tried to "pick up" a girl in a bar or public place; if there's one thing I knew, it was that people in bars had problems, and why take on someone else's. One day I was talking to my mother who said, "You know, Chris, the girl next door is very cute, smart, and a perfect lady." An instant flash of the blonde, to whose parents I'd sold a fan, with the warm smile and the sparkling, blue eyes, jumped before my mind's eye.

"Do you think she'd go out with me? She's three years older, and smart."

"You're smart too, when you apply yourself."

"Where could I take her?" I must have been affected by the idea of seeing her; I had never fumbled about how to date a girl before.

"She went to UC, how about a football game?"

*　　　　*　　　　*

"Martha, this is Bob Christopher, Joy's son; you know, I sold your parents a fan."

"Sure, I remember you. How are you?"

"Great. I uh...I uh, was wondering if I might take you to see UC play Kentucky next Saturday? I'd really like to."

"I'd love to go. Should I call you Bob or Chris, like Joy does?"

"Chris."

"I enjoyed meeting your girl, Carolyn, when you sold us the fan. How is she?"

"I don't know. I don't see her anymore."

"Mmm. My folks enjoyed the fan this last summer. It runs so quietly."

"Good. What are you doing, now that you've graduated?"

"I'm working in Mother's office as an administrative assistant to a sales engineer with the Dravo Corporation. They make large centrifugal pumps and steam turbines."

"Great. I'll call for you about one on Saturday. Is that okay?"

"That'll be fine. I'm looking forward to the game...and seeing you."

"Me too, thanks. See you Saturday."

At last Saturday came—my first date with Martha. I carefully brushed my blue suit, as the other one was frayed at the cuff line. I'd sprung for a new white shirt, which I married to a maroon and navy tie. I looked in Grandmother's full-length mirror and said, "Buddy, you could model for Brooks Brothers." On the way to Martha's, I gave old Punk Brewster at his shoe repair shop a half-dollar to shine up my one pair of cordovan leather shoes. Pop let me borrow his Cadillac because my Jeep had no side curtains. I was afraid of rain, which always poured in on the seats. I had had curtains but they had torn, and I didn't have enough money to replace them. Gosh, if it rained on Saturday, that would be some first impression on Martha if she got soaked! Funny thing, though, three months later this did happen, and she laughed about it as she sat on her wet stockings and feet in the movie. Sharing our "wet night" told me she was the girl for me.

Grandmother Allan was of the same cut; she knew how to laugh at little mishaps, like the first time I invited Martha home for dinner. We were having rib-roast-of-beef. The three of us were in the kitchen when Grandmother took the roast out of the oven. It slid off the platter and skidded all the way across the kitchen floor like a hockey puck on new ice. I started to feel embarrassed, until Grandmother, after watching the slide, had to sit down and hold her sides, she was laughing so hard. Martha did the same, then me. It was wonderful. When I took Martha home, she said, "Chris, I love your Grandmother. I hope I can always have an outlook on life like hers." I went all fuzzy inside.

Going back to our first date, I nervously rang the Surnbrock's doorbell after smoothing my hair for the twentieth time. When Martha answered, wearing a medium blue suit that matched her friendly, sparkling blue eyes my heart ticked some extra beats. I stood there looking like some country bumpkin or, at best, some outlander from the Mill Creek Valley, where I grew up. She smiled and said, "I'm ready—it should be a good game."

I held open the door to Pop's Cadillac, noticing perfectly shaped legs as Martha slid in. Within minutes, we were talking about Walnut Hills, teachers we'd shared, and of course, I had to tell her about my football playing, and about UC. I tried to sound erudite, knowing how bright and well-educated she was, though she was the height of modesty. I felt completely comfortable after the first hour and as the afternoon wore on, even more so. Whenever we talked, she looked directly into my eyes with an infectious sparkle that made me feel I was with someone with whom I would always be able to share things. I also noticed her spontaneous enthusiasm, whenever UC did something good on the field she'd jump up and cheer. She understood football more than any girl I'd ever known. I was in a whirl when I took her home, where we had dinner with my mother and Pop. At her front door, I asked if I could call her. She said she'd like that. That night I had trouble going to sleep, my mind was filled with warm fantasies, unlike any I'd ever experienced. The theme of them was seeing me in a new, elevated light, sharing things with Martha.

That date led to nightly phone calls, another football game, a downtown lunch on her break, and a pattern of three dates a weekend. By Christmas I had kissed her, and our families shared Christmas Eve at my house. Martha had started going to Holy Trinity with me. She began working with the girl's section of our interdenominational club and taking confirmation classes. What was so neat was that all of this happened so easily. There wasn't much discussion, no pitches; we just flowed, a united pair, into whatever came along. We didn't have dominance issues (power struggles). We were a natural team, despite vastly different backgrounds and lifestyles. Martha tended to be shy, but when she expressed herself with her unique and meaningful succinctness, everyone nodded yes. Brains, modesty, a thirst for knowledge, kindness, enthusiasm, and deep loyalty were the qualities I saw in her in the first three months we went together.

Was there a cloud floating between me and my new-found rays of sunshine? Yes, I wasn't making a dime on my commission-only job. The recession of 1949-50 was on, and I wasn't the best door-to-door salesman. At twenty, I'd had so many turndowns and doors shut in my face, it was hard to charge out in the rain to ring another fifty or sixty doorbells per day. Even with Martha's expressed support and demonstrated love, I felt I was back in Walpole's "The Land of Lacking All Things." Hell, I loved this girl, but what could I offer her? A college drop-out with a bank account under a hundred, and a job that didn't earn me any money. "Yeah, Moose, you're a real triple threat," I thought as I parked at the church one night for an Ash Wednesday service.

One of the scriptures read, "Ask and it shall be answered for thee." I thought about this line the rest of the evening. I guess I sounded sad on the phone with Martha. She asked me if I was all right. I couldn't tell her what was worrying me; that I was afraid I'd lose her because I was near broke and didn't have a profession or a good education. She sensed something, because she said, "Chris, you have made me very happy. You've given me confidence in myself. You've helped me into a church I like, and I just like being with you."

"I love you. You're the best thing that ever happened to me."

"I love you too."

"I need to see you, how about a movie Friday?"

"Sounds good, can't wait. Good night, Chris, I'm here for you."

I hung up the phone feeling great, but also more worried about how to keep her. I knelt down by my bed, "God, what should I do? How can I have Martha? You know the spot I'm in, I need you God. What should I do?" I thanked God for letting me back into his house, and for bringing Martha into my life. The next night after a movie and a mouth-watering double burger "Big Boy," we went to Martha's house. We sat on the couch in the living room, dark, save for a sliver of light from the gas street lamp that backlit her soft face. I held her tight, as if she might slip away. My throat was hoarse, but I burst out with, "Will you marry me?" Without hesitation, she looked up at me with her warm blue eyes. "Yes." And then she kissed me.

The next day I awoke in whirl of thoughts—joy, fear, excitement, dread, wonder, and hope. What had I done the night before? The reality of my emotional proposal started to sink in. After some wild thought-chasing, I knew I was happy about "keeping" Martha with me, but how was I going to support her? In the euphoria of our acceptance of each other, there had been no timetable set for a wedding. Thank goodness! I had time to do something, like find a steady job, pronto!

Over the next few weeks, Martha never said a word about jobs or income. Her parents and my mother were happy for us, and they never mentioned the economic side of our proposed marriage. I began to realize that they all had faith in me. Together with my return to Holy Trinity and my work with the boys club, that did something wonderful to me. About a month after my two a.m. proposal, during my prayers, I suddenly stood up and said aloud, "I'll do *whatever* I have to do to support Martha." The next day I caught a streetcar for downtown Cincinnati (I had sold my Jeep to clean up some debts) and went to the employment agencies.

Miss Grady looked to be about thirty. She really listened to me tell her why I needed a job. I'll always remember her big brown eyes focused on me while I told her my entire background. As I was leaving, she touched my upper arm and said, "Robert, I'll do all I can to find you something. I believe you have potential."

She walked with me to the elevator and pressed the number one. As the door closed I saw her smile and a brown eye wink at me.

The next day I got all three Cincinnati papers and studied the want ads. I answered seventeen of them. Nothing happened for a week, but I kept up this daily discipline. Then Miss Grady called and asked me to come see her. "Robert," she said, as again those brown eyes held mine, "I have an opening for a quality control engineer. I believe with your good grades in the sciences you could handle it. Are you interested?"

"Yes Ma'am."

"Good. It's with a company that makes building materials. Can you go there this afternoon for an interview?"

"Sure, where is it?"

"Lockland, it's with the Philip Carey Manufacturing Company."

"Philip Carey!" I exclaimed.

"Yes. Do you know them?"

I told her how I had stood across the street in my father's Gulf gas station as a little boy, and how I had once ridden in the switch engine because its engineer lived up the street from my Grandmother Christopher's house.

"Good. You should be right at home. Our fee is two weeks pay, but you can send me ten dollars a week if that will help you."

"That would help, if I get the job."

"I'd bet on it! And, Robert, if it doesn't work out, please come see me. I'll help you any time."

I did get it. It was shift work with a weekly rotation. I was to start on the graveyard shift at sixty dollars a week, plus overtime. And there was plenty of overtime. The recession was fading and there was a nationwide demand for building materials; a Depression and war-starved nation was trying to fill pent-up demands for houses and cars. Carey, besides making building materials, also made sound deadening for automobiles; a work experience that served me handsomely in later years. I ran tensile, deflection, specific gravity, pliability, and bursting tests on the sound deadening materials; and weight, length, percent saturation, color, and strength tests on two building products of saturated built-up roofing and linoleum base. I reveled in the association with factory men as I had at U.S. Shoe and Cambridge Tile. I was in awe of the process machinery that took raw material in at one end and turned out a finished item at the other. I told Martha, mimicking Saint Peter, "On this rock, I will build our future." To this day, whenever I write about my career, I capitalize the word Industry; my love of it overrides good grammar.

*   *   *

"In the name of God, I, Robert, take you, Martha, to be my wife, to have and to hold from this day forward, for better or worse. This is my solemn vow."

On that August 12th, 1950, six months after my proposal—spontaneously made out of total love and respect—Marty and I were united for life. Her immediate, unconditional acceptance of jobless, broke me, gave me my life. No greater love could I ever be given.

As we walked down the aisle between smiling faces, I heard a whisper from somewhere "…for this son of mine was dead and is alive again; he was lost and is found."

~

CHAPTER

10

"For the things we have to learn before we can do them,
we learn by doing them."
Aristotle 384-322 B.C.

I was 22 years old and struggling with "electives" in the freshman year of my adult life. Marty and I had been married for almost two years and we were approaching parenthood. Besides holding down a new job as a graveyard-shift foreman at the Philip Carey asphalt roofing mill, I was carrying three subjects at evening college.

My wife and I had just learned that our first baby (I had already told over thirty people in two days), was due in seven-and-a-half-months from this late January date. We'd spent over half of our checking account to buy her two maternity dresses in an economical three-season weight of spring, summer, and fall. Marty said one would suffice, but I insisted she needed two. "What will you do when one of them needs washing?" I asked. I thought maybe I could get some overtime pay to help cover the increased expenses. I was excited about the baby, and loved the look that life inside Marty brought to her clear face, but twinges of fear, whenever I thought about the responsibility, tightened the muscles in my stomach. The basement-store salesclerk, who patiently waited on us as we deliberated, said the dresses were on sale. We decided on a blue one like her eyes, and a brown one like mine. The three-and-a-half-room apartment we had just rented cost a week-and-a-half's salary, so I worked out a deal with the landlord. I kept the grass cut, the halls clean, and handled minor maintenance in the four-unit building for a fifteen-dollar-a-month rent reduction.

A few weeks earlier I had been in my new superior's office. "Robert," division-superintendent Gilbert said to me, "You will start a week from tomorrow at eleven p.m., where you will be the sole supervisor of the shift. But first we will give you a week on the day shift to learn all you can. Incidentally, you are the youngest foreman we have ever had in the asphalt-roofing division. I know you will do your best to make the midnight shift a productive team. Good luck." With this terse directive, I started my first supervisory position, charged with directing a crew of fifty some men, all ten to thirty years older than me. The shingle mill had three, two-hundred-yard-long, asphalt-roofing machines, each carrying a crew of seventeen men. The products were asphalt-roofing shingles of various weights and designs, and asphalt-roll roofing, almost always misnamed "tar paper." I learned that tar came from the destructive distillation of coal and in the sixties was proved to be carcinogenic, but asphalt was the bottom product from crude oil that had been destructively distilled in an oil refinery.

During that first week I was left alone in the plant to walk around all of the machines and observe the details of making roofing. The sum total of my tutorial education came from a grizzled old general foreman named George, who once a day when he saw me eating my lunch, would bristle up and bark, "Get off your ass and get something done." George would then quickly exit the mill office. He was of the old school who felt any young foreman should have to learn his job "the hard way," as he had. He knew the operations, and by God he was going to keep the secrets.

I was excited about my first supervisory job, though of course I didn't have a fully formed concept of what I wanted to be. I carried in both my heart and mind a blend of Grandmother's admonition, "Bobby, believe in God, and get ahead," and the guilt of knowing I had dropped out of a pre-med program after only one year. "You're a loser," I had told myself on that black, gut-twisting day when I received my card full of D's and incomplete marks. Marty must have married me on faith, certainly not for my ninety-four-dollar bank account or my lack of a college education. I didn't even have a job when I proposed. Gosh, I'm lucky she said yes. Why she did is still a mystery.

"Remember, *you're* in charge," were Mr. Gilbert's parting words to me that day in his office. His words made me proud, but also a little nervous. I remember how excited Marty was when I got home and told her about my promotion. It felt good to be a boss.

I didn't tell her what the senior foreman on the day shift had delighted in showing me. It was a bullet hole in the wall of the foreman's office. My predecessor had just missed being hit by a soft-nose slug from a thirty-eight pistol fired by a disgruntled fork truck driver whom he had fired for drinking on the job. At supper I shared with Marty my thoughts about how I was going to handle being the boss of the night crew. I had never even been a supervisor on any summer jobs I held in high school. My head was filled with thoughts about the night shift union steward whom I heard was a real "locker room lawyer," always able to get the better of management personnel in grievance settlements. I guess my youth and enthusiasm for this first chance had made me blind to the negatives I had been fed by the other foremen, who were at least fifteen years older than me and probably destined to remain in their present jobs until they were retired.

Marty praised me that night. "I know it's just the first of many. Do you have the right clothes?" she added. I had decided to wear a white shirt, even though it was a dirty environment, because I wanted to set myself apart from the men I was to supervise. Grandmother had told me on several occasions that to be a leader one must "stand tall." I wasn't quite sure what that meant, but thinking about this made me remember the vice president at Procter and Gamble. Mr. Pleasants was tall and wore a three-piece suit, a homburg hat, and a cashmere overcoat, and carried a leather briefcase. I also remembered the image of a hero, General George Patton, with his shiny helmet, polished boots, ivory-handled pistols and form-fitting coat. These leaders did seem to stand tall in front of their charges.

During high school summer jobs at a shoe factory, ceramic tile factory and the freight yards, I saw bosses giving orders, bawling people out, walking around with a serious glare, pointing to things that were to be moved, and signing papers. Once, at the tile factory, I overheard my boss and the plant manager talking about how they had to get rid of a certain man who worked near me, because he was a "troublemaker," somebody who might start a union. From this, at seventeen, I deduced that a union guy must be a bad person. Gosh, I thought, the mill where I was going to work had a union, the A.F.L. Papermakers. How will I supervise unionized workers? No one in our family had ever been in a union. My uncles and grandmother had always said negative things about them. Our family, with deep New England-English roots, and as Americans, Episcopalians, and Republicans for decades, was not in the labor movement. I had assimilated many of my family's values and beliefs, including those on organized labor.

As I reflected on my lowly and taxing situation I thought of my former classmates, now at Harvard, Yale, Williams, or other fine schools where they were studying medicine, law, political science, or business administration. Many of these guys in time would receive masters and doctorate degrees. Thinking about them didn't do much for my self-confidence. Here I was on a graveyard shift with a high school diploma and nine night school credits, realizing someday I'd be competing for a top management job with these educated guys. Higher education was common to the early Silent Generation. With the Korean War drawing only a minimum of soldiers and marines compared to World War II, many young men were going to school. Also, the changing attitude toward available and ambitious women, caused by their necessarily heavy participation in formerly "men only" jobs during the war, gave them the confidence to "go for it." And the economic strengthening of America which followed the Depression and World War II, made more funds available for tuition, as did the GI Bill.

I knew my former classmates were a long way from my night shift foreman's job at Philip Carey's roofing mill, which paid $275 a month. Well, I had nobody to blame but myself. But maybe someday I'd make it to a better job. Every time I thought about my screw-ups, I'd remember Marty and the coming baby. She was great. No matter what I did, leaving her alone for school or work, or trying to sleep in the day, she was always smiling and had some encouraging words. Jesus, I had to take care of her, I just had to.

*   *   *

The first night, at about ten o'clock, dressed in an old white shirt with frayed collar, tan pants, and heavy work shoes, I grabbed my lunch box and headed for the streetcar. Riding along I opened my lunch box, and there was a sandwich made by Marty, an orange, a cookie, and an "I love you" note stuck to the inside of the lid. She had sat in the winged chair in front of the window waving as I walked toward the streetcar stop. At the plant the second-shift foreman introduced me to my fifty-three men. Superintendent Gilbert had posted a notice on the board announcing my appointment as new third-shift foreman. Someone had written, "Here comes another one." When the second-shift foreman went home at three a.m., I walked the two floors and the outside areas of the mill. The men looked at me quizzically, uttering a terse hi ya, or yeah. A couple said more friendly things, like "Hi ya, boss," or "Welcome to nights." Many of the guys looked sleepy. My crew was a mixture of blacks, usually on the less-skilled jobs, a lot of whites from the low-income part of town and a lot of hill people from Kentucky who had come to the big city to work in the defense plants during World War II. They all wanted to earn that "time and again" for countless overtime hours making engines for the P-47 fighter planes. The union shop steward said nothing when I met him. I extended my hand, which he did not touch. I took this as an omen of possible animosities to come.

The two machines scheduled to operate were running. I checked time cards, made several more rounds, told the mechanic about a couple of minor items, entered my comments and production quantities in the log book, and headed for the streetcar. This supervisory stuff wouldn't be too bad. I was the boss, and on that first night we met standards! I couldn't wait to get home and tell Marty.

After the first few nights of sailing through on the exhilaration of being a boss, I found my new routine becoming a struggle. I'd get home at seven-forty-five in the morning, eat a bowl of cereal, and go to bed with light pouring through the window shades, and sleep till three-thirty, get up and study for an hour, then leave by streetcar for evening college. After school, which ended at ten o'clock, I would catch another streetcar for a forty-minute ride to the plant in Lockland, and get there ten minutes before my shift started. I was attending evening college at the University of Cincinnati two nights a week, and working six. On non-school nights I would spend the few hours before leaving for the plant with Marty listening to music, playing chess, or once in awhile, when our budget allowed, going to a nearby movie.

As I settled into the job, the newness of a "new boss" wore off with the men. Almost every night I would be confronted or tested by someone. "Hey Boss, how should I do this?" Of course their knowledge of the process was far greater than mine. I was only an observer so far. These men had worked there for years. They knew the minute details of how the dry felt would react with the 450-degree asphalt, or how to set the slate blender cams to achieve the desired colors. But when there was a saturator break, the dread of any roofing machine foreman or crewman, the men became suddenly very sluggish in their pace to fish out the pieces of torn felt from the saturator pan, clear the coater, and clear the slate and press sections of the machine before rethreading the machine and restarting production. As incidents became more numerous and downtime increased, I became frustrated and hollered at the men, "Come on you guys. Let's get going!" To which they just looked blank or said, "Yeah Boss, whatcha want us to do?"

Production suffered. My nightly numbers were in descent. Mr. Gilbert started calling me at eleven each night to see if there was anything I might want to share. My daytime sleep was fitful, interrupted by the realization that I wasn't making it as a foreman. The more my shift fell behind the other two, the more tense I became. I was threatened by the glaring low numbers in the production log and by my own inner knowledge of how I couldn't seem to cope with the men.

My confidence was ebbing fast. I was sleeping only three or four hours a day. My school work was becoming a greater load with each passing week. I was carrying Accounting I, Labor Economics, and Purchasing. Trying to balance T accounts after three or four hours of fitful sleep was a high hurdle. In my first year at school I'd been on the Dean's list. Now I saw that goal slipping due to my worry and fatigue. I was always exhausted from lack of sleep and constant tension. I was not myself with Marty, but she never complained. Her perception of what was bothering me was accurate. One night before work she told me that if I thought working at nights was not good for me, she'd help me scour the want ads for another job. She also said that she knew I could win out where I was. "I never doubted your intelligence or effort, Chris," she said as she and our baby she was carrying sat on my lap. My tiredness melted away, and I balanced all ten of those damn T accounts.

Because of our decline in production, Mr. Gilbert scheduled Ford Hopper, the second-shift foreman, to stay two hours into my shift. Ford was to help me get the men off to a good start. Naturally, the machines ran well for these two hours; then when

Ford left, trouble would begin. Paper would break at the press roll section. Next, the-early morning cold drafts in the rear of the sixty-year-old building would chill the top saturator rolls, and the dry felt would stick to them and cause a pan break. This caused a half hour of downtime, plus sullen bitching by the crew as I pushed them to get the machine going again.

One night I asked Ford what was wrong with my crew. He responded, with a cynical, lip-curling, "It's the fucking union, pal—the fucking union. These guys need a strong hand or they'll eat your lunch. Look out there at that nigger shop steward, he's just always around behind your back tellin' the guys to mess up. 'Cause if they mess up enough, the old man'll move your ass outta here, then he'll be the big ass hero with the men. Ya need to fire one of the son-of-a-bitches. Then you'll get the respect ya need." I tried to digest this advice remembering Ford's twenty-five years on the job and his good production record. Somehow I just couldn't quite accept it. I was troubled for days, so I stayed over one morning and talked to the level-headed General Foreman, John Miller, about what Ford had said. John was a solid guy, and Mr. Gilbert's right-hand man. He just looked at me while I talked. Then he said, "Bob, Ford's bark is a lot louder than his bite. He doesn't act like that on his shift. He's firm, but I think he was giving you a little stuff with that advice. You run around trying to fire everybody and it'll blow up in your face. Just hang in there. You're learning."

"Thanks, John. Can I call you if I get in a jam?"

"Sure."

I felt better after my talk with him. When I shared all of this with Marty, she said, "Chris, maybe Ford is jealous of you."

"Jealous of me? Why?"

"Cause you're young and probably going somewhere one day. He's stuck where he is, I'd guess from what you've said."

"Thanks, babe, you're the best."

"Just trust in God, Chris. You're smart and strong, and I believe in you." I felt better, and vowed to try harder.

A week later I was walking on the second floor where the various colors of slate granules were being blended before being fed to the machine below. As I rounded the corner I found Evans, the slate hauler, asleep behind the warm coating mixer. I shook Evans' shoulder and told him he was fired for sleeping on the job. When the ensuing grievance was filed, the plant manager told me I was wrong. On a night shift, one had to use a little sense. Yes, if a man was a chronic on-the-job-sleeper he could be dismissed, but in this case Evans must be given a warning because it was his first time. Firing Evans was too severe. He was put back to work and given the two days pay he had lost. The settlement earned me sneers and derisive grins from the shop steward and his allies.

I continued to struggle. I got my first below-A grades in two subjects. One night, dreading going to work, I was looking in the drawer for socks and came across my *Book of Common Prayer*. It had been given to me by Bishop Hobson at my confirmation. Memories of Grandmother Laurie and her wise words, "Believe in God and get ahead" came rushing back.

"Huh, I'm not doing either. I haven't been to church or said my prayers for more than a year, and I'm sure as hell not getting ahead." Seeing Marty, now four months pregnant, in the next room, I sucked in my breath with the realization that I may even get fired if things kept going the way they were. I remember closing my lunch pail with my left hand, and instinctively placing the prayer book on top of the wax-paper-wrapped sandwich. Marty made meatloaf once a week for me. "Thanks for the sandwich," I called from the bedroom.

"I love you, Chris, please be careful tonight," she smiled as I left her alone for the night.

About two a.m. as I was eating my lunch at the desk in our foreman's office, Frank Waddy, the saturator operator on number three machine came in. "Need new gloves, Boss. Dees ain't good no more. I got burnt last night when I was fishin' that break. See the hole here?" I dropped my sandwich and got a pair of the long gauntlet gloves that were issued to the men who worked around 450-degree asphalt. As I turned back, I noticed that Frank had picked up the prayer book next to my lunch pail. When he saw me, he placed the book back on the desk and looked up into my eyes. His look was expressionless. "Thank you, Boss," he said as he exited the office with the new pair of gloves. I noticed a smudge of dried asphalt on the small gold cross embossed on the front cover.

The next day, Mr. Gilbert asked me to stay over in the morning and come to his office. He asked me to tell him what I saw as the trouble with my shift. He quizzed me: Why was my downtime so high? Why did my crew take twice as long as the other shifts to get the machine going again after a break? I didn't have definitive answers, so I alluded to the union steward, cold weather, sleepy men, being reversed on my firing of Evans, and other generalities. To all of my weak answers, Mr. Gilbert said very little, but he concluded the meeting with the thought that maybe my talents lay in other fields than line supervision. He said he'd review our conversation and talk to the other foremen. "I'll see you again in a week, Bob." Our meeting ended with this curt directive.

I almost threw up in the streetcar that morning as I felt the weight of Mr. Gilbert's words. Was I a loser again? What could I do to support Marty and the new baby if I was fired? I opened my lunch pail in case I did throw up. There was my prayer book, with the asphalt smudge still on the cross. I flipped through it just to take my mind off the wave of negative thoughts that consumed me. On page fifty-seven I read a collect for guidance, and reread it so intently that I went one stop too far on the streetcar and had to walk a quarter of a mile back to my stop.

When I arrived home Marty was gone, but there was a note saying she was with her parents so she could do some shopping downtown for baby clothes and supplies. God, I wished she were there! That afternoon I overslept, so I had to eat supper on the run in order to make it to class. Marty entered the apartment as I was cramming a banana in my mouth. As I ran out, she called down the stairwell, "I love you. Please be careful."

I hardly heard my professors that night. I kept thinking about the meeting with Mr. Gilbert. I knew I was in trouble. The worry preyed on me, knotting my stomach. I half wished the streetcar would never get there. But at the plant, with a lot of inner talk, I mustered up a poker face, checked the men in, set the color schedule for the shift, got the mechanic to adjust the P.I.V. drive on the shingle cutter, and started my walk around the plant. The machines, for once, were all running okay. I felt a ripple of gratitude that I didn't have to immediately jump into a troubled situation. I guess when you're adrift in a sea of worry, any twig of good fortune looks like a raft. When I got to the back end of number three, I saw Frank finish splicing a new roll of dry felt on the exhausted roll, which meant he had twenty minutes before the next splice had to be made in this continuous roofing process. Frank turned when he saw me, and said in a hesitating voice, "Bob, I see by that book you got dat you're a God believin' man. Dat's right, ain't it?"

I looked down at my feet, and then looked up. "I think I am, but I could work harder at it."

He asked me to sit with him on the asphalt and limestone-stained bench next to the saturator. "Bob, you workin' yourself to death, but you ain't gettin' nowhere. It's like you tryin' to reap somethin' good from a whole field of dem tares dey is always talkin' 'bout in the good book."

I asked Frank what he meant. "Boy, let me tell you somethin', not that I should be doin' it, but you seems like you wants to be good. I heard you got a wife, an' is goin' to have a baby some time. Dat right?"

"Yes, that's right. Baby's due in early September, we think."

"You probably need this job to support your family."

"Yes, I do," I said and sagged down on the bench, searching the face of this fifty-five-year-old black man.

Frank very hesitatingly reached out his hand and put it on my shoulder. "So do all of these men workin' here. Most of 'em ain't got more'n a few dollars saved. But, dey need to be led. Dey ain't neither cattle, nor sheep. Dey is men, just like you an' me. You want to be driven?"

"No, I guess I don't."

He told me he had been raised by his sharecropper father and mother along with eight brothers and sisters, fifty miles east of Memphis in a dirt-floor, shotgun house. He never went to school, just worked on the owner's farm till he came in 1942 to Cincinnati with his older brother to work in the Wright Engine plant.

I asked him. "What do you think I need to do to lead the men?"

"Be good to 'em. Find out how dey live. What's botherin' them. You know dis asphalt is dirty stuff. Dat cheap old soap dey got in both the locker rooms ain't no good. I hear dey got some good Lava soap in the storeroom over in twenty-seven. How about gettin' a few bars an' passin' 'em out? Hey, time to splice the next roll," He jumped up and hobbled back to the felt stand.

The rest of the shift I thought about what old Frank had shared, then all the way home. I talked about it with Marty at breakfast, where I also fell asleep over my cereal bowl.

When I awoke at five in the evening, I was still thinking about it. I knew I was at one of those forks in life's road. Firing people and fighting unions wasn't what I wanted to do. That stuff wasn't about being a leader. As I look back to that April, I can say my life took a different turn from the ten minutes I spent with Frank Waddy on that dirty bench by number three saturator. I learned a lasting lesson from a man who couldn't read and signed his pay check with an X.

There was no school that night, so Marty and I spent the next few hours listening to some good music and talking about the baby and the things she had bought. "Chris, you don't seem as tense tonight. How are you feeling?" I told her I felt better, but I didn't know why.

"Hey, can you believe it? I'm looking forward to going to work tonight!"

That night at the plant I walked around the plant at a much slower pace. I stopped at every station and talked to each man, asking about something that was not work related. It was a Friday night, and I knew they were going to have Saturday and Sunday night off, so I thought I'd try the soap idea. I filled out a requisition for Lava soap, sent a man to the storeroom with it, and had a case put in my office. About a half hour before quitting time, I went around the plant and handed each man a bar. The looks on their faces were something I had never seen. As I passed it out, I smiled, "See you Monday night, I need you."

On Monday, I stopped on my rounds and pulled up a keg to sit next to Bill, a press roll operator, who was divorced and suffered from hemorrhoids. I couldn't get him to talk at first, but finally I asked why he was always frowning. Bill told me he needed an operation for his condition, but couldn't afford it. I told him I had just heard at the foreman's meeting that there was a new medical plan. "Bill, maybe the new plan will help with the expense. I'll check on it in the morning and get back to you."

Later, I went to the second-floor slate room where I saw Evans sitting behind the coating mixer, just about to doze off. I went up to him, gently kicked his foot, and said, "Hey, old timer, how about a cup of coffee. Here's a quarter. Run up to the canteen and get us each one. The fresh air'll wake you up. I'll watch your job while you're gone."

"Yes, sir, yes, sir," Evans replied with a smile that displayed shiny white teeth. That night our shift made eighty-seven percent of standard instead of the usual fifty percent.

A few weeks later, I stopped by Frank's post and thanked him for what he had taught me. "But Frank, I think that Carter, the union steward, is still trying to work against me."

"Don't you mind that uppity, high-toned nigger. You just keep doin' what you're doin.' Workin' man needs a union sometimes, but not when dey fill dem stewards full of ideas about dem bein' da real boss. You is doin' some good things now." This was better than all the "good runs" Mr. Gilbert had written in the log book for the last two nights. I felt lighter than I had in more than a year.

A few nights later, Mitch, the fork truck driver ran into my office. His wife had burned herself at the laundry where she worked and he needed to go home. "Bob, there ain't no one else can drive the fork truck, but I gotta go!"

"You go, Mitch, we'll cover for you some way or other. Go on!" I ran out of the office, grabbed the warehouse driver and my machine relief man and asked if they could cover for Mitch in addition to their regular jobs. "I'll give each of you guys your lunch break and I'll drive if you don't laugh at me for driving slower than you do." They agreed. The next night there was a note from Mr. Gilbert saying he was glad to see the production improve, but curious about why I had been requisitioning so much Lava soap.

As April faded into May and June, my shift production slowly improved to acceptable levels. Then in July, we had the highest percentage against standard of all three shifts. I had made some simple charts and graphs showing production, downtime, and scrap percentages, which I shared with the men, praising them for excelling over those other guys. I told them even though they worked at night, they were really THE FIRST SHIFT. When we set a new record for the whole month in August, I bought everyone a hamburger and a coffee, even though it meant I didn't get that set of Civil War books I wanted. When the baby came in the middle of a shift in September, one of the men loaned me his car to get home quickly. He told me, "Just leave it in front of your apartment with the keys under the mat."

The next week I passed out cigars that said "It's a Boy." I thanked my crew for completing that shift when I left them without any supervision at three-thirty in the morning. "I owe you guys." Most of the men smiled and said something to the effect of now that I had a son, I better get started on making another, just so I didn't forget how.

By December, the third shift was the talk of the company. That was when Mr. Gilbert called me one day and said there was an opening in the Industrial Engineering department, and that I should consider it as it could be a step to higher management. He told me I would continue receiving promotions if I continued going to college and demonstrating the leadership I had shown in turning around the third shift. I accepted the job.

On my last night as night shift foreman, I put a note on the board thanking the crew for helping me to achieve this promotion. Frank and five others came into the office and gave me twenty-five dollars to buy something I wanted. No supervisor before had ever received a collection from the hourly work force. As I walked around the plant where I had struggled but grown so much in the last two years, I had a hard time saying goodbye to each man. I couldn't help crying. My throat was sore from the unsuccessful attempts to suppress my tears. Not a single man laughed at me.

~

C H A P T E R

11

Experience teaches slowly, and at the cost of mistakes.
J. A. Froude, 1818-1904

It came to me as I slid out of our double bed. It was my first day in an office; my last night as a graveyard foreman in the shingle mill was just forty-eight hours ago, and now I was going to work in the daylight, dressed in a suit and tie. No more working all night and then trying to sleep in our one-bedroom apartment with Marty a nervous wreck trying to keep two-month-old Bobby from crying. She almost wore the Taylor-Tot out walking him around Pleasant Ridge. No more trying to stay awake from six-forty until ten after ten in evening college classes. I could go after work, then go home and sleep—gee, like normal people!

Agog with curiosity and excitement-induced stomach butterflies, I entered the industrial engineering office on the second floor of the plant office. It was going to be a new world for me—no roaring machines, no mica dust in the air, no pungent fumes of asphalt—just a somber room full of twenty desks, all occupied, save one, with intelligent, articulate, college-trained engineers.

"Gentlemen, this is Bob Christopher, our newest addition. Bob comes to us from line-supervision in the shingle mill. I know you will welcome him and show him every courtesy." In less than a minute, the manager introduced me and assigned me to the empty desk. I walked down the aisle between the two rows, as a captured pioneer might have done through an Indian gauntlet on the plains of the West. My new associates looked at me with expressionless faces, which I later learned masked their incredulousness at how this twenty-three-year-old, untrained college dropout from the factory floor had the audacity to mix in with their mature and educated group. Most of them were graduate engineers, some with master's degrees. I thought to hell with that; I had a wife and son to support, and I was going to "get ahead," just like Grandmother Christopher had told me to. I'd had enough failure—enough sitting on the outside looking in. Philip Carey was the rock on which I would build the future for me and my family. Hadn't I just gotten my second promotion in a little more than two years— why not more?

I started making time studies, in hundredth parts of a minute, of many labor-intensive operations in the plant. Luckily, I didn't have to include any of my former night shift crew. The objective of my work was to see if we could improve the units per manhour as well as set the standards for incentive pay. Usually the workers tried to make the work take longer than it should in order to get a loose standard. I had to learn how to rate their pace to arrive at a reasonable standard. To help me learn, I was taking a night school course in time and motion study from Mr. Gilbert, my former boss.

Three weeks after starting my new job, we celebrated our son's first Christmas. At three-and-a-half months, he didn't grasp it, but I appreciated the spirit of new birth—both abstractly and personally. Was our new child destined to make a mark, no matter how small, on the world, as did that ancient birth in Bethlehem? As I thought about the turnaround in my life since rejoining the church and marrying Marty, I thanked God. At an Epiphany Sunday service (my mother was watching Bobby) we sang *We Three Kings*. Singing (?) in my flat, non-musical voice, I thought about my three personal *Magi* who had brought me gifts finer than frankincense, myrrh, and gold—Grandmother Christopher, Marty, and Harold Gilbert, who had brought me hope, love, and my earthly resurrection.

I worked extra hours, quizzed everybody in the department about techniques, and practiced timing things at home; I was determined to be the best in our group. Soon I was working on job combinations and eliminations. The common touch I had picked up in my factory floor days stood me in good stead—I was able to talk the language of the workers being timed—simple, practical, and very concrete. These men couldn't afford to dwell in abstractions—they dealt in how to earn enough to feed their families. There were a few four-letter words, but not as many as today's movies would lead us to think. It was a real test for me to be talking and working with a machine operator or laborer, as my studies were aimed at reducing his job or raising the bar on his incentive earnings. I worried about being fair to the men while keeping the company efficient. There had to be a balance—the worker needed a job to live, and the company had to keep its costs competitive or there would be no jobs. Industry, like nature, survives on equilibrium.

I noticed that many of my college-trained associates did their work from a theoretical approach, seldom leaving the office or delving into the nuts-and-bolts details of the floor operations as I did. In fact I spent so much time in the production departments, the boss used to ask me about it. When I told him, he said, "Good, Bob, that's where it is." At the end of the year I had saved the company more money in the labor area than anyone else in the department—roughly twenty times my salary!

I was charged up by the realization that I was making it in this higher-educated playing field. I ate up night school, taking four subjects at a time, and being on the Dean's List every semester. However, without a very supportive wife, none of it would have happened. When I went into the industrial engineering department, I lost my shift differential and overtime pay bringing a net result of a thirty-percent cut in pay ($5,000 to $3,500 per year). My promotion and its valuable experience was one Marty and I paid for, but never regretted. To paraphrase Henry Ford, a man should only invest in himself until he's forty. With the cost of better clothes for my office job, a new baby, and night school tuition, there was no money for clothes for Marty. She never complained, only quietly encouraged me and took care of Bobby while I worked and attended school. We were truly following Ford's advice, as every extra penny was going into things that educated me—there were no savings, stocks, cars, television, or frills in those early years.

Things were rolling along. After a year I got a three-hundred-dollar-a-year raise, and our son continued to amaze us with his brightness and fine looks (another objective parental opinion). But in the late winter of 1954, a recession hit the building materials industry. Cutbacks in personnel were the order of the day. Our department, on a "black Friday," went from twenty to six. I was one of the six who remained! I had a new boss and many added duties, which allowed me to not only work on labor savings, but material and process ones too. I went for this—it was an opportunity to show what I could do.

Besides taking four courses in school and picking up more responsibilities on the job, I was teaching Mr. Gilbert's time study class at evening college for ten bucks a week, which helped Marty and I buy our first house in Silverton. It was a forty-year-old, two-bedroom frame house next to the house where seventh-grader Roger Staubach lived. We'd see Roger and his dad tossing a football in the backyard, never dreaming how far those early passes would take him in the world of football, the Navy, and a Christian-based, exemplary life. I ran into him in 1978 at the end of his Dallas Cowboy career at a trade show in Texas, chatted with him about the old neighborhood, and returned home with autographed pictures and a football. What a great role model he is!

In the spring of 1955 our second son, James, came into the world at 10-3/4 pounds. When I told my boss, he said I needed a day off. Marty's response was, "You, how about me?" We were happy with our growing family. With Jim's birth I started a bi-weekly campaign for a raise. Finally, after three months of lobbying I received a $600-a-year raise, the largest one-time raise in our department's history. This allowed us to buy our first car, a second-hand Plymouth sedan, which we called Chauncey.

One May morning, Mr. Bush, the Lockland complex's manager, called me into his office. Would I take over the inspection force of the quality control division, the one where I worked in my first five months at Carey? The forty inspectors had unionized eighteen months earlier, and in that time had filed over two hundred grievances. The aged chief inspector was very limited in people skills and only knew black and white when it came to the rejection of materials or dealing with people. Quality had suffered in all nine production divisions, and labor problems were taking a lot of management's time for dealing with petty gripes, many of which were aimed at the chief inspector. He was known by this: when an inspector needed a new red pencil to highlight a rejection on his control sheet, the chief wouldn't give him one unless he turned in a stub less than an inch-and-a-half long. And, woe to him who lost his red pencil; he had to buy a new one.

I liked the opportunity to try my labor-handling skills, plus cover the entire mega-complex of the Lockland plant, as well as earn overtime. In the year that I held this job I had one grievance and saw the percent of rejected material drop from ten to four. I spent a lot of time with each inspector, regardless of the shift, stressing the importance of his job as a preventative force, not just a remedial one. From this experience, I learned a principle I have carried with me the rest of my life: people respond to a sincere personal touch. No one wants to be a number or to be categorized as "the help." I learned that an informed work force was a powerful and responsible one.

And what was the price of my steady advancement and credibility with management? Not enough time with my family, and zero knowledge of what was happening in the world. I missed the Korean War, because I was Three-A: married with child. The Korean War was in fact the Silent Generation's war, and ironically, both history and large segments of the population are *silent* about it. But many of my classmates and friends found nothing silent about the gunfire of the North Koreans or Chinese Communists. Jack Rogers, a good buddy from Walnut Hills distinguished himself as a Marine platoon leader, risking his life to save his men, for which heroism he received the Silver Star. I always admired Jack at school. We had a bond—the attraction of opposites. Jack came from a refined Southern family, lived in a large Georgian-style home in Hyde Park, and was active in Big Brothers and student council, as well as being a champion swimmer. Despite the difference in our social and economic backgrounds, we did a lot together on weekends and later shared a lot of stories at a class reunion.

*   *   *

The first half of the fifties were times of widespread mistrust. Fear of communism had pervaded our country like a gut-gnawing virus. Senator McCarthy was acting as the grand inquisitor of any and everybody, even one of America's greatest and most effective servants, George C. Marshall. In time McCarthy was exposed for the demagogue he was. But, real time communism was in many countries and being widely disseminated by the U.S.S.R., causing the cold war to escalate. There was much spying, counter spying, and single and double agents, many of whom just disappeared. The phrase "covert operation" became a part of our vocabulary. But Marty and I were insulated from these global and national actions in the bubble of striving to raise our family and make good on my series of job promotions.

And in America, another war was escalating: the fight for racial equality. Many Silent Generation people, both black and white, were a vital part; leading sit-ins, nonviolent marches, and finally forcing government intercession against segregation. These actions became foundation blocks in the integrated house our country needed to build. I can't say honestly that Marty and I were activists in the civil rights movement. We were both humbled and sad when we would see pictures of dogs unleashed on innocent black people who were seeking only the most basic of rights that poor whites take for granted. And we wondered what God thinks when He sees the "ultimate Christian" in a white sheet and hood with a Bible in one hand and a hanging noose in the other. Ethnic cleansing isn't a new practice with Iraq or Kosovo. We Americans have our own brand—ask any Native or African-American.

Marty and I, and our families, never practiced discriminatory actions toward other races or religions, but as a teenager I had told my share of ethnic jokes. Over time we assimilated the message brought forth by passive and militant voices alike— Martin Luther King and Malcolm X, both of whom died for their beliefs. If only man could minimize his penchant to dominate, to play God. But, as William Faulkner expressed in *Intruder in the Dust*, the poor southern white needed the black to push himself up in his own esteem. And this need isn't just confined to the redneck from the south. Yes, progress has been and is being made in the civil rights movement, but it is largely because African-Americans fought for it. There would be no progress without the courage of thousands exemplified by Rosa Parks, King, and Malcolm X. But for them and their followers, we'd still have segregated washrooms and eateries. Through a slow evolutionary process, Marty and I have become supportive of any movement that works for equality. We can do more, both as a society, and personally. We keep trying, and we feel good about how free of prejudice our three sons have grown up to be.

*   *   *

After a year as chief inspector, I was again called into Mr. Bush's office, where he introduced me to the general manager of Carey's Eastern Division, which included the entire East Coast sales area and a manufacturing plant in Perth Amboy, New Jersey. Would I now consider taking the job of assistant plant manager at the Perth plant? I knew I would that very instant, but replied, "May I talk it over with my wife tonight?"

"Certainly, Bob," Bill Bush (who was to become one of my stronger mentors) said. "Let Clarence Howard [the general manager] tell you more of the details." Mr. Howard was a tough-talking salesman who never minced words about what he wanted or thought. But he was most cordial to me, and I looked forward to learning from him. He told me the Perth plant had made a lot of progress under his guidance as general manager.

That night Marty and I got out the atlas and found Perth Amboy. She smiled with tongue-in-cheek, "Chris, where you go, I go." I guessed she must have just been reading the book of Ruth. Then she asked about the job, and did I think it was an opportunity. Finally, at midnight, we said yes. The next day I told Mr. Bush we would go. I didn't tell Marty that the Perth plant had had thirteen plant managers in thirteen years, and had never made a profit—it was called the Siberia of the company. Having just turned twenty-seven, I didn't know corporate fear—I saw it as an opportunity—as in, where the risk is high, so is the reward.

I had six weeks to get things in order: train a replacement and make sure Marty, Bobby, and Jimmy had what they needed while I was fitting into the new job and finding a home for us in far-away New Jersey. I also had to attend my graduation from evening college. Dressed in cap and gown, I stood with hundreds of others in Nippert Stadium and was presented my Certificate in Factory Management. I had earned twenty-four grades over six years—twenty-two A's and the two B's I received during the days of stress and trial on my night shift foreman's job. Armed with fourteen management subjects, I set out, like David with his handful of stones, to slay the Goliath of no profitability at the Perth Amboy plant. But my sling of tough on-the-floor experience was strong.

*   *   *

"Now the Lord said to Abram, Get thee out
of thy country...unto a land that I will shew thee."
Genesis 12

I boarded the dull red Pennsylvania Railroad car of the Cincinnati Limited at the Norwood station and found my roomette. Through the window, I saw Marty and the boys waving at me. My heart contracted and my eyes welled with tears. Marty's beautiful face had a sadness I had not seen before. She was fighting back her tears; I was going to be gone for at least six weeks, maybe longer. We had never been separated a single day in six years—I worked a lot, but we had some time together each day, even if it was only a few minutes and sometimes at three in the morning after I had solved a quality problem at the plant.

The engineer released the air brake and pushed the throttle forward on the diesel engine. My family still waved as they were left behind by the accelerating train. But the picture of them standing on that platform has stayed with me to this day. The click-click-click of the wheels passing over the track joints told me we were rolling into a major new chapter of our lives. We were going into a land that we hoped God would show us, as He had shown Abram.

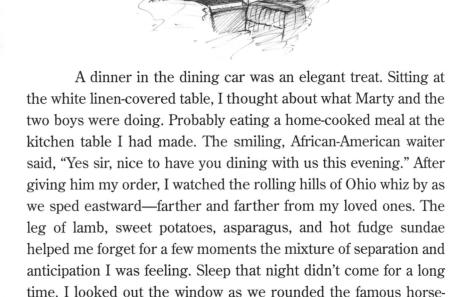

A dinner in the dining car was an elegant treat. Sitting at the white linen-covered table, I thought about what Marty and the two boys were doing. Probably eating a home-cooked meal at the kitchen table I had made. The smiling, African-American waiter said, "Yes sir, nice to have you dining with us this evening." After giving him my order, I watched the rolling hills of Ohio whiz by as we sped eastward—farther and farther from my loved ones. The leg of lamb, sweet potatoes, asparagus, and hot fudge sundae helped me forget for a few moments the mixture of separation and anticipation I was feeling. Sleep that night didn't come for a long time. I looked out the window as we rounded the famous horse-shoe curve at Altoona, Pennsylvania and could see the end car of our train from my head-end one. It was appropriate—I thought, "I can see where I've been, but I can't see where I'm going."

After ten days of working (more like observing and learning) at the plant, and going back to my single room at the motel for a lonely dinner, I told Mr. Howard I didn't want to stay any longer. He listened, then said, "How about a weekend back in Cincinnati at company expense?"

I jumped at this, casting aside my ill-based decision to quit. I called Marty that night (a rare thing in 1956—people, particularly struggling young families, didn't spend long-distance money unless it was an emergency. Wires and letters were still the major means of communication.) "I'll be home Friday night!" We almost wasted the weekend just trying to decide how to have a super time. Finally, on Saturday evening we simply started living our previous lives, and it was great, although leaving for the airport on Sunday for an all-night, four-stop, piston-engine plane ride was very hard. But, we knew I'd be home in two more weeks, and every other weekend until the house sold; nothing much was happening on that front. I always brought the boys something, like the Uncle Remus book that inspired me to try to say all the Brers: "Rabbit, Terrapin, Fox" and of course, "de tar baby" in proper dialect as I read to them. It always tore me up to see their faces when I left again. After I'd been at Perth six weeks, the plant manager resigned to go with a competitor. This of course ignited my expectations, but I also knew I had no experience at that level of management.

Three-hundred-and-fifty employees were spread over three shifts in four major production departments and several service functions: a paper mill (the felt from it was the substrate for asphalt roofing); the roofing department with three machines; the asbestos shingle department; and the asphalt-based paint and emulsion department. Additionally there was plant engineering with thirty-four mechanics, electricians, and pipe fitters; a quality control force; shipping and receiving department; and the office functions. I understood many of the intricacies of roofing, but the other production units were new to me. Nothing was said about who would replace the departed manager until a senior production consultant from Lockland was assigned as interim manager.

We finally sold our house with the help of a company subsidy and moved into a $15,000 tract house that, except for the color, looked like every other house in the sixty-unit subdivision. We celebrated Christmas of 1956 with Marty's visiting parents in our new seven-room split-level, where three rooms equaled one in our Cincinnati house. But we were together. I took Marty's father on a tour of the plant. He said, "Bob, you sure will have your hands full managing this old plant." I saw through his eyes, not my ambition-filled ones, that it was a hodge podge of old, unrelated buildings. The warehouse was a former sweatshop-like shirt manufacturing plant; the paper and roofing mills had been a late nineteenth-century, terra cotta tile molding and firing plant; the asbestos cement operation had been a roller rink; and the office was an old three-story house—a real heterogeneous admixture of architecture, degrees of decline, and configuration. It was truly "a house that Jack built."

I learned that buildings do not an operation make. Within that homely assembly of buildings was a hard working supervisory staff, diverse in ethnic background—Italian, Polish, Portuguese, German, English, Slovene, and Hungarian—but carrying a strong belief in themselves and a good knowledge of their operations. I took to them, and they took to me. I wouldn't have traded that favorably reactive chemistry for all the new buildings in the world. Then it happened—I was told I would be the new plant manager at $9,000 per year, with the hope (slim) of a small bonus.

The plant was still in the red when I received my new responsibilities and it stayed that way for the remaining nine months of 1957. I worked twelve hours a day plus eight on Saturdays. Every department superintendent cooperated with me, showed me things, and made sincere, thought-out suggestions, but we couldn't fight low selling prices and erratic production. Asbestos cement-siding shingles were a nightmare to make, and the variable quality of the dry felt from the paper mill caused a lot of downtime and scrap in the roofing machines.

With all of the hours I was working, Marty was alone a lot. Every couple of months she'd break down and cry out of loneliness. But, God bless her, she'd quickly wipe the tears away and support me all the more. She truly was the backbone and spirit of my life—without her I'd have failed. Besides my being away from home so much, we got news of her father's untimely death while she was eight months pregnant. We flew back to Cincinnati for the funeral. Again, Marty showed her strength of character in how she handled this deep loss. She said, "He was a wonderful man and always kind to me. I guess our soon-to-be-born child comes into our lives as Daddy leaves." I know she mourned deeply, and privately, for this quiet, gentle man, but she never let her grief come between her and the boys and me, or her duty to the family. She was, and is, a rock of stability.

A bright spot that fall was the birth of our third son, John—a happy child, who scared us to death when he contracted a severe bronchial infection at two months. For days we'd sit up with him round the clock taking turns sleeping. One night we thought he had stopped breathing. I grabbed him and jumped into a steamy shower in my pajamas. The steam helped him breath, and he started to heal. All parents go through scares with their children—mental, physical, and psychological. But what would life be without our children?

As 1957 closed on red numbers, my old mentor Bill Bush would come to Perth every other week for a two-day visit. He gave me invaluable counsel. "Robert, you're running yourself to death, but you're only half effective. Now just sit here with me. Take a yellow pad and list the first ten things you need to accomplish tomorrow—then do them!" I did, and after a month of this discipline, and charting some of our troubled areas, (the same way I had as an enlightened night shift foreman) things grudgingly improved. By April of 1958, thirteen months after my promotion, we were slightly in the black for the first time in the fifteen-year history of this plant. And except for a break-even year in the deep recession of 1960, things remained that way until I was promoted back to Cincinnati in 1967.

Achieving and sustaining profitability did not come with a keystroke or in a couple of over-simplified sentences, but I think it was best said in a poem, written by an unknown author, and titled *The Mills of the Gods*:

"The mills of the Gods grind slowly,

Yet they grind exceeding small."

The mills that grind success in old plants, in cyclical industries, grind even slower and smaller. The turnaround of the Perth plant was like filling two large sacks of flour, one micron-sized grain at a time.

I could write reams about the hundreds of issues I confronted and solved to allow the evolutionary growth that spawned sustained improvement at the Perth plant, but it would take an entire book. Just to name a few: low selling prices; capital-starved equipment; bad habits from the "old days"; poor people-handling practices in the unionized workforce; and lack of continuity in plant management—thirteen managers in as many years. But, while we were challenged by these things and more, we showed up every day (and many nights) and met them head on.

My gruff old paper mill superintendent, who called me "Slim," said, "Slim, you came in here and literally picked this mother up on your back and carried it." His eloquent praise was more than I deserved. But I did put in twelve-hour days, spending very little time in the office, so I could be out with "the troops," encouraging them, helping them to solve our problems, and learning what was needed to carry out my foundation-stone principle of management: "Okay, we had this happen, but what do we need to get or do so it doesn't happen again." We always came up with a plan, equipment changes, or new procedures, often deriving them over coffee in cardboard cups and Marlboro cigarettes until midnight.

I had a capital budget, always woefully short of what we needed, so I learned how to kite and finagle capital funds. One practice was to call my boss in Cincinnati at three in the morning and hurriedly say something about an emergency breakdown. He'd mumble something like, "Take care of it, Robert. Call me tomorrow and send in a capital request." The new stuff was ordered by eight a.m. A couple of times he asked me if anything ever broke down in the daytime! In the request, I'd always say that this was outside of our budget, and could we just approve it that way. After a few years of wheedling and "stealing" extra capital out of a tight management, we had the fastest-running, most productive machines in the entire company! But, more important than the many major machinery changes and equipment was mainspring roofing superintendent, Manuel Martin.

Manuel was an immigrant from Portugal, with a third-grade education, but an intelligence level as great as anyone with whom I have ever worked. Coupling his inherent smarts with a strong work ethic and a rare savvy for mechanical things, he tripled our roofing production per hour over the eleven years he worked for me. Our relationship was perhaps the most educational and synergistic one of my entire forty-seven-year work career. He taught me that big things are solved by the cumulative effect of making every tiny component the best it can be. I taught him how to handle people—that good machines were not efficient if the people running them were not motivated and relatively happy with their job.

We traded off on each other—people skills for mechanical know-how—year after year, usually after five p.m., but the sun never set on a day's production problem without our having resolved what we would do differently from that night forward. I wish I had a nickel for every problem we solved. Thirty years after I left Carey and Manuel, I flew a red-eye special, coast to coast, to hold his hand in an Edison, New Jersey, hospital as he died of cancer. I owe him so much—he taught me most of what I know about machinery and problem-solving. I was the boss, but he was the teacher. Together, we proved that two plus two can equal five or more if it has to. Ironically, and symbolically, a few months after Manuel died, the Perth Amboy plant died—closed down from the cancer of age and obsolescence, after sixty years of providing hundreds of jobs and roofing for millions of houses.

And while I waged the "war" against the enemies of competitive price cutting, union negotiations, new pollution laws that
were way ahead of existing technology, industry-wide recessions
every few years, and overtaxed facilities, I was trying to help out
on the home front as well.

No country ever won a war without the full support of its
civilians. My civilians were a very supportive, non-demanding wife
and loving, obedient kids. Nothing I have accomplished would
have been possible without them. If daddy had to work, they
understood. I couldn't articulate to them at that time what it was
like being raised during the Depression in the poor end of town,
or how the bitter taste of previous failures made me want to spit
out a gush of determination not to fail. I hadn't as yet read about
the force of overcompensation, which I now know was a throbbing
dynamo, relentlessly driving me to succeed.

I know they were disappointed that I never ate dinner
with them Monday through Friday, but I always tried to do as
much as possible with them on weekends. We went to parks, made
things together, played games, and went to Sunday school and
church every week. The first one we attended was Grace
Episcopal in Plainfield, New Jersey. It was an old established
church, resembling a cathedral in England, and whose rector
looked and sounded like he had just stepped out of an Anthony
Trollope novel. One fall morning we were approaching the church
when a chauffeured Rolls Royce pulled up and a well-dressed
dowager alighted to the sidewalk with, "I say, does anyone know
what the Haavads did yesterday?" And every Sunday as the kids
arrived for Sunday school, a kindly old gentleman with white hair
was there to greet them. He stood on the walkway into the church
in rain, snow or shine. He would smile and say "Welcome," to
everyone and pat the smallest tykes on their heads. He was as

much a tradition and dependable pillar of the church as the rector. When John was about four, he went up to him and called him God. I guess we all felt that just a little bit of God did shine through this man. Despite the spiritual atmosphere of this Gothic, Anglican sanctuary, one Sunday I pulled a gaff. We were all standing in our pew when a well-dressed and coiffured blond, clad in a leopard skin coat, glided up the aisle. When she was even with us, I said to the family a little too loudly, "I wonder if she shot it?" The blond turned red, people around us snickered, Bobby blinked, and my wife choked back a laugh as she poked me in the ribs. Hey, even Henry the VIII let his court jester in his churches!

New York City, the Big Apple, was only a forty-minute train ride for us. We'd take the kids into the city to visit museums, see buildings and movies, and ride the ferry to Staten Island. Cub Scouts also were a part of our life. Marty was a den mother, and I was a pack chairman, while young Bob earned all of the badges. Jim was a leader of his seven-year-old neighborhood group, and John followed me, imitating me as I painted, cut the grass, or washed the car. They got along fine in school, except for one year when first-grader Jim had a lack of chemistry with his teacher. In his first week of school, he ran out of the room calling her a big fat pig. I always had tried to teach them to be honest, but after our "bay of pigs" incident, I introduced them to diplomacy. And Mommy had some teacher cajoling to do.

Roofing and siding are cyclical businesses. They were particularly so in the early sixties. With the ringing in of 1963, our industry saw a recession. During the first five months of that dark year, our orders dropped to forty percent of normal, which made me have to curtail entire shifts, cut days worked, and often shut down operations for a week at a time. When we had layoffs, the hourly workers got no pay, just a small amount of unemployment

insurance, and only if we were down longer than the required waiting period. Most of the time we weren't down long enough. To
help our men survive I had them do a lot of painting, track repair,
clean-up, and minor maintenance. I got hell from the president in
bi-monthly reviews about my high indirect labor costs in a recession period, but I kept our trained crews alive and never had a
strike in my eleven years at Perth Amboy. After a serious two-day
review by the president about why I was spending so many indirect labor dollars, I sulked for a day, felt sorry for myself, talked to
God, and went right on trying to take care of my crews. I survived,
and so did our team, but I could write an essay on sophisticated
"ass-chewing." It would be authentic too; I was on the receiving
end—no pun intended.

    1963 was a bad business year, and it was also tough on the
home front. Marty had major female surgery, which scared us
both. I stopped smoking cigarettes, after twenty years of inhaling,
which gave me some depression from withdrawal. As I fretted
(without nicotine) about no business, I was also having anxiety
about how Marty and I would handle the aftereffects of her hysterectomy. We'd heard all of the tales about mood changes and
poor sex. Fortunately we had a good surgeon and estrogen! As
always, Marty's strong character helped her sail through this with
flying colors.

    I took to walking around the block after the kids were in
bed, counting stars as I dialogued with God. I had had several spiritual experiences by this time in my life, but now I faced a deeper
one. I knew I was in a wasteland without confidence and was bur-
dened with worry. This was the first time I totally let Him into my
life. There was no, "Please get me out of this," or "We need this."
No, I had been bowed by all of the weighty realities I was carrying—I guess having one's ego and confidence confounded by

suffering and worry that strips away the consuming thoughts of self, is the rite of passage to true spirituality.

After a month of the daily discipline of serious prayer and trying to provide for the men at the plant, something led me to take the family on a Sunday ride through a new housing development. We rounded a corner and saw, on that gray February afternoon, a wonderful two-story colonial home. Martha's breath let out in a huge sigh, the kids' eyes popped, and I thought, "Can we?" It was a brand new tree-lined cul-de-sac with sixteen lots. The three models were all different—not like the Monopoly-board houses of our neighborhood. "Should we?" Marty tentatively asked. "Sure," I replied with a bravado that covered my mixture of excitement and fear.

We entered the front foyer and were greeted by a smiling lady Realtor, who put us at ease—what a psychologist she was! We were in wonderland as we toured the nine rooms, all of which were twice the size of our split-level. The house sat on over half an acre. Finally, I got enough nerve to ask the price. "$27,500, sir." Armed with pamphlets and the Realtor's card, we went home in a whirl of longing.

My mind was a seesaw. On one end no business at the plant, on the other wanting to bring our family into a better neighborhood and fill Marty's days with a home of which she could be proud. I went back to see the lots on a Saturday on the way home from Perth Amboy, and met a man who had bought one on the street. He was a doctor and exactly my age. We talked for an hour, after which, in a burst of wanting to live near people like him, I picked up an offer sheet from the Realtor. Marty and I signed it that night. Four months later we were in our new home on a street with fifteen other wonderful families, all about our age, and in their first big "move-up."

We started going to a new Episcopal church in the "brainy-borough" of Metuchen, New Jersey. The rector, Doctor Fryer, was warm, an excellent administrator, and a good judge of people. He had us leading stewardship drives, teaching Sunday school, getting the boys into youth activities, and I was elected to the Vestry. We bought a secondhand car for Marty from a superintendent at the plant. The boys made friends quickly in the neighborhood, where we had several block parties, get-togethers, a bridge club, and inter-family birthday parties. It was the American dream neighborhood, one which could have been painted by Norman Rockwell and received the Good Housekeeping seal of approval. Things at Perth Amboy started humming in 1964. We were leading the company, and I started receiving bonuses—a mixture of company stock and cash.

And something new started happening at the plant—every two weeks a man came and garnered samples of the water effluent from our paper mill. Roofing felt is the shirttail relative of fine papers. Both are made from wood and wastepaper fibers carried in water to a forming machine; formed, pressed, and then dried on high-pressure revolving steel drums which are part of a three-hundred-foot-long machine; at speeds up to 250 feet per minute for roofing felt, and over 1000 for toilet tissue. Although the system that carries the processed fibers at a one-percent concentration to the forming machine is supposed to be "closed," a balance is almost impossible to maintain. This causes excess water to be discharged into a sewer, river, or in our case, the Raritan Bay. The dumped water contains wood and paper fibers, both high in BOD (biological oxygen demand) and COD (chemical oxygen demand). These oxygen demanders take oxygen from the water, rendering it stagnant, and in extreme cases, non-supportive of marine life.

As I mentioned, the laws prohibiting this type of discharge were ahead of the technology to effectively treat paper mill effluent. This condition was also true in other industries. The treating of effluents liquid, gaseous, and solid is expensive. There is generally a reluctance to spend money to do this unless it is a matter of survival. To paint the industrial companies with the broad brush of "murderers through pollution" is not fair, but there are many published cases of deliberate negligence by some companies regarding their treatment of waste and employee environments. Without laws demanding the elimination of pollutants, our world would become uninhabitable in time. Cynicism aside, volunteer abatement is desirable, but highly idealistic and improbable. It is not a profit-motivated activity—the short term costs of pollution controls are not readily embraced by CEOs under pressure to please stockholders and keep their businesses viable.

Our lifestyles and economies are geared to industry—no industry, no jobs! And if an industry does not show a profit—the scorecard of commercial and industrial life and death—it no longer exists, nor do the jobs it has created. Huge sums spent on pollution controls can wipe out profits unless, wisdom and creative engineering are used in the solution. Often when effluents are treated, wasted materials can be reclaimed or the waste reduced, if not eliminated, rendering a payback for the investment. When our country is attacked, as in World War II, we finance the armaments required to preserve our liberty. The attack on our lives, and those of generations to come, by toxic pollutants, is also an enemy we must defend against. Tax credits for pollution eliminating equipment are a help, as well as "you're a good neighbor" praise for complying companies which results in better consumer recognition and product preference. The tug-of-war struggle between pollution laws and slowly evolving technology is a check and balance, and I believe we must press on with the laws. However, they must be administered with diligence, firmness, and fairness. The answer: what's-best-for-society-oriented leadership by our government, the clergy, caring citizen's groups, parents, and our teachers. The facts of what we can do to our Garden-of-Eden planet must be taught to every citizen, and our laws must have teeth. If the monies spent on armaments could be used for pollution elimination...I guess I dream.

At last I received a notice to "cease and desist." I had a visit from a young assistant state's attorney, who demanded a timetable for correcting our effluent. I was at a loss. Contacting the corporate office brought an engineer who fumbled around for a month without developing a plausible correction. Now the heat from the state was on. An editorial in the local paper cited us, and referred to me as a felon who was harming life and limb. But we had to keep going—we needed to stay in business; our customers and employees needed us. Sometimes I'd wake up in the middle of the night from a nightmare about a flood of dirty water flowing over me as I reached for a big bag of money just out of reach.

One night when I came home early (a rare event), Bobby asked me if I was a crook. Marty had shown him the editorial so he would be prepared if any of his friends mentioned it. I explained that I was not, and shared with the family what was up. "We want to do the right thing—we just need to figure out how." In the following weeks I received more pressure from the attorney, who was juggling his duty, his political office goals, and the poor politics of shutting down a plant and seeing three-hundred-fifty men without a job. Finally, I wrested a commitment from corporate that they would do what had to be done, but they needed time. So, I went to downtown Perth Amboy to see the attorney we had put on retainer. This was an experience I'll never forget!

David Wilentz was the state attorney general who had prosecuted Bruno Hauptman for the kidnapping and murder of the Lindbergh baby. Mr. Wilentz had become one of the most powerful men in the Democratic Party—a virtual kingmaker. When I entered his surprisingly plain office, it was like seeking an audience with "The Godfather." The waiting room was filled with shabbily dressed people, who were all seeking state jobs with the racing, liquor, or other licensing agencies. As each one came out of his office, they didn't exactly genuflect, but they expressed gratitude in various ways.

Finally, my turn came. Mr. Wilentz, said, "Christopher, I see you're making a name for yourself—editorials and all." I explained why I was there; we needed time to solve the effluent problem.

"Is that some crap to stall with?"

"No, sir, we will correct the problem. It will take about a year and three to four-hundred thousand dollars, but our management has committed to do it."

"You're not kidding me?"

"No sir."

With that, he bellowed at his secretary, "Get the governor on the phone." In minutes the governor of New Jersey was on the other end of the line. "Jim, these people at Philip Carey need their jobs. They'll clean up if they have the time, about a year. Okay?"

"Okay, Christopher, you got a year. Don't fail to meet it."

I went back to the plant on a curtain of air. I could tell our employees that their jobs were safe, and I could tell our three little boys that their dad wasn't a crook. I set up a frequent follow-up system for the project. I became a pest to the president as I wrote or called every week to secure the engineering from corporate to solve our problem. I also gave Mr. Wilentz unrequired monthly status reports. He had extended himself for us—I wanted him to know we were doing what we said we would.

I had just seen, and benefited from, quiet, invisible, far-reaching power flowing from a little office in Perth Amboy like pulsating alternate electricity on a high-voltage wire across the state. As I learned more of David Wilentz's history, I realized that his quiet influence had been nationwide. In World War II, one of Henry Kaiser's liberty ships bore his name. Wilentz's office was lined with pictures of him with several democratic presidents. This power and influence helped save jobs as well as reach into many corners of the Democratic Party. For our part, we designed and installed several separators, filters, and chlorine treatment stations, as well as a further closing of the paper mill system. This installation brought our effluent into code. The dedication of the system was attended by local officials and the assistant state's attorney, who had a couple of photographers there to take pictures of him and me shaking hands in front of the largest filter. Whenever I hear about the Lindbergh trial and the state's prosecutor, I smile and say a small thanks for David Wilentz and his far reaching influence.

*   *   *

During the summer of 1967 very violent race riots broke out in Newark and Plainfield, just five miles from our home. The riots were fierce—property was looted, damaged, and burned. In Plainfield a policeman was hacked to death, and a mile from our house a white man was pulled from his car and beaten. The anger and fury of the African-Americans who lived in these towns, as well as those in Los Angles, Detroit, and Cincinnati, erupted into violence that cost several lives and millions of dollars in damage.

Why was this happening? Hadn't some gains been made in the civil rights movement and anti-segregation laws of the early sixties? Yes, but the economic status and living conditions of the majority of African-Americans had not improved. It was one thing to be able to drink from the same fountain as an Anglo, but that didn't guarantee a job, or equal treatment by an employer. The color lines, like indelible dyes, hadn't just blended together overnight.

The gains of Selma, new anti-segregation laws, and the legacy of Martin Luther King would take decades to pervade a society imbued with hundreds of years of prejudice and white supremacy. Even the Bible flows from a white, male "top-down" origin. The unleashed frustration that burst forth on the streets of many major cites, during "the long hot summer" of 1967, was a crying-out for equality and a chance. It was a demand for release from the debilitating shackles of selfish bias. It came from people who had no access to wealth, political sway, or legal recourse— anyone backed into a corner will lash out with his or her most primitive responses. Murder and looting can never be condoned, as Mr. King preached, but neither can the imprisoning of one race for the selfish gain of another.

When we learned of the mutilation of the Plainfield police- man, saw army tanks parked in the streets, and heard about the man pulled from his car, I did something I have done only once— carried a loaded forty-five automatic in my car. This was my prim- itive response to the fear that my family or I could be harmed. At the peak of the tension, on a Monday evening, I was driving home on a single lane road. I could see several hundred yards ahead, a beat-up car partially on the dirt shoulder with the two left-side wheels several feet into the driving lane. As I neared the car, I slowed down; another car was coming from the opposite direction.

Then I saw five African-Americans by the right rear wheel of the car. We were in the general area of where a man had been pulled from his car a few days earlier. I felt my stomach cramp and my mouth go dry. I didn't know what to do. It was impossible to do a u-turn. I moved—it felt like I was in slow motion—reaching for the glove compartment. I opened it, keeping my eyes focused on the road, and slowing a little more. I fumbled until I finally felt the checkered stock of the forty-five. I pulled it to me, cocked the exposed hammer, and held it in my right hand at one-o'clock on the steering wheel. The oncoming car passed, and I swung into the opposite direction lane, as a couple of the men by the old car sidled toward the road. I think they saw the gun in my hand, because they glared at me while I passed just a few feet from them. I'll never know if I would have been able to shoot a human being. I thank God for not having to make that decision. I have kept this incident to myself until now; my family didn't need to know this.

As the summer passed and the weather cooled, the rioting subsided, and I put the gun away. But, the needs of African-Americans were not as easily put away. Progress is still being made, but there are many miles to go before we reach racial equilibrium. Men like Colin Powell, Secretary of State, and women like Condoleezza Rice, the President's National Security Advisor, act as good role models, as do many other prominent African-Americans. The more men or women of this caliber that emerge, and that white people allow to emerge, the more progress will be made. We had a black cub master in Bobby's pack, who was such a good leader and gentleman we were never aware of our differing colors. Time, education, and love will dim the color line.

*   *   *

Our company, founded in 1873 by a farmer from Hamilton, Ohio was acquired by the Glen Alden Company in the summer of 1967. In any takeover, organizational changes are made. To my surprise, I was promoted to a vice president's position and given the responsibility for several plants. My new office was to be at corporate headquarters in Cincinnati. I was ready—eleven years as a plant manager had grown old. And we were excited about moving back home to where our families were. Yet on the day we drove off in two cars, we cried for miles. We were leaving the font of our baptisms as self-sufficient adults and as a family unto itself. We were leaving friends, the genesis of our family spirituality, and the workplace of my industrial growth. To stand still is to wither, but moving forward demands the price of dear things left behind.

⤴

C H A P T E R

12

If men could learn from history, what lessons it might teach us!
But passion and party blind our eyes, and the light which
experience gives is a lantern on the stern,
which shines only on the waves behind us!
Samuel Taylor Coleridge, 1772-1834

On a cold December day in 1967 we moved into a large colonial home in Montgomery, Ohio, just five miles northeast of Cincinnati—Marty, me, Bob, Jim, John, and some new specters. The Beatles, the Rolling Stones, and a host of records that spewed out the "new music"—the beat that changed the mores of a nation, helped grow a male's hair long, and freed America's youth from the conventions of the GI and Silent Generations. Boomers (those born between 1943-1960) would grow up in relative affluence and readily absorb the thumb-your-nose-at-the-establishment vein that now appeared on television. Many of their thoughts and wants were expressed in free-verse poetry and protest songs, or in dress ranging from very casual to pure sloppiness and grunge. Draft card burning and noisy demonstrations echoed the prevailing disillusionment of America being in war, after war, after war. Viet Nam, a politician's war, was the flash point for a social revolution.

As the disillusioned voices of the Lost Generation—Hemingway, Fitzgerald, and Dos Passos—had fled to Europe after World War I, a wave of wild living had followed in the "Roaring Twenties." As the voices of post WW II—Dylan, Baez, Spock,

Freidan, O'Leary, Kesey, the Chicago Seven, (which included Walnut Hills grad, Jerry Rubin), Cleaver, The Beatles, and Rachel Carson—sounded in the coffee houses, and in mass protests in the streets, a wave of wild living followed in the sixties and seventies. The country was being forced to hear a cry for change, whether it wanted to or not. Hippies and flower children expressed their disillusionment at repeated wars; the glass ceiling over women; suppression of blacks, Native Americans, and other minorities; and the abusive exploitation of the environment. GI and Silent Generation folks began to look at things differently, albeit grudgingly.

But any tide that comes in also has a backwash. With the flower children it was illegal drugs and promiscuous sex; freedom was being interpreted as license. I believe the restlessness of the Boomers, whose world view was not shaped by Depression economics, led to a surge to "find themselves," outside the boundaries of the Establishment. The justified protests against the Viet Nam War were a galvanizing agent in bringing a generation to their perceived destiny, but who brought with them the hangers-on who saw an opportunity to do as they damn well pleased. This social upsurge, which seemed more like a runaway flywheel without a brake, spawned, as the country had in the twenties, the social revolution of the Sixties and Seventies. America again looked at things differently. It's a shame that drug use, loose sex, and a shirking of personal responsibilities diluted the energetic core of the movement.

Did all these voices of protest—intellectuals, both sincere and phony—enter our conservative, Republican, Episcopalian home? Yes, they did. Son Bob was an avid reader of the social commentary of the day, as well as Gandhi and King. Upstairs, stereos continuously issued the tunes of the Beatles and Rolling Stones.

And when Bob wanted to take an African-American girl to a dance in Ault Park on the heels of "the long hot summer" of riots, we felt we had to say no; but in reflection, we admire his lack of prejudice.

In the upsweep of the social changes of the Sixties, the loosening of heretofore moral codes about no sex before marriage, extramarital sex, and sex-filled cohabitation without commitment, was not confined to just the "under-thirties." My generation, while outwardly denouncing Hugh Heffner, read and fantasized over his *Playboy* publication. As folks hit their forties in the nineteen-seventies, they faced middle-age issues, such as the "syndromes" expressed in the film, *Bob and Carol and Ted and Alice*, or the switching of sexual partners though random selection in the "key clubs" of Long Island. Some started growing their hair longer too, dressing in the current "mod" style, and indulging in affairs that offered sex-for-the-sake-of-sex. Why let conventions like love and marriage nix the ecstasy of forbidden-fruit orgasms in a no-tell-motel? Such behavior promised temporary assurance that middle-aged, Silent Generation males, and females, were not "out of it." What a turnabout! As youngsters, we of the Silent Generation had copied our forerunners, the heroic GIs; now, as middle-aged men and women, we were copying our offspring!

Our family, like so many others, faced the long-hair issue. At first we stayed rooted in our feelings against it, but the boys would say, "Jesus had long hair." Gradually we accepted the style. Peer pressure can be tough, and if long hair was rebellion, we thought there were issues and habits that were far worse. But we did wonder at humans' historical obsession with hair—from Sampson's shearing to the rigid stand by American parents on how their offspring should wear their tresses. The nation's "crowning glory" had been forced into prissy curls, a bouffant, flapper bobs, Charlotte Ford Niarco's do's, Afros, and GI burrs. There was even a Broadway play, *Hair*. It was truly "the age of Aquarius." We middle-aged males worried about not having enough hair, while our sons worked to have more than their sexual opposites. At the time, it seemed a large issue, but it was a pretty innocuous matter.

*   *   *

What we thought would be a great move to Cincinnati turned out to be not so good. The kids were unhappy in the new neighborhood. Here the children of the nouveau riche seemed to have lost their sense of how to act like normal kids. John had a teacher who carried a paddle in a shoulder holster, like a private eye with his piece at the ready. We did have some happy reunions with aunts, uncles, and some cousins. My mother, Pop, and half-brother Buzz, came out to our home every other weekend. I think the size and beauty of our house gave Pop a little heartburn.

But this new life in the "old hometown" was hard on Marty. The winter of 1967-68 was one of the coldest on record, with temperatures dropping to below zero. Respiratory ailments like flu, heavy colds, and pneumonia abounded. During one of my extended trips, Marty had the flu, and my mother cared for her. I was traveling ten days out of twenty, leaving Marty home with the three boys—two teenagers and fifth-grade John—and the fast-approaching senility of her mother. She had the torturous decision of whether to place her mom in a nursing home or let her continue to bumble along, possibly hurting herself, in unassisted living. In view of her mother's declining mental and physical condition, Marty made the tough call and put her in a nursing home, but not without guilt-racked sleepless nights. Aging parents, due to the increased longevity of our times, forces the onus of how to care for them on most families. It was not a happy time.

Again coincidence (God remaining anonymous) opened a road to better times for us, but the event, though good, came from a dark plot—as night leads into the light of day.

Intrigue has been with us since the guile of Eden's serpent. And history reveals its presence in the-ever-so-subtle, ecclesiastical position-maneuvering of the Vatican. Intrigues, often imbued with guidelines as expressed by Machiavelli in *The Prince*, are most often devised to seek gain for the devisor at the expense of the duped. And how did the spinning web of intrigue come to our family? The origin of the cabal started months before its manifestation—back in Perth Amboy, a few months before my job promotion and our move back to Cincinnati.

In my last few months at Perth, after the sale of the company, I had been assigned a new boss—a good guy, about five years my senior, but not well grounded in operations. He was the corporate type that handled his superiors with quiet, don't-stick-your-neck-out-too-far charm. He was with me on the last day of our labor contract negotiations which, eight hours before the contract expired, had not yet been settled. An earlier merger with Glen Alden had brought a wave of insecurity to our work force. Now the union was pushing for a dime-an-hour raise—a psychological threshold, as well as a smidgen of economic security. Prior to 1967, settlements had only been reached on single-digit numbers. The union negotiators, my personnel manager, my boss, and I were in my office, stalemated at 8.5 cents, a number my boss had told corporate Cincinnati was his opinion of where wages should be for our plant—even though this was his first visit to Perth Amboy. The clock passed six a.m., one hour before the men would strike if there was no contract. Many were gathered in the parking lot awaiting word. Serious bargaining had already stopped at an impasse at two a.m. After that, we drank coffee and sat looking at each other—neither side offering anything. Finally at six-forty my boss went to the men's room. With him gone, I asked the international rep how much the men would lose if they were out for a week. He told me a hundred more than the penny-and-a-half they were holding out for. He then asked me how much the company would lose if the men were out for a week. I said, "Thousands more than the penny-and-a-half."

"What can we do, Slim?" (my Perth Amboy sobriquet)

"What can you do with a penny-and-a-half, Steve?"

"I can settle this with no strike."

I saw the minute hand click to six-fifty-seven. "You got it, Steve, go get 'em."

Smiles broke out all around, as Steve ran for the parking lot, and my boss returned. Seeing our faces, he wanted to know, "What's up?"

"We just averted a costly and damaging strike."

"How?" He stammered, turning a bit red.

"With a lousy penny-and-a-half! A cost of less than ten minutes compared to a potential week-to two-week strike—a ten-thousand-dollar annual investment to save a million in sales. Plus you'll have the best plant in the company running like a jeweled watch. I think our new owners will like that."

"You had no right to go that high!"

"My job is to see that this plant is run profitably. I do all that's required to carry out that responsibility, whatever it is—you want to change that?"

He was quiet. "Well I guess that's best at that. Let's go have breakfast." In that moment I began to write my corporate tagline—one that future employees would articulate over and over—"tough on bosses."

From that day on, particularly after I moved to corporate, he showed deference to me in meetings. He never interrupted the discussions if I was addressed or reporting. The plants for which I was responsible were profitable, and the new president had taken a shine to me, which he showed in general meetings by asking my opinion on companywide issues. When he did this, my boss, who reported directly to the president, would blush and look at his feet. We got along, but it was a corporate version of the *pax Romana*. (Coincidentally, my boss was of Roman descent.)

One day he and the human resources manager (formerly called personnel manager, back when janitors were not yet called sanitary engineers) came into my office and shut the door. They hemmed and hawed, but finally the boss said, "Bob, we did some industrial scouting for the company and took the liberty of using your name."

"How's that?"

"We saw a half-page ad in the *Wall Street Journal* for a seasoned manufacturing manager at a national building materials company. It was a glowing ad, but only gave a box office. So, we sent in a sketchy resume on you to see if it was a competitor."

"And?"

"We got a favorable reply, and it is not a direct competitor. It's Evans Products—lumber, plywood, railcars, and hundreds of retail building-supply stores. We wanted to alert you in case they contact you." After a lengthy pause, he added, "You can just tell them it was a mistake." With that they left—and I was left in a quandary. What was this really about?

A week later I received a call from the personnel manager at the Evans Products manufacturing and distribution center in Chesapeake, Virginia. "Mr. Christopher, we were very impressed with the experience and accomplishments outlined in your three-page resume (three pages are "sketchy?"). Would you visit with us for an exploratory interview? We're really interested in you."

That night Marty said, "What do we have to lose by you just talking?" I agreed. I'd been at Carey eighteen years, and I had been told the Evans job could lead to a general manager's position, which included sales responsibility, something I had not yet had at the VP level. I arranged to go to Virginia on a Saturday and Sunday. But I couldn't stop thinking how strangely this had all come about.

My interview with a corporate vice president and the regional vice president, whose office was at the plant, went well. The complex was eleven acres under roof! It produced pre-finished plywood wall paneling and moldings and particle board furniture components. Although two years old, it was still in start-up mode, having not hit a profit as yet. The six-hundred person work-force was fraught with inexperienced help. Agrarian Sussex County didn't produce educated or skilled factory workers. Most of the men had been day laborers who picked the seasonal crops of peanuts and other farm produce.

There had been two manufacturing managers already. That fact, the profit picture, and the size made me think of 1956

Perth Amboy—times three! The annual sales volume was greater than all of my roofing plants combined. This realization started a flow of adrenalin and creative juices—maybe I could do it! Maybe I could pick up much-needed sales experience, as well as new manufacturing techniques. I wasn't forty yet, so why not invest in on-the-job education that would sustain me more than the stock or bond of the day?

I went back to Evans for a final interview, the salary package—which was thirty percent higher than my present one—and a starting date three weeks hence. Back in Cincinnati I told my boss I was accepting the Evans job. He said, "Damn, I goofed!" But he didn't sound convincing. When the president heard about my leaving and how it had come about, he raked my boss over the coals for an hour, according to his secretary. I was sent to two other Glen Alden operations to see if they could offer me something that would keep me with the company. But my mind was set. When I told the family, they cheered. They had never been happy in Cincinnati. In later months I had to tip my hat to my former boss for how smoothly he erased a hard-breathing rival without showing his hand or alienating any of my supporters—Machiavellian intrigue at its best! But, as Grandmother Allan had said many times, "Things always happen for the best." As usual, she was one hundred percent right.

We drove to the Norfolk-Chesapeake-Virginia Beach area, where every other family was in the Navy. The night before I was to start we bought a house in Virginia Beach. When I told my staff this the next day they were incredulous. "What if you don't like it?"

"I have to like it," I replied. "I resigned my previous position." Like Cortez who burned his ships on the shores of Mexico, I had burned mine at Philip Carey by refusing the extended offers of the president. I thought also about God's admonishment to Lot as he fled Sodom—I had no intention of turning into a pillar of salt!

Marty and the boys stayed with me in a motel for a week before they flew back to Cincinnati to try and sell the house. Putting them on the plane reminded me of the sad parting we had made twelve years earlier when I left for Perth Amboy. I felt like a part of me was leaving with them—I was not a whole man without them near me. I knew I could exist in the daily demands of my job and even in the lonely motel living, but the joy—the fullness of life—left me when the Piedmont Airline's turbo-prop flew off carrying those dearest to me.

Partings leave a hollowness that seldom goes away until there is a reuniting. It brings to mind how many times in my life I have experienced a parting from God. Yet He is always there when I let Him into my life again—usually after a trauma. The love of our maker, who always returns, no matter how many times He is shut out, is a love and forgiveness far beyond human comprehension— at least beyond mine. I still cry in church every time we sing *How Great Thou Art*—"Then sings my soul, my Savior God, to Thee; how great Thou art; how great Thou art!"

* * *

I had a lot to learn. I didn't know a piece of plywood wall paneling from any other piece of wood. Getting into the operations, I witnessed the fascinating process that started in the Philippines and ended on one of our trucks bound for a warehouse in any one of a hundred towns. Briefly, Philippine mahogany logs were cut in the forests, hauled to the coast by oxen, put on a Japanese vessel, shipped to Korea, and then floated into the harbor of a Korean village where a plywood plant was located. Once in the mill, the logs were rotary peeled into thin pieces, which were glued and then laminated into a three-ply sheet of plywood. The mill was manned (?) by hundreds of tiny Korean women, all wearing size four red, low-cut gym shoes and a colored cap designating their job. The finished stacks of the plywood were loaded on an Evans Products-leased ship run by a Greek captain, destined for shipment to one of three Evans plants in the states.

When we received the raw plywood, we converted it to decorative wall paneling, usually a four-by-eight sheet for conventional houses, and four-by-seven for mobile homes. The panels were three-sixteenths or a quarter-inch thick. The process for this conversion was a quarter-mile long. The raw panel was fed through two coarse-grit high-speed sanders and then a roll coater that filled the open pores with calcium carbonate. The quick-drying filler was sanded just before the panel had grooves cut into it by a tenor—to make the panel look like it was a series of six-to eight-inch planks. After grooving, the panel was "painted" with a color-coordinated base coat. The toned, opaque panel went into a temperature- and humidity-controlled print room where a wood grain in three colors was applied by three in-register rotogravure presses. The last phase was a nitro-cellulose-based topcoat (the equivalent of the outer coat of varnish on furniture) on the panel for durability. The topcoat was so well engineered that fifty panels could be stacked and banded immediately after the top coat was applied without any sticking in the stack. All this was done at two-hundred-feet-per-minute. We printed about thirty patterns—oak, hickory, elm, walnut, cherry, and teak, in various colors. The print cylinders were photo-engraved from pictures of actual trees. These panels retailed in 1970 for $5.98 to $15.00 each, depending on the quality.

We had fifty percent of the 500,000-unit per year mobile home trade, and about twenty-five percent of the conventional home and commercial business. We were number one overall in market share compared to Georgia-Pacific, Weyerhauser, and three smaller private companies. Evans had been the developer of the Korean plywood mills in the sixties. Ordering the raw plywood from these mills was an art and science both. We had to work with five-month lead times, Longshoreman's strikes, and worldwide price fluctuations in plywood futures. Buy high, you lose money; not order right and you had either inflated, dollar-binding inventories or no material to supply customers. My material manager, Frank Herbert, was a whiz at this. We never had a goof in my six years at Evans. Frank was also a brother, a confessor, and a true friend. Together we turned the roaring Chesapeake plant around in a year.

I'll never forget the second week I was there. Frank and I knew we needed to make a total assessment to be certain that when we started our watch, the books were in order. Inventorying three million dollars worth of raw and finished wood with three hundred "counters," many of whom couldn't read or write, was a challenge of monumental proportions! The weekend we selected for the inventory presented us a one-hundred degree day with humidity almost that high. We knew we had to keep the employees in the plant until the count was completed and verified. So, we said we would feed the crews on site. Frank and I strode into the local Burger King and matter-of-factly ordered, "Three-hundred and twenty whoppers and the same number of cokes." The clerk blinked his eyes and came back in his tidewater drawl, "Let me see your money!" We slapped five C-notes on the counter and got back a dollar and eight cents in change!

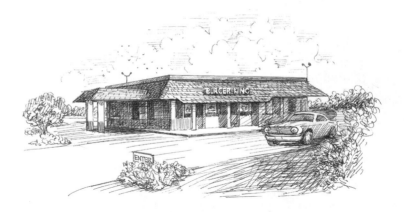

Besides learning the process, distribution channels, and customers, I had to learn how to be both diplomatic and firm, to avoid alienating my boss. Well, thirty-nine isn't too old to walk a tightwire. My boss, at fifty-one, was rumored to be having an affair with his twenty-four-year-old secretary. He was also used to having everyone in management fawn over him, regardless of their reporting relationship. One day on the plant-wide public address system I heard him paging one of my superintendents to come to his office. Telling the man to stay where he was, I plowed into my boss's office saying that my employee was on the job and that was where he would stay. I'd be dead if looks could kill, but I held my ground. I explained that to maintain discipline and the correct line of communication, he should go through me for his needs. It took a couple of weeks for that to sink in, but it did.

The next incident happened when his secretary came to me with some directives. I pointedly replied, "Honey, I don't take orders from intermediaries. Tell him if he wants something to come to me directly." Another two weeks of strained relations, but in time he became more discerning in his orders and communications.

Those first five months were not easy—fencing with the boss; learning a new process; facing production, quality, and profit problems; not to mention horrendous inventory losses from accounting manipulations by previous management. I worked long hours, and had to quell the resentment of a couple of supers who were used to doing as they wanted without overseeing. But thanks to our strong home base of Marty and the three boys, I started to make headway. The big boss from Portland, Oregon, (corporate headquarters) came out for a year-end review. We had posted a small profit in November for the first time, but most importantly we had cleaned up over eleven-thousand reject panels and had balanced our inventories. We had eaten all of the sins of the past two years and were poised to make 1969 a winning year.

After I had been with Evans for sixteen months, the top boss of my division, Don Gardner, came for a visit. He took me to dinner without Bill, my immediate boss. The entire two hours was a quiz. Don was not happy with Bill, despite our being in the black. He probed me in sixteen different ways over a prime filet mignon that I never tasted. He even touched on Bill's personal relationship with his secretary. Finally, he asked me if I wanted my boss's job. I thought for awhile. Sure I wanted it; but this didn't feel right. I remembered something Uncle Stanley had said to me when I was about twenty-one, "Bobby, always play things straight, and you'll never lose any sleep."

"Don, I want to move up, but I think you need to give Bill another chance. How about issuing him a strong warning and telling him he's on the edge of going."

"You're sure you don't want to move up now?"

"Not today."

The next morning, I went into Bill's office and related most of what was discussed the night before. "Bill, they're down on you. I'll help you all I can, but you better make peace and a new pledge to Don." He thanked me. Later Don said he admired my not putting ambition ahead of my integrity. I was never sorry, and I guess leopards don't change their spots. Two months later Bill was fired, and I was given the job. What a waste; Bill was intelligent and charming, but his sensual and egocentric drives got in the way of doing the job. When he left, Frank Herbert said, "Bob, you're tough on bosses."

While we were winning the battle at Evans, our family was changing too—growing up. The boys had been in three schools in two years. It was tough on them, but they adapted, making new friends and picking up some ocean-related sports. Bob was in drama and dancing on the fringes of the new mores of the seventies. Jim was again a quiet leader in his group, and John was playing baseball on a Little League team at the Little Creek Naval Amphibious Base. We attended Old Donation Episcopal Church, taught Sunday school, and sat on the vestry. There was a small lake near our house where the boys used their little, square-ended boat. Marty had a neat cadre of ladies with whom she played tennis. But sadness crept into our lives; between November and July we lost Marty's mother and uncle, and my mother.

These deaths affected the kids, who had lost both Grandmothers in eight months. It seems that kids have a special relationship with grandparents; I know ours did. They gave the boys love and attention, but didn't impose daily disciplines on them. My mother had called me on my fortieth birthday in May, wishing me well, wistfully telling me how proud she was, and how much she loved me. She ended with a casual reference to a scheduled hospital visit for some tests. When I hung up I was crying, and I told Marty my mother was going to die. How I knew this I'll never know. It was as if her sweet talk carried an encoded message—a prophecy of death. Six weeks later she would be gone. I flew back to Cincinnati twice to see her, to thank her for her love and tell her about the kids. The last time was a week before she died. She was a beautiful woman, who had struggled with our nearly lifelong separation, but had always put on a smiling, caring face. I will probably never completely fill the void of not having been with her for the biggest part of my life. For me, her funeral was mostly a replay of all the others—my dad, Grandmother Christopher, Uncle Stanley, Grandmother Allan, and Marty's family. When it was over, I once again felt empty. But Marty stepped up so beautifully with her support—she has always been there for me—spiritually, mentally, and physically. Now we were alone as a little cell of our forbears. But we had each other.

Six months after the promotion, I was given the added responsibility of the Memphis panel plant, which was at best a break-even operation. I began going there for two days every month to set up programs for its turnaround. The assignment of Memphis to me was part of a major change in the organization of the division. Heretofore the division was organized with a general manager at each location, responsible for both the sales and manufacturing for his region. Now, I was to assume the responsibility for all plants as VP of manufacturing, absorbing a new plant every three or four months. The general manager and the sales manager at Memphis were being reassigned to full time sales jobs, with no more responsibility or authority for the plant. This upset their previous cloister of autonomy. In transition, they met my plane on my first visit. Shaking hands with one hand, I carried my leather attaché in the other, which prompted what I later heard, *"Yankee carpetbagger."*

This signaled that the one-month transition period would present a challenge to get true information, let alone cooperation. They were cordial off the job, entertaining me at night, but close-mouthed at daytime meetings at the plant. On my first night we

went to the Rivermont, overlooking the Mighty Miss. When the
band played *Dixie*, they jumped up on their chairs, waved their
napkins, and yelled, "The South will rise again!" As a lifelong,
culturally imbued northerner, I figured there were a few fences I
would need to jump over.

On another night, after a day of trying to get information
from them with little yield, four of us went out to dinner at a
Memphis rib place, then to a "club." At the club we sat at one of
several round tables that had attractive girls in hot pants that barely
covered their rears standing in the middle of the table. They were
in high heels and danced to the three-piece band. I was agog—my
eyes darting from one pair to another in this eye-level sea of shapely, bare legs. The flashing-black-eyed local manager peered at me
and said, "Damn, Christopher, you're like a blind dog in a meat
house!" I guess I was.

I got a lot of laughs and good dinners, but what I learned
about the plant I got on my own. I was appalled at some of what I
picked up. For instance, the black factory workers were paid an
hourly rate if they worked, but the white workers on the same jobs
were considered salaried, and got paid whether there or not. I got
this changed, and received a mixture of praise and a few whispered "nigger-lover" comments. But, I ploughed ahead, getting
some quick capital money from my boss that allowed us to put in

some needed improvements. In six months the plant improved its efficiency, safety record, and quality, as well as the morale of the workforce in both the factory and office. I included more of the staff in the decision-making process, which brought their enthusiastic devotion—a team was emerging and we were comfortably in the black.

Before 1970 ended, we had put the Memphis plant permanently in the black. One big reason our pre-finish division was ahead of our competitors was our designer, Fran Dreazy, a rare combination of artist and engineer, whose designs were unique. He could envision wood grains, colors, and ticking (small indents in the wood to resemble pores) in an artistic mode, and convert his vision to commercial reality. I would meet him at the Chicago Art Institute and spend a couple of hours walking the rooms, never mentioning our needs for a new design—no need to, he perceived that. After our time in the museum, he would say, "I got an idea." We'd go to a gravure house and he'd translate his new idea to a set of three print cylinders and a ticking roll. In a few months, Evans would grab more business with Fran's new panel. We enjoyed the increased profits and market share, but they didn't come easily. Fran reported to me, which was a challenge because he could not be guided like a production man, engineer, or administrator. He carried a lot of psychological baggage, and had to be handled delicately. He drank a lot and could become morose.

One night he called me from Los Angles saying he was going to commit suicide. I asked him why even though I felt I already knew it was from guilt and lack of personal discipline. He had accidentally dropped scalding water on his two-year-old son's arm, causing it to be permanently deformed. I listened for awhile and finally, clutching at a straw, I said, "Fran, you kill yourself, I'll never talk to you again, and I'll stop your pay right now!"

It worked; he was good for another six months and three new designs—whew! On Christmas morning, 1970, the phone rang at seven in the morning. I picked it up and heard *I Never Promised You a Rose Garden* being played over long distance. Fran had a sense of humor!

*   *   *

In 1971, Evans was a decentralized company. There were five major groups: Transportation, Retail, Forest Products, International, and our Pre-finish/Interior Products. Each had its headquarters away from corporate, which was located in Portland, Oregon, because that was where the chairman lived. There's an old saying, "if it ain't broke, don't fix it." There's also an American penchant, "If one aspirin is good, take the whole bottle." These conflicting clichés came into play that summer. The entire company was doing well. So why not tinker with it? We might make it better—the whole bottle theory was applied!

The company decided to centralize. Hundreds of people, division centers, and staffs were moved to Portland. The Forest Products and Pre-finish divisions were merged into one group and organized on functional lines: sales and manufacturing became separate entities, thereby setting up adversarial roles. I was promoted to Vice President in charge of seven plants and told to move to Oregon. We settled in Lake Oswego, just south of Portland. This was a hard move for Jim who was going to be a junior; but even more devastating was leaving his first real love behind, as well as some very close friends. John was more adaptive and said little, and to his credit quickly melded into the new community. Jim and John had now gone to four schools in four years. Our many moves taught them how to adapt to new environments, but at the cost of their growing no roots.

The move was eased by the warm reception we received from the company's attorney Dick Kent, his wife Laurie, and their four kids. They invited us to their home for Thanksgiving dinner, which practice we shared every year for our entire stay in rainy Portland. They also introduced us to a tennis club and many people. Warmth extended by a caring family like the Kents can greatly enhance the lives of all those they touch. If everyone would do more of this, our world would be safer and free from much conflict.

The competition between newly created staff positions was fierce. Georgia-Pacific was easy to compete with, but the in-fighting about transfer prices from our own company plants to company stores and warehouses was a gut-wrenching ordeal. Didn't Pogo say, "We've seen the enemy, and he's us?" Every top guy was trying to get more turf and be the hero. The direction from the top was laid-back. Planned conflict was the mode—put the guys in an arena and let them duke it out—the best will survive. The word teamwork was not a watchword of the new organization—it was every man for himself.

But, we mercurially soared to new heights in sales and profit. The economy in 1972 and 1973 was robust. Conventional and mobile housing starts were at an all-time high, and "do-it-yourselfers" were flocking into our stores and warehouses in droves, buying our products. And the top brass, like the gods of Olympus, said, "See what a good organizational move we made."

With all of my operations in Virginia; Memphis; Southern California; Missoula, Montana; Philips, Wisconsin; and Jasper, Florida (one traffic light), I was away more than I was home.

This was not good for raising two teenage boys. Bob was still in Maryland, but Marty had her hands full. Reluctantly, and not without some deep-seated guilt, I didn't mind going off to my plants, as the Portland corporate office was sterile to a hands-on manager like me—I never lost my love of talking to hourly workers, patting them on the back, and showing them how much they were needed. At that time I was responsible for over fourteen hundred employees and a hundred million in sales.

In May I was asked to give a report on the progress of my division and my outlook for the future. It was only my second summons to the "big poker table in the sky"—my name for the sixteen-foot in diameter, inlaid teak, conference table in the Chairman's top-floor, skylight-lit private conference room. Many a weighty decision and deal had been made at that table, most of which were as dicey as betting into the dealer's two aces showing in a game of five-card stud. The meeting was attended by selected major shareholders, the chairman, president, my boss, and a couple of my staff. At this point in time my division was the jewel of the company. Our sales and profits were higher than ever, plus we had picked up huge gains in plywood futures by buying millions of board feet at the right moment. Those particular profits might better have been held prudently in reserve for future price declines, but our youthful president wanted to wow Wall Street, so we took up the purchase price gains as operating profits—some really big months, but no umbrella for a rainy day!

As I projected my array of colored slides and transparencies, passed out product samples, and flipped graphic to-the-point charts in Technicolor, covering every phase of our division's success and glory, the American Dream of business was unfolding. Exciting to even the most seasoned I've-seen-it-all-before business-man. As I flipped over my last chart with a climactic swish,

I felt a slowly building apocalyptic shudder under my feet. It was if a quake was making its first reverberating tremors in the foot of the mountain of attainment I had just described and documented. The smiling and appreciative faces around that table exhilarated me with a flush of pure joy. I had reached an apex of my career with Evans. I was accepted as a peer of the company's top echelon of ownership and management. Yet, despite the joy and satisfaction of that meeting, I seemed to hear a distant and mournful train whistle somewhere in my subconscious, like the one from the slow freight that had slipped past my house on the day after my father's funeral. It hung in the air of my mind as it blew its warning call. Was I hearing a prophetic warning?

In mid 1973, President Nixon lifted price freezes, unleashing a torrent of price increases that built to flood stage by the second quarter of 1974. The foundation of the nation's economy was washed away in a surge of unchecked inflation. When the tide receded, deflation followed. Interest rates hit twenty percent; orders fell off; and for Evans Products, plywood market prices decreased. But there was no reserve to offset the high value of the wood we had on our books—it had been squandered in a euphoric spree of profit reporting. The situation was compounded by a lot of speculative wood buying at the chairman's directive. Now the piper must be paid. Cash was tight, bills were stacking up, and payrolls had to be met. Competition had gotten tougher, and Evans had its front line troops at headquarters. As turf-grasping middle managers, these guys had built huge staffs to "fight" the specter of internal competition for recognition. Edward Gibbon, in his compendium, *The Decline and Fall of the Roman Empire*, defined four causes of that fall. One was "the domestic quarrels of the Romans," i.e., internal strife. And so it was with Evans—we were collapsing from within. As Abraham had taken his son Isaac to the

altar to sacrifice him to appease the Lord, the chairman
discharged his hand-chosen, "you're-like-my-son" president—but
no angel stayed this sacrifice to the gods of Wall Street.

And where did the millions of feet of high-priced speculative plywood bought by the chairman end up? You guessed it—on
my balance sheet. The directive came down to unload it to raise
cash, so I sold as fast as possible at fifty to seventy cents on the
dollar. The hit to my division's books was like black Tuesday and
black Thursday in October of 1929.

When things go wrong in a company, usually two things
happen. First, there's the idea, "Let's put things back like they
were before the fall." Then comes, "We need," (like the cavemen,
and other early humanoids) "some sacrifices to appease the gods."
This dual strategy was accomplished in a single stroke! We decentralized, putting troops back on the front lines. But in the process
many were let go. To the company's credit, severance packages
were generous.

The family and I moved back to Virginia Beach, where I
set up Division Headquarters in the Chesapeake plant offices.
I was now a Vice President-General Manager, with both sales and
manufacturing responsibility. Just before we left, the chairman
stopped by and asked me why we had such high losses two
months running. I replied, "Sir, it's from dumping the plywood that
was bought on speculation before the price plummeted." He
winced, left my office, and I never saw him again.

Marty and I were "empty-nesters" back in Virginia. Two
of the boys were now in college, and John stayed in Portland to finish his senior year in high school. It felt like we were living in the
airless vacuum that precedes a tornado. Of course, we had church
activities, good fishing on the Outer Banks of North Carolina, and
we were working hard to bring the division back to profitability.

On the surface things seemed normal. But the storm hit at eight a.m., the day after Christmas. An arch rival, acting on a management directive, had flown a redeye night flight in from Portland to tell me I was fired. I asked him how soon he wanted me to leave. He said, "How about in a half hour."

I said, "No way, dummy. I need to brief you on the things that are happening and pending. Do you want a big slippage in the transition?"

Red in the face, he stuttered something about he guessed not. I worked eight hours that day, laying out all of the issues. I introduced him to the group as my successor and urged them to cooperate. I even bought him lunch, and not on the company expense account. At four-thirty I packed my personal effects and left the office. As I waved a final goodbye to the guard, I made a vow: "I'll never again let anyone meddle or intrude in what I run without full documentation. Short of that, I won't accept any responsibility, without *carte blanche* authority"—and I never did again.

"Fired! Hey, this is new—what do I do?" I prayed as I drove home in the company car I was allowed to keep for a month. On the way, I passed an employment office that was just about to close for the day. In the grimy, dimly lit room there were a dozen large-armed, writing-desk-chairs occupied by some African-Americans, and an alcohol-smelling Anglo in dirty clothes. I set my leather attaché down, opened my cashmere topcoat, and approached the clerk sitting at a paper-littered desk, "Can I help you, sir?"

"Yes. I want to fill out an application for employment."

He was surprised. "Sir, we mostly fill jobs for domestics, and day-by-day laborers."

"Are you refusing to take my application?"

"Why no, sir. It's just that…uh, it's just that you don't look like our normal applicant. What is your field?"

"Industrial management."

"I see. Well, if you really want an application, here."

I sat between two ladies who stared at me until I said, "Hi, girls, how's the job market?" They smiled, and I got to filling out the forms. I heard one of them suck in her breath when she glanced at my paper and saw the customary salary figure.

Over the years, when I have lectured or spoken to college kids, I've been asked, "What was the most growing experience you've had in your career?"

My reply: "Getting fired…oh, yes, and applying for a new job a half hour later with a group of minimum-wage day laborers and cleaning ladies. When you're out of a job, my friends, there's no room for pride or past glories."

CHAPTER

13

In the day of prosperity, adversity is forgotten and in the day
of adversity, prosperity is not remembered.
Apocrypha, Ecclesiasticus 11:25

The day after I was fired from Evans Products, I gathered my family around me. The boys were home with us in Virginia Beach for the Christmas holidays. I explained to them what had happened, and what corporate politics and scapegoatism were. Marty and I also told them to watch expenses—my severance package was only three month's pay, and Bob and Jim were in West Coast colleges, while John was finishing his senior year in high school in Portland. Bob, who had worked one summer for Evans asked, "But, Dad, wasn't your division one of the best in the company? How come they fired you?"

"Well, Son, for six out of the six-and-a-half years that I had it, the division was the best. But some risky gambling in plywood futures by the chairman and a rival of mine, plus the recession, tarred it with two bad quarters. Also, my salary package was deemed high if a decision was made to sell the division to pecuniary Weyerhauser." (The event happened a few months later.)

I wasn't sure how I should handle my dismissal with the boys. They hadn't reacted with much feeling when I broke the news. Then it came to me—they had never wanted for anything materially. They all had had summer jobs, and were given allowances. We regularly asked them to do things around the home, such as grass mowing, room cleaning, and errands, but they never had to depend on their labors for their daily bread. They seemed to sense my emotional letdown, and said things like, "Hang in there, Dad." Or, "Don't let the bastards get you down." But in a few, too short days they would be off for the West Coast to continue their schooling and their search for identity. My growing up in the Depression had moved me, right or wrong, to protect them from what I remembered of my grandmother's scrimping in those early years. In hindsight, maybe they, maybe everyone, would benefit from some tough times. I sometimes feel affluence produces apathy—or said a different way—depressions, if not totally debilitating, produce determination.

In spite of the dampening effect of my firing, we had a good time, and the boys, before they left, hung out with friends they had made earlier when we lived in Virginia. As they walked up the open-air stairs at the Norfolk airport, we smiled, waved, and looked at their near shoulder-length hair. Marty and I still thought it way too long, but had kept our feelings to ourselves—that ground had been ploughed too many times.

Even before they left, I started a rigid program of job hunting—a first-time experience I did in a feel-as-you-go manner. Each morning I sublimated my feelings of rejection, anger, and anxiety and followed a daily regimen of making calls, writing letters, and answering ads. Hearing the boys and Marty talking in the next room kept me motivated. After they flew away a quietness that was like an airless vacuum permeated the house. In it, I had to push myself hard to work at ad answering and letter writing. I thank God for Marty's ever-present love, support, and cheerfulness. It was an unending source of strength and inspiration. The only negative word she said about the entire situation was to characterize Evans' management as "stupid."

Living in non-industrial, Navy-oriented, Virginia Beach didn't offer any local opportunities, so I contacted everyone I knew who might be able to guide me, or give me a lead—maybe even a job. I took the *New York Times, Wall Street Journal, Chicago Tribune,* and *Los Angeles Times,* devouring the want ads daily. This produced a couple of interviews with companies competitive or ancillary to Evans, but no job offers. Next, I started calling on headhunters in Chicago, New York, and Washington D.C. The last thing a headhunter wants to see is a guy who needs a job. They are looking, as one of them said, for fresh meat. But I was determined, and talked my way into a few. Walking up and down Wacker Drive, on zero-degree, twenty-five-mile-an-hour-wind days in the Windy City wasn't exactly fun.

These exhausting and discouraging trips netted zero, but they were all part of the enormous effort I was pouring into the hopper of job search. So far, nothing was coming out of the bottom. The longer the search went on, the more my emotions pulsated like sine waves on an oscilloscope—not quite a 60 cycle, but often. I'd have days when I was upbeat and eager to write and call; and then there were dark, confidence-sapping days when I had to force myself out of bed and to my desk. Sometimes I'd sit at my desk just staring out at the bare winter trees, denuded by forces beyond their control. I sensed the graphic metaphor of the trees that symbolized my present status—stripped of purpose, employment, and self-esteem. When I looked toward the cove near the pond that Marty and I fished, I saw a grouping of three stark trees. In their singular, naked, and horizontal bare branches, side-stretching like a tee, I saw the crosses of Golgotha, cleared of the faltering life once pinned on them. Was the dormancy of the trees their echo of death, like my own dormancy? I knew from memory that they would bloom again in spring, but would I bloom again in useful endeavor?

I tried not to spend much time, or waste much effort and emotion, feeling sorry for myself, but, I did think—maybe even brood—a lot about being out of work. And with every passing day I heard the clock ticking off the duration of my severance pay. I had ten weeks remaining—then my income ceased! I thought about the times when I had had to lay off hard-working men and women to reduce expenses so that my operations would survive a recession. I always told my conscience that the sacrifice of a few to save the whole was justified. My logic and sworn responsibility was irrefutable, but since I was now the recipient of some "irrefutable logic and expedient sacrifice" I could empathize with the trauma of anyone who was unemployed through no fault of his or her own.

Most of the people I have known or studied, sought, in addition to survival, purpose in their lives; not being able to earn a living or contributing something to society through goods and services, can destroy one's dignity and confidence. I felt mine was being slowly eroded. One has only to see a Dorothea Lang black-and-white, Depression-era photograph, to sense the total despair of the unemployed. Being out of work deprives one of both physical and mental sustenance. Many philosophers and psychologists have said man's life is a search for meaning—it's difficult to find meaning in the rejection and ensuing idleness of being sacked.

After seven fruitless weeks, filled with yo-yo like emotions, on a dark February day that matched my mood, a "good" call came. It was from a headhunter I had been referred to by an old Evans-Portland associate. Funny how things that I did for him that I couldn't even remember, came back as fruit from a spontaneous seeding of friendship. How did a distant memory of me drive this man to recommend me, instead of himself, for this promising job offer? Was it divine intervention or coincidence? It was truly manna from heaven as I plodded across the shifting sands of a jobless desert, not knowing where I was headed. People have laughed at my desert metaphor, but I can't think of anything that more accurately describes being out of work. A desert is barren—no water, no food—and it can generate a heat that dries up a person's soul and spirit. There are no route signs, no milestones of success, just slogging ahead with the dimmest hope of finding sustenance. Receiving this positive sign was like stumbling onto an oasis just before I expired. The call was in no way related to any specific letter or call I had made. True, in the big scene, I had worked hard at trying to get a job, but this offer was not from any of my efforts—why did it happen?

The company was the Susquehanna Corporation, a mini-conglomerate. One of its subsidiaries was Rockwool Industries Inc., a five-plant manufacturer and distributor of thermal insulation. The job called for a CEO of the subsidiary. The headhunter asked, "Mr. Christopher would you be interested in meeting me to discuss it?"

I tried not jumping into the phone, and came back with an enthusiastic yes. We met in Chicago for two hours. Then the president of the parent company joined us. After two more hours with him, I was scheduled to spend a couple of days with a consulting and testing firm in Philadelphia for a thorough evaluation. And was it ever thorough! I didn't have to strip my clothes, but I was stripped mentally, emotionally, and psychologically—everything from ink blots to extensive psychological inventories and probing interviews.

My testing was all positive, and I was told to start in three weeks at a forty-percent increase in pay over my Evans job! I thanked God, and vowed I would always try to avoid laying people off, or firing anyone, unless it was a dire situation. I had tasted the wormwood of idleness and the hollowness of rejection—may I never inflict these curses on others.

Before actually starting however, I had one more interview. The major and controlling stockholder, Studebaker-Worthington Corporation, held forty percent of the stock, traded on the Amex, currently with very low volume at two to three dollars a share. Both the parent company and the insulation subsidiary were not profitable at that time; the recession of 1974-75 had hit their businesses hard.

Additionally, there was a two-million dollar preferred stock overhang (dividends not paid over several quarters), thereby blocking any common stock dividends until the preferred had been paid. This kept the stock price down, which didn't please the major stockholder. Studebaker-Worthington was a marriage of the old car manufacturer—no longer making cars—and Worthington Pump, maker of pumps, compressors, valves, generators, STP, and other industrial products. They had acquired the controlling stock of Susquehanna as a diversification acquisition. S-W was run by a hard-driving, astute chairman named Ruttenberg. His president was Les Welsh, a man with one arm who could play any sport. The president of Susquehanna was a man several years my junior named Jerry Kean.

Taking a job with a company in the red was nothing new to me—I guess I had either enough confidence or naiveté at forty-five to believe I could turn it around. I also had, as Adam Smith wrote in *The Wealth of Nations*, "the natural confidence which every man has more or less, not only in his own abilities, but on his own good fortune." And then, there was the consideration that I didn't have a job. So profitable or not, this opportunity looked even rosier than the red numbers. I flew into LaGuardia for my interview with Ruttenberg, Welsh, and another large shareholder of both Susquehanna and S-W stock, Richard Colburn, the acting chairman of Susquehanna. I didn't know the combined, personal net worth of these three gentlemen was several hundred-million-dollars. It was an hour-long interview with many questions about my past experience, what I hoped to achieve at Rockwool, and my five-year personal goal. I must have done okay; I saw them occasionally smile at each other. When it was concluded, they shook my hand and wished me good luck. I took the elevator down, but I could have floated down on the emotional cloud I was riding.

Walking down Fifth Avenue, hearing the toot-toot of taxis, recalling the opening bars of *Rhapsody in Blue*, I enjoyed the purposeful hustle of the fashionably dressed, scurrying New Yorkers who passed me. I began to whistle *New York, New York*. Peering into the inviting shop windows, I felt whole again. In my exuberance at being employed, and as a CEO yet, I bought Marty a Fifth Avenue cashmere cardigan and my first pair of hundred-dollar shoes. Later I sent each of the boys fifty bucks.

The first week of the job I spent at the Sunset Boulevard headquarters of the parent, Susquehanna. Rockwool was based in Denver, where I was scheduled for the second week. I spent a lot of time with Jerry Kean learning the background of both the parent and my subsidiary. Then I spent a week touring the plants in California, Colorado, Texas, Missouri, and Indiana. When I left the Alexandria, Indiana, plant on a Friday afternoon, I had to drive at eighty-miles-an-hour to catch a plane in Indianapolis for Portland, Oregon, where Bob had remained. He was scheduled to graduate that afternoon from the Portland Institute of Art. I made the plane by leaving the rental car, its engine still running, at the entrance and running to the gate with a security officer hollering after me. Bob, John, and I spent a happy weekend together before I headed back to our home in Virginia Beach, hoping the offer on the house had closed.

*   *   *

Rockwool insulation is made from slag, the dross or residue of metal smelting: iron, copper, or lead. Metal-bearing ores are heated to plus 2500 degrees, unleashing the metal as a liquid, which is poured off the top of the magma. The residual slag or clinker contains traces of the indigenous metal, but is useless to the metal smelter. Rockwool insulation manufacturers buy this slag at relatively low prices. The slag is charged with coke (destructively distilled coal) into a smelter and again heated to a liquid state. The molten rock pours from the bottom of the smelter onto a high-speed spinning wheel circled by a perforated ring ejecting high pressure air or steam. The molten rock is spun into fibers similar to cotton candy. These fibers are sucked into a large room-like chamber and fall onto a moving, perforated belt that is under suction, which action creates a moving blanket of rock fibers about six inches thick and eight feet wide. A phenol-based binder is applied to the fibers, binding the wool prior to being paper encased into a blanket, or bat, as it is called in the trade. If the wool is to be applied in the home by blowing it in loose, a dust inhibitor is used instead of the phenol-based binder.

We finally sold our Virginia Beach house, and Marty and I moved to the bright sunshine and freshness of Denver. On our first Sunday morning there, we looked to the west and saw the snow-capped Rockies against a brilliant blue, cloudless sky. We were together again, in mile-high, clear air—symbolic of the new lives we were to begin. Gone was the dank, dark depression of job-less Virginia. A whole new life was opening up for us. I wasn't a fired executive begging for a job; I was a CEO of a company that needed me. Marty looked at me over our breakfast of bacon and eggs. "Chris, remember twenty-five years ago when you started on the night shift at Philip Carey at a dollar-fifty-an-hour?"

"Yeah, I do, and I'd still be there if it wasn't for your love and support and God's grace."

We liked the people at Rockwool. There was an instant bond with the five general managers and the small corporate staff. One general manager in particular became my confidant, ally, and friend. Lanny West was a big Texan with a mouthful of pearly-white teeth and a grin as wide as his native state. Clad in a conventional suit, cowboy boots, and a University of Texas belt buckle, he could sell anything to anybody. He always called me "Chief." My secretary, Barbara MacLean, was an excellent assistant. I chose her after screening several highly qualified ladies, but B.J. had the most important talent—she could speak for my office to customers, suppliers, and employees, with perfect tact and clarity, and never caused a ripple. She became the communication center for our entire company and a master at scheduling my time.

It was easy to build a team; the people were eager for solid leadership and a feeling of purpose. I laid out three goals: return to profitability by reducing costs ten percent through a documented, bottoms-up cost reduction program; increase sales fifteen percent by expanding our geographic shipping areas to pick up incremental business allowing our plants to run at least six days a week for maximum burden absorption; and define some new higher-margin uses for our products in areas other than the predominantly residential ones to which we were tied. The team responded enthusiastically to this new plan, and with a lot of long hours of planning and execution, we were profitable six months later!

Jim and John came to Denver a few months after we arrived, and took jobs that lasted a year before they both entered college in Oregon. As a family, we did a lot of trap and skeet shooting, loading our own shells—not blowing up the house despite our ample supplies of gunpowder and percussion caps! It was difficult for an eighteen-and twenty-year-old to live with Mom and Dad and try to be independent men. We saw them grow a little as the manual work they did taught them some of the reality of the workplace. That year honed their desire to get an education and live on their own. When they left for school we cried; yet we found a new peace in just being with each other. Everything in life, it seems, is a trade-off.

*   *   *

In January of 1976, Jerry Kean, the CEO of Susquehanna, resigned. A week later, Mr. Welsh asked me if I would consider becoming president of Susquehanna. I couldn't believe this! My incubation in the company had just completed its nine months, and I was being selected to run the parent of six diverse subsidiaries. CEO of a substantial publicly traded company—was this the "getting ahead" Grandmother Christopher had told me to do? Of course, I said yes.

I had to be interviewed by the six directors, including Fred Carr, CEO of Executive Life, who later soared to financial heights before plummeting off the charts in the collapse of the junk bond market. Fred told me over lunch on Rodeo Drive that he would approve me, but the time clock was ticking on the time left to turn Susquehanna back to profitability and into paying dividends again. He said my predecessors hadn't done it. We shook hands—I liked him.

Richard Colburn, who had been acting chairman of Susquehanna, was going to step aside. I was to be CEO, and Les Welsh, president of S-W, the chairman. I had a lot of autonomy and authority, but S-W maintained a thin string on me.

I had to go to Mr. Colburn's office on Sunset Boulevard and ask him for his company car and credit cards. This man could have bought and sold me a hundred times or more. So, I hemmed and hawed in front of his desk. But he smiled and said, "Bob, no problem. I've been relieved by far worse people than you." I always appreciated his graciousness. He was a generous man. For example, his multi-roomed mansion on Doheny Drive, next to Eartha Kitt's home, had a room with controlled humidity and temperature filled with Amati, Stradivarius, and other fine violins and cellos. Dick would loan these to deserving musical students at Southern California schools.

Together we worked out a plan to merge the L.A. Susquehanna corporate office with the Rockwool staff in Denver. This move saved us nearly a quarter-of-a-million per year. Dick remained a supporter and friend during my entire tenure with Susquehanna.

Two of our subsidiaries were involved in highly classified defense work. We designed and produced rocket engines for missiles used by the Army and Navy, particularly the rockets fired at an enemy's jets. They sought either infra-red or heat. We jokingly called them high-powered suppositories—I guess they were. We also made radio-controlled radar decoys for the Israelis, and signal flares for all branches of the armed forces. I'm sorry we made the latter. One week after I took over, I got a call telling me we had just killed eight women at the flare plant.

Flares are made with materials that can flash at forty degrees. In our plant in Camden, Arkansas, they were packed mostly by local African-American women in individual concrete cells. There was a lightening storm in the area, and they had left the steel door open for more air circulation. A bolt hit near the cell and the electrical charge ignited the flare chemicals with a resultant explosion, killing all eight. When I got the call, my response was two-fold—the instinctive human reaction of sorrow and pity, and the company executive's concern about liability. Could these deaths ruin the company? Was I crass? No, I don't think so. If there were no company—there would be no jobs for fifteen-hundred people. Later, after three months of investigation and serious negotiations, our insurance and workmen's comp took care of the families of the deceased. No, we couldn't replace wives and mothers, but we did help the surviving families financially. And we devised more secure locking devices for the doors to try and reduce human error.

All of the S-W subsidiary presidents and a couple of their staffs were asked to attend a three-day meeting in the Dominican Republic (one of Ruttenberg's four houses was there) to present our business plans and forecasts for the balance of the year. Wives were invited, and we were flown there in luxuriously furnished private jets. The first two days boggled my mind and made me squirm. Each guy put on a film or slide show with tons of data based on research—projections of world-wide market trends, and new innovative products. Not having been on the job more than a couple of weeks, I had no data, slides, or films. All I had was three transparencies made the day before we flew, and a yellow pad with some notes.

Each night in our room, after seeing beautiful professional presentations full of dramatic visual aids, I stayed up till three in the morning rewriting my report. Finally, it was my turn, the last presentation of the session. I got up and told my story, interspersing my talk with my three little transparencies. I stressed the priorities I was following and our goals—short, medium, and long term. I finished with a projection of profitability by June (it was February), and concluded with how I would accomplish this through my people. My words were the simple words of action: costs, sales, collections, new uses for products, and people motivation.

I sat down feeling I was the lame duck, but to my surprise Gus Levy, a well respected leader of one of the nation's largest and oldest brokerage houses, who had worked with Ruttenberg for thirty years, came up to me and said (no kidding), "Bob, I liked your presentation the best of any. You know the ground level basics of business—no fluff, no pie-in-the-sky stuff. Congratulations."

I was stunned. This man had spent thirty plus years advising, underwriting, and financing multi-million-dollar mergers. He'd been around the corporate financial area all of his business life. I stammered, "Thank you, Mr. Levy."

That night at the closing dinner by the pool at the Caso de Campo complex, Mr. Ruttenberg reported Mr. Levy's comments to him. He added, "Good show, Bob." Mr. Levy to Mr. Ruttenberg was like Abraham to Isaac.

Marty and I flew back to Denver on a cloud of emotional exuberance. I'd made it with the "big guys." But upon reflection, I knew there had to have been guidance from a source beyond myself. I didn't have an MBA like my colleagues, and I had only been a CEO for eight months. I had devotion to the job, and sincerity, but there had to have been an influence I didn't see.

After about five months on the job, I was feeling fairly comfortable. I looked forward to going to work, as it seemed that each day we accomplished something to improve and grow the company.

Then some dark clouds floated across my bright sky of success. At a board meeting in New York, Ruttenberg and Welsh told me that S-W wanted to sell their holdings in Susquehanna. "Damn," I thought. "I just found a great job with people who are treating me great. I see a future of growth, and they want to sell it to who knows whom!"

Ruttenberg said, "Bob, you have some contacts in industry. Find someone you like, and they can have our shares for sixteen to eighteen million."

"Mr. Ruttenberg, I believe we're going to see a steady increase in profitability, and we'll pay off the arrearage in dividends before a year passes. You ought to consider keeping your shares; in time you'll make a lot more than sixteen million."

"Perhaps, but bring a friendly buyer, and we'll make an intelligent decision. In the meantime keep on the way you're going; maybe we'll reconsider."

"Thank you, sir. I will."

*　　　*　　　*

The principle of cause and effect, like the law of supply and demand, is a firm reality. Remember the OPEC-induced gas lines of late '73 and '74? The oil shortage, contrived to drive up prices (supply and demand), brought about programs in America aimed at conserving fuel—55 mile-per-hour speed limits, airfoils on the cabs of semis, and the conservation of heating oil by tax-incentives for the re-insulation of residential and commercial buildings. This program and awareness greatly benefited Rockwool Industries, and of course the parent, Susquehanna. The home and commercial re-insulation program took a while to gain the public's acceptance, but by early 1976, our insulation plants were on seven-day shifts resulting in soaring profits. The eleven Rockwool insulation machines became twenty-four-hour-a-day, seven-day-a-week "money machines."

*   *   *

I would go from Denver every other month to Chicago and meet with Les Welsh, president of S-W, to review our results and just talk for a couple of hours. Les was a remarkable, brilliant, and kind man. He pushed raises and bonuses for me; after I had held the Susquehanna CEO's job for only eight months, I crossed the six-figure salary line. He had lost an arm above the elbow in a farm machine accident when he was in junior high. His determination to not let this tragedy hinder him was extraordinary. He became an all-state guard on his high school football team. As a fifty-five year-old executive he ran companies, played tennis, golf, and shot shotguns.

In the summer of 1976 he told me that S-W wanted me to streamline Susquehanna into a building materials company— meaning four of our subsidiaries were to be spun off. The company would be comprised of Rockwool Industries and R & G Sloan, a molder and distributor of plastic plumbing fittings and pipe. What could I say? I didn't like the idea of shrinking my base of control and reducing the dollar revenues, but I knew the reduction of profits was a very small percentage of the anticipated revenue reduction. I had no choice—ownership has its rights—something I tucked away in my arsenal of business ammunition. Sometimes we just have to march, like good soldiers—we grouse as we march, but we march! After a day of sulking, I realized I would gain the valuable experience of selling whole companies: two defense companies, a plastic compounding company, and a mineral processor.

Like everything in 1977 and the first half of '78, these divestitures went smoothly. I never felt I had the Midas touch, but our sales and profits just kept accelerating, as did the return on the sale of the four subsidiaries. In reflection, our success, which was almost disproportionate to my efforts, started to breed an insidious cancer—apathy. Our team worked their jobs every day, and we never stopped trying to improve, but our profits were double the industry's average! However, I feel that humanity, and I in particular, are at our best when the motivation of survival and challenge are ever present.

Report by Susquehanna Shows Sales, Earnings Up
Rocky Mountain News

In late spring of '78 another grenade was thrown on my table of happy success. S-W announced they had a buyer for their forty percent holding. It was a Belgium company. I started receiving weekly calls from Mr. Ruttenberg cajoling me about how to handle the Belgians when they came to look us over. "Bob, I'm counting on you to be your usual professional and personable best. They'll like you...and, Bob, they'll need you."

I met the Belgians in New York, and we had an amiable meeting. Within days the transaction was completed, and guess what? S-W received $43,000,000 for what they had been willing to sell for $16,000,000 two years earlier. I guess my team had done some good—for them. In the transition nothing was said to me about a position. I floated in a nether land of undefined responsibility. Did I have a job? There were no more calls from Mr. Ruttenberg—no calls telling me he was happy with the sale, or that our growing of the company had meant another $27,000,000 for S-W. Finally, one day Les Welsh called and said he had detected unhappiness in my demeanor, and he figured it had to do with my unsettled status. He called the Belgians, who apologized over and over. They took it for granted that Mr. Ruttenberg had told me I was to continue as CEO. Les got me a three-year contract at an increase and a year-end bonus recommendation of sixty percent of my salary. All of these items were honored. The first six months of the new marriage were a honeymoon *extraordinaire*. Marty and I were invited to Brussels several times, royally feted, and told how great we were. Profits kept rolling in, and like stock prices in mid 1929, they were spiraling ever upward. My perks were spiraling upward as well—frequent raises, bonuses, stock options, a company-paid membership in the prestigious Denver Country Club, chartered Lear jets, a Cadillac company car, and a respectfully endowed thrift plan. Life was good. We were riding a soaring crest of success, yet we began to wonder, is this real? After being raised in the Depression, working up corporate ladders in slow steps, watching expenses for the first twenty years of married life, we found ourselves riding a bubble of worry not—if you want it, just get it!

Soon I was asked by the Belgians to look at other businesses as possible industrial-growth acquisitions in Europe and America. But the American economy in the spring of 1979 started to waver. Japanese and European imports of cars, steel, and other items were flooding a nation that had let its postwar efficiencies and productivities wallow in the apathy of earlier successes. The term "rust bucket America" was being whispered in the corners of the brokerage houses, as well as showing up in the journalistic jargon of the *Times* and *Wall Street Journal.* More and more cars without the name of GM, Ford, or Chrysler were showing up on our roads. Tons and tons of off-shore steel were rolling into American factories. These imports reduced American jobs and the available purchasing power for American-made products. Like a slowly developing fungus, recession was creeping into one industry after another.

Heavy layoffs caused people to stop buying houses that required insulation and plumbing fittings. The demand for the re-insulation of homes dropped off as incomes shrank. Suddenly, Rockwool was in a competitive firefight with the giants: Owens-Corning, Johns-Manville, and Certain-teed. Price wars were raging for the reduced market. Susquehanna's profits in 1979 dropped to thirty percent of 78's. This was not what the Belgians thought they were buying into. Mr. Ruttenberg's timing was excellent! The next year, 1980 started out with a continued downward trend in the building materials industry. Our profits had slipped to a minor loss position, which meant a reduction of cash for dividends that the Belgians needed to make payments on their financing of the S-W shares. Where did this trend lead? It led to a meeting in New York in early March.

"Mr. Christopher, the board would like you to resign as President and CEO of Susquehanna."

I was stunned by this bolt from the blue! Caught in a wave of shock and disbelief, my stomach contracted sharply, as if I had been hit in the solar plexus by Muhammad Ali. I could feel a gush of underarm perspiration dampening my custom-made shirt as I fought for control. This is not what a fifty-year-old executive, with two sons in college and a comfortable lifestyle wanted to hear as the country headed into the recession of 1980-82.

Looking at his feet, the Belgium-headquartered chairman of the company I was running continued in a quaking voice, "I am prepared to stay and operate the company for the next six weeks until your replacement is on board." Obviously fearing I would bolt from the room, or perhaps hit him, he backed away adding, "I have brought enough clothes. I can stay . . . I can stay even for six weeks."

"Fired for what reason?" I asked myself. True, the Belgians had paid a high price for the previous owner's majority holding of the Denver-based Susquehanna Corporation, a mini conglomerate of building materials companies that was to be their entry into the American industrial arena. That wasn't my fault, nor was the decline in business brought about by the current, nationwide recession, I rationalized.

In a rush of disbelief, I wondered: Why me? Why now? Having for thirty years managed industrial companies in cyclical businesses, I had faced a lot of trials, including tough union leaders, demanding and fickle customers, recessions, mechanical breakdowns, gut-wrenching layoffs of innocent people, and all of the rest that being the responsible party demanded. I had been criticized, shot at, challenged, yes, and even let go, but not this way; rejected, defrocked and cast off by a man who couldn't even look me in the eye! This man, ten years my junior, in his eagerness to score an acquisition triumph, had not prepared his owners for the reality of the American business cycle, the ups and downs of industry. He was intellectually very bright, but came from a European bureaucratic culture lacking in American "business savvy."

In times of crisis, I have always been amazed by the funny, often unrelated, thoughts that pop into one's head. Something my grandmother had said about, "praying for one's enemies," flashed on my mental screen. As the gravity of my position (or lack of one) sank in, I went toward the man, put my arms around him and said, "Charles, don't fret. I can still run the company for you until your new man is ready. It would be difficult for you to be over here away from your other operations for that long." Reinforced by this remark I added, "I don't hate you for what you feel you have to do." With this, he sagged, as a look of disbelief and relief crossed his flaxen, Flemish face. I helped him onto the settee in my sitting room at the Waldorf=Astoria, site of tomorrow's board meeting which I had just been requested to refrain from attending.

Disbelief slowly evolved into cautious hope, and he half stammered, "Yes, yes, that will be fine. Are you sure that you can do this?"

Donning the happy facemask of a Greek actor, I said, "No problem." I really wished that this tragedy was being played on a Hellenistic stage . . . I surely could have used a little *Deus ex machina.*

We finalized the details of our new temporary arrangement in the blase elegance of that now infamous Waldorf Suite. Looking around, I mused, "I guess as an out-of-work executive, I'll be staying in Motel Sixes, straw mattresses and all, while I'm on the job hunt."

After Charles left, I called my wife in Denver to share the news. As always, she was supportive and solicitous of my well-being. "I'll be waiting at the airport. Don't worry, Chris. We'll talk it over. Remember, God has always provided. Just be careful, and I'll see you tonight. I love you."

My plane to Denver didn't leave JFK for three hours, so I ordered coffee and brioche from room service. My stomach needed something in it to quell the butterflies. Signing the check, I thought longer than usual about the tip, but in a grab for self-assurance I put a handsome 25 percent on the tab. Pouring some coffee into the fine china cup, I reflected on what incidents might have led up to today's traumatic event.

I quickly put my finger on two factors; one, major and general, and the other, personal and more specific. The general picture was one of the new European owners feeling that they had been bilked by the former owners. When they bought the company in 1978, things were at an all-time high. However, the OPEC- triggered, energy-conserving, reinsulation boom of 1976-79 had started to cool dramatically, as had building activity in general. This trend strongly impacted our sales and profits. This was nothing new in the building material's industry. It would rebound in a couple of years, as it had always done. But, to a new owner who had just stretched financial capacity to meet the price of this

American opportunity, logic was quickly smothered by a blanket of emotional resentment.

The other reason, I conjectured, was a personal one, dating back some five months. A two-day meeting had taken place here in New York. I remembered the day well. Charles, the chairman, and a couple of his toadies met with me in their suite at the Carlisle Hotel in upper Manhattan. The recession had reduced our sales by 30 percent. To keep our plants running on a four-day schedule, thereby covering fixed overhead and keeping our employees working, I met many tough, competitive prices. This, of course, reduced profits to a mere break-even or small-loss basis, but it was better than losing more business and having to lay off hundreds of loyal people. These people had worked long hours during the busy years, helping to make the profits that everyone enjoyed—and bragged about.

During that meeting, the chairman said, "You should raise your prices to improve your margins and profits."

I replied, "If we do, we will lose more business to competition and be forced to shut down some of our plants. This will let the fixed burden eat us alive."

He continued with, "We know, but you should consider raising your prices to restore the margins that we bought the company on. We have made commitments to our shareholders and lenders."

"I can appreciate that, but if I raise prices, we will have less business and lose more money. At present, I believe we have balanced demand and pricing at the best point possible in this recession."

"Yes, but you are not achieving the margins that were present when we bought the company."

"I have done what I know from experience is best for the

current condition. This condition will pass, and we will have retained our customers and our trained employees, at a minimum of loss."

Again, he came back with, "But, to improve your margins, you must raise prices."

"I can't do this in good conscience. However, if you order me to, I will."

"We will not order you to. It's your decision, but we recommend that you raise prices," he told me in an unfamiliarly firm voice, as the two toadies nodded.

"I can't do this, unless you say so. What's it to be, Charles—yes or no?"

"You must resolve this. We are not telling you what to do, but we recommend that you raise prices," he said in his dull monotone.

I knew that all would be well for me, at least for a few quarters, if I did what he recommended. I started to agree, "I'll . . . I'll . . ." No! I couldn't say it. I thought about all of the good people I had touched, known, and with whom I had shared many challenges. "That's doubletalk and bullshit. Either say yes or no!" I blurted out in a fit of frustration, showing the lack of respect I had for this poser of authority who couldn't say, "do it, or don't do it."

Surprisingly, they said nothing. They changed the subject to other items on the agenda. The next day we started the pricing discussion again. It was a repeat of the earlier one. "Was this 'Belgian brainwashing?'" I asked myself. If so, it stunk. I was always a believer in clear-cut decision-making and leadership, not this kind of doubletalk.

Finally after five hours of this no-resolution discussion, I left the room recommending that the chairman try and have intercourse with himself, if he couldn't make a decision and be responsible for it. I heard very little from him after that meeting, until this morning in March of 1980.

So here I was, out in the cold with no job prospects, sitting in solitude on the principles of leadership in which I had long believed. I had a wife, three sons, some pride, and a lot of bills to pay. "What price glory?" I said aloud to the Iranian cab driver, as I left the Waldorf for JFK and the next chapter of my life.

Riding through the Midtown tunnel, I realized that what any executive fears most; getting fired, had happened, and besides, I'd trod this ground before and come out ahead. I felt my pulse. Yes, I was still alive and breathing! Actually, I had a flush of feeling free. I'd gotten this far; I could rebound and go forward. Brushing any semblance of false hope aside, I said realistically, "I have God, a supportive wife, and experience. What else do I need?"

~

C H A P T E R

14

*It is the characteristic excellence of the strong man that he bring
momentous issues to the fore and makes a decision about them.
The weak are always forced to decide between alternatives they
have not chosen themselves.*
Dietrich Bonhoeffer, " Miscellaneous Thoughts"

Out of work at 45, out of work again at 50—would I survive
this "tender age" trauma? Would anyone hire a fifty-year old "fired"
executive?

The tires on the McDonnell-Douglas DC-10 squealed as
they hit the runway at Denver's Stapleton Airport. Through the
first class window, I saw the puff of gray-blue smoke that always
accompanies 160-mile-an-hour rubber hitting static concrete, visu-
ally announcing, "We've landed." My flight from New York, where
I had agreed to tender a peaceable resignation as President and
CEO of Susquehanna and had committed to run the company for
six weeks, had been smooth. During the four-hour ride, I'd
thought about how I'd made a fortune for the previous stockholder,
Studebaker Worthington, created hundreds of new jobs, accomplished several profitable divestitures, and had given the plumbing
fittings subsidiary new direction into the higher margin markets
of industrial fittings.

But I hadn't been able to adjust to the European style of
management (the free will and self-governance that I was imbued
with, due to the early death of my dad, precluded being a toady to

management that evolved from imperial hierarchies), or convince them that the American economy was a cyclical thing. I had soared to the giddy heights of industrial and financial success, and I had just plummeted deep into the abyss of an involuntary resignation. I recalled my days at Evans when I swore I'd never let anyone force me into making a business decision I felt was wrong. I was still true to my oath. The price? No job!

I deplaned into the passenger corridor and was immediately absorbed into the hubbub of milling passengers and seemingly endless rows of concessions. The first one dispensed booze to fearful flyers, tired businessmen glad the day was over, and those who just couldn't pass up a bar. Next was the snack stand with dozens of reddish hotdogs reeking of garlic, cooking on heated stainless steel rollers, waiting to be speared, slapped into a bun, slathered with mustard, and gobbled up—indigestion to follow. I watched harried travelers shoveling them into their mouths as they scurried to their planes, remembering the elegant restaurants and fine dining halls I had enjoyed over the last five years. I wondered how soon I'd be happy just to have one of those economical, fat-filled "tube steaks," as W.C. Fields called them.

Exiting the terminal into the contrasting colors of approaching dusk, I saw the sun setting behind the snow-capped Rockies. I mused grimly, was my industrial sun setting as well? Then my spirits lifted—I saw Marty sitting in our new Jeep Waggoneer, smiling. How many times in our thirty years of marriage had she put that comforting and supporting smile on for me—masking lurking fears or concerns? No matter what the crisis, she always said, "Chris, I've got faith in you."

I tossed my bag into the rear, "Move over, Babe, let's see how this thing drives."

"Sure, you'll like it," she mumbled as she kissed me. "Glad to see you home safe. Wanna go to the Marriott for supper?"

"Okay. I'm starved for a steak…and you pal."

Marty had picked up our "mountain-trip-buggy" that same afternoon. Believing we would be in Denver for a long time, we bought the Waggoneer for trips into the Rockies. Now I was thinking, the car is only three hours old, and I'm wishing I had the twenty grand in the bank.

"Why so quiet? You like the car?"

"Yeah, it drives great; like the color too. Sorry if I'm quiet. Guess I'm trying to figure where to start on the job search."

"I know it's easy to say, but, Chris, you handled it before. You'll find something, and I'll help you with resumes or anything else. You're strong, good looking, experienced, and a hard worker—something will turn up. Remember, God has led us out of trouble before. We'll make it, and like your Grandmother Allan always said, 'Things always work out for the best.' Don't worry, please."

"Thanks, Babe. What would I do without you?"

"That goes both ways, you know."

On the way to the restaurant we talked about the future. I would be running the company for six more weeks, as a resigned, but not a lame-duck, CEO—pride sometimes is an ally. I still had a year-and-a-half on my contract, which would be paid, so we had income for a while. Also, we'd been able to sock some dough away from several lucrative bonuses and the exercising of Susquehanna stock options in the stock's run-up from three to ten dollars a share. But no asset pile lasts forever if there aren't new funds added from income. "Bottom line, buddy, you need a job," I said aloud.

Sunday's sermon touched on how one needs to occasionally stir his roots, expressed through the metaphor of the fig tree needing its roots cultivated for healthier growth—disrupting the hard-packed ground of the *status quo*. As Marty and I heard this, our hands met on the hard oak pew. We turned to each other and smiled through teary eyes, not sure where we would be in the future, or what lifestyle we could afford. Inwardly we were filled with apprehension, but outwardly we wore the armor of daily duties—deflecting the arrows and stones of anxiety. People's resilience under stress is usually exhibited by clinging to what is at hand—the concrete presence of tangible demands, not the abstract of what may or may not happen.

Our daily chores were carried out, but no matter how deeply we tried to immerse ourselves in them, there was a lurking queasiness. We felt detached from the mainstream of being at work, of being useful, of being like our employed peers. As a twenty-one-year-old, newly married breadwinner on the rock of Philip Carey, I'd taken a stand about dedicating my life to supporting my faithful wife. I felt complete only when I was working to accomplish this. I read in a book, *The Way of the Wasp* that the burden of white, Anglo-Saxon Protestants is that we can't do anything that doesn't have purpose. I found no significant purpose in taking out the garbage, running errands, or cutting the grass; it wasn't earning a living—I wasn't accomplishing the things I knew I could do.

I mounted my job search with fervor—two kids in college, bills to pay—no time to waste on self-pity, or what might have been. As I had after leaving Evans, I called everyone I knew. I was able to get a few interviews after running an ad about myself in the *Wall Street Journal*, but they were in fields I didn't think I could grab a hold of. Marty and I also looked at some local businesses, but realized we didn't have enough capital to buy anything larger than a "mom and pop" operation that would take a lot of floor time on our part. To paraphrase Adam Smith, we can only earn so much from our own labors, but wealth is earned when we add to our labors the earnings of other laborers (as in owning or directing large work forces—the career path I had walked for years.) My experience was corporate management of manufacturing companies, not running some back-alley candy and nut packer, custom packaging shop—or worse.

My six-week tenure of running Susquehanna as a resigned CEO was interesting. I made decisions as if I were permanent. When my replacement arrived, I showed him around Denver, helped him find a home, turned my desk and loyal secretary over (ouch!), and told him my wins and sins. On the last day, Charles from Belgium (who had asked me to resign in the Waldorf) showed up. I had assembled fifteen key managers in the conference room. I introduced each one with three sentences about their virtues.

I walked around the room putting my hand on the shoulder of everyone, remembering all that we had built together. Forcing back tears, I said, "Charles, this is a top quality team. If any mistakes or bad decisions were made, I made them. These dedicated and capable men carried out my plans, and if the plans did not work, I am responsible." Opening the conference room door to leave, I turned back around. "Farewell, my friends. May God go with you from here on out." Passing through the outer office, I saw my secretary and several women clerks crying. To them I blew a kiss.

Driving home in the company-owned Cadillac, which I would keep until I found a job, the tears I had held back in the conference room burst forth in a spate of longing. A longing to belong, to lead, to build, to feel I was doing something with purpose. When I got home, Marty put her arms around me, and her warmth triggered a few more tears that had been pent up since that March day at the Waldorf when I was first asked to resign. I'd never have made it as a Native American—stoicism isn't one of my virtues.

Finally, I said, "It's over, Babe. I guess we're going to stir our roots like the rector said."

"Yes, and we're going to get through this, and I know you'll...we'll make out better than before. Denver isn't the only nice place to live. We've been here for five years—that's a long time for us—time to leave. Anyway, the drapes need cleaning."

Six weeks went by and no luck. I called an old high school buddy, Ted Poor from Cincinnati, who was now with a national headhunting firm in Chicago. We had a good relationship, having shared Walnut Hills High School. We had been seeing each other over the last four years, as I had given him several lucrative searches at Susquehanna. When I had told him of my present plight, he asked, "When are you coming to Chicago, Bob?"

"Tomorrow," I decided before he inhaled from his question. What he did for me then was something I will never forget— the next day he rode a smelly, crowded bus from the Loop to O'Hare, where we met for two hours. His firm was trying to fill a job for a Chicago-based company that made asphalt roofing and automotive sound deadening. I couldn't believe it! Over half of my career had been making asphalt shingles, and I had done quality control work on automotive sound deadening at Philip Carey.

The parent company was International Bank, located at Seventeenth and Pennsylvania, diagonally across from the White House. International Bank was a "merchant bank," a term new to me. In effect, it was a conglomerate of diverse companies, but heavily into off-shore banks and on-shore insurance companies. In addition to the financial companies, it owned three industrial companies, one of which was Chicago-based Globe Industries.

International Bank had been started by retired four-star general George Olmsted, a former commandant of West Point, who served as America's liaison with Chiang Kai-Shek during World War II. When I entered the office of my prospective boss, Frank Taylor, a retired two-star general, I met my last boss from Philip Carey coming out from interviewing for the job I sought. We said hi—I held no resentment toward him for his Machiavellian end-play in getting me to leave Philip Carey. I had benefited more than he had from his ploy. In later years, I saw him at industry meetings, where he always asked reluctantly, "How's Globe doing?"

My interview was with General Taylor, and a Mr. Bourne, who ran one of the industrial companies, but held a lot of clout with International Bank's management. Before I could even sit down, Bourne asked me, "Have you ever cheated on your wife?"

"Never on company time, sir, and *if* I had, I'd be sorry for the rest of my life." I saw him wink at General Taylor and caught just a glimpse of a "thumbs up" signal he tried to hide. Where my answer came from I'll never know—except I felt an inner glow, as if I had been the transmitter of an innate thought. The kind of thoughts Plato said exist randomly in the universe; that Carl Jung said are part of the "collective unconscious;" or that Grandmother Christopher told me came from God.

The interview lasted an hour. They said they'd call me in a few days. A week later, we met at O'Hare and they made me an offer. Since the company I was to run was sustaining severe losses, their offer was below my last salary at Susquehanna. But it was a six-figure number. They had called two former directors of Susquehanna, who had given me a good recommendation. I guess a fifty-year-old canned executive can get a job!

Whew! Only six weeks after I exited from Susquehanna, I had a job, an income, and a year-and-a-half of pay still coming from Susquehanna! I guess having our roots stirred, like the fig tree in the sermon, did help us to become healthier. The following Sunday in church, Marty and I again thanked God for leading us to a new job, and to a new segment in our odyssey of life—back to the midwest of our youth and to the comforting smell of asphalt. We were going eastward to the city about which Carl Sandburg wrote:

Hog Butcher for the World,
Tool Maker, Stacker of Wheat,
Player with Railroads and the Nation's Freight
Handler;
Stormy, husky, brawling,
City of the Big Shoulders....

We were excited about moving to Chicago and about the challenge of turning around Globe Industries—a task that would take a lot of "brawling" and some mighty "big shoulders."

*   *   *

From the moment we hit Chicago on July 1, 1980, I couldn't wait to get started. I went immediately to the office, while Marty went with a Realtor to look at houses. We met for dinner, and decided we didn't like any of them. So by ourselves, we drove around Flossmoor, a commuter town, twenty some miles south of downtown Chicago—that famous area called the Loop because the elevated commuter trains from three directions make a "loop" to return to their suburbs of origin. After living in the West, arriving in Flossmoor was like returning to the womb. It resembled many suburbs in Cincinnati—in architecture, flora, lifestyle, and established solidness. We were so happy driving the tree-lined streets, seeing the many churches, and taking a stroll in the one-block "downtown" with its Illinois Central train station and cute shops. After five years of high living, flitting to New York, Europe, and Los Angeles, and dealing with European owners, the down-to-earth values and solid middle-of-the-road ethos of this town gave us a familiar good feeling—a feeling of permanence, of belonging, and of security.

We stopped at an old fashioned ice cream parlor, just like the ones we knew as kids in Ohio—marble top tables and chairs with wire legs. Again we felt we had come home. We walked past the circa 1920 commercial buildings, eating our cones and holding hands. Then we went up one street and down another until we saw a sign advertising new homes of colonial design. Luckily we caught the builder on site, and two hours later we owned one. Like our home purchase in Virginia Beach, we did this without any experience on the job. Why wait? We were here and we had to make it—had to like it—had to make good. Marty went back to Denver to sell the house, and I spent the next six weeks in a motel, my loneliness assuaged only by a couple of weekends with her.

Each morning I took the company's three-year-old Chevrolet to my office at the end of a street lined with ten-feet-apart "Chicago Houses," those archetypal six-room, one-floor brick bungalows with no garage that dot the Chicago landscape with a density like tokens on a Go board. This Southeast Chicago suburb was known as Hegewisch—odd, a German name for a predominately Polish (as in the front steps were scrubbed daily) neighborhood. That peculiarity was typical of the distinct, ethnic neighborhoods of Chicago.

My office was in a hundred-thousand-square-foot, wire-cut brick building that also contained a warehouse, idled from a defunct operation. Walking up the cement steps I thought, "We gotta turn this into something productive." Office space is great, but it doesn't produce any revenue.

Inside I encountered a mishmash of design, in truth, an absence of design, except for a few prints of Chicago scenes. The women all wore long pants—a sad scene for a "leg-man" like myself. The furnishings, like the women's clothes, just looked tired; no snap or brightness to any of it. To my relief, none of the accountants were wearing green eyeshades, nor did they sit on high stools in front of small, inclined desks. I saw no quill pens either.

Given the historical culture, the neighborhood, the office, and the dress and decorum of the staff, I knew it might be a while before I saw a Cadillac company car, chartered jets, or heard sophisticated lunch conversation. But, within a few days I discerned the dedication and goodness of these hardworking, ethical folks. They were not encumbered with the need for status symbols—their priorities were a job and carrying the responsibility of raising their families with solid, home-grown values. And it was obvious they had never been empowered by being allowed to participate in the management of the company.

They weren't drones—they were just not in the "inner circle" of management. Together we made a few plant trips and I took several of them to lunch. Definitely, this was new experience for them; whoever heard of clerks and secretaries accompanying management to lunch? I began to know more about them and their backgrounds. The entire group could be led to greater heights if given tools, encouragement, and good direction, and allowed to become a part of the management process.

This would be my first priority—to employ the full potential of everyone in the company. Right now we were in the red, and current sales were a measly 18 million dollars in automotive and 20 million in roofing. The sum of these came to only a third of what I had managed at Susquehanna. And we had a total of three-hundred-and-fifty employees, one fourth of my Susquehanna crew. How far up could these sales and employee numbers go? The thought strengthened my resolve to increase both, which would help to bring a sustained profit and provide work for more people. The sales had to come first, then the jobs.

Looking at the present conditions of the company, and the country too, I wondered if I was up to the task. By any standards or experiences of the past, turning this company around in the present economy looked impossible. God, if I didn't, where would that leave me—out of work again, at an even more vulnerable and unemployable age? *Aw, hell, I can do it. I've pulled things together before. I have to do it here, what's the alternative? But, there sure aren't any clear signs—no light on the horizon. Low prices in roofing, low market share in automotive, and a bunch of scrap at every plant. I just gotta do it one day at a time—each day I have to do something that's positive—little steps, but consistent. I'll go to Lowell today and pull the guys together and get them fired up by letting them lay out a step by step program for each machine. I'll call what we come up with by some name that reflects them—none of that government acronym crap, but some title to give them a buy-in, and some pride of authorship.*

That night at home, I told Marty about my concerns, sharing how I had come to the conclusion that we had to just plug away one day at a time for a few months. She agreed, assuring me she'd do anything she could to help. Whenever my confidence was ready to flag, Marty was there again to bolster it. It dawned on me I had to do the same for all of the guys in the plants who must be wondering if their jobs were going to be there. They had to be as discouraged with the scrap as I was. Too many times shallow managers think hourly workers are not human—don't care about what they turn out. That's bull, the workers I'd known for thirty years cared about what they made, about their future—they weren't some lump of humanity. You couldn't pigeonhole them into some demeaning category like "the workers" or "the help."

If I did nothing else at Globe, I was going to make the team—workers, salespeople, supervision, anybody—develop and utilize as much of their potential as possible. *I'm no genius, nor am I a god. I need every one of them, and I'd better give them the tools and leadership they deserve. Hell, this is a challenge, but what opportunity isn't? God's given you this chance, so, buddy, don't doubt what you're going to do from this day forward—you're going to build the best damn team the roofing and automotive industries ever saw!*

Somehow—maybe through divine intervention, some early values Grandmother Christopher had instilled in me, Marty's faith, the response of my new associates, or a pinch of ego inspired by son Jim's admonition of, "Don't let the bastards get you down," I never lost the fire that flamed within me that day. I wish I knew what it is in us humans that breathes renewed determination—maybe even wisdom, or at least direction—into us when we have lost all but a deep encoded faith that makes us take another step, when we thought we had lost our way.

Globe had known some brilliant days when the auto industry used their simple, heavy sound deadening that had a good margin. But, since the gas crunch of '73 the car makers wanted high acoustical performance with considerably lower weights per piece and lower costs as the ever-tightening pinch of Japanese and German imports sapped their market share and profits. Globe had addressed these new demands by structuring a technological license with a European company that would provide the company with the new technology of making lightweight, but effective, deadening. So far, the absorption of the new designs and materials was resulting in huge losses. Globe had slipped in market share at GM, Ford, and Chrysler to fifth out of six acoustic suppliers.

Globe's single-machine roofing plant in Whiting, Indiana, had seen the sun set on the heyday of asphalt shingle profits due to reduced demand in the recession of 1980-82 and severe over-capacity in the asphalt roofing industry. Price cutting was rampant as over one-hundred plants, nationwide, struggled to get enough business to survive on. Together, the two businesses were suffering a sizeable loss. One bright spot, there was a debt-free balance sheet that yielded sufficient cash flow to meet all payrolls and supplier invoices—at least for a few months.

I knew I had a major challenge ahead when I started to hear a lot of watercooler provincialisms about the "good old days," and how this "new stuff from Europe" was messing things up— "why can't we go back to the old materials?" There were three plants that made sound deadening: the "main" plant—a term that reflected a parochial mindset that would have to be changed—in Lowell, Indiana. Another one was described by old guard employees as the "one we shut down to help Lowell" in Oregon, Ohio (east Toledo), and a plant that Globe owned half interest in, was located in Tillsonburg, Ontario.

When I toured Lowell, it was a sea of scrap on the various department floors, as operators tried to make the new machines and materials perform. I asked the VP of Manufacturing to wire Europe at once to send three technicians for an indefinite stay— no technicians, no fee-paying on the license! They arrived two days later. I assigned one to each shift and demanded a daily report of changes, problems, needs, and recommendations. In one month we went from fifty percent efficiency to eighty percent.

I never got a clear or objective answer as to why the Oregon plant was shut down. I asked for the calculations that proved it should have been closed. I heard, "We just know we needed to put all the business in Lowell to soak up overhead."

I came back with, "How about the sunk fixed costs of an idle plant in Oregon?"

"Well, they'd be there anyway."

"That kind of fuzzy thinking stops today; or you do! Now let's talk about what we have to do to get that sucker running again, pronto!" I quickly learned that there was carpet underlay business—one specialty of the Oregon plant—available. It had been dropped because there were complaints from the carpet customers about quality, and who needed that kind of grief?

I got the Detroit rep on the phone and told him to call on all four auto carpet manufacturers by the end of next week. He did and got some orders—in one month the plant was running again—a hundred hourly people were recalled. We also picked up two large, multi-layered, and unwieldy floor coverings for a mini-van, and a sedan. We got them because our competitors bid them high due to the difficulty in manufacturing them. With these two parts and the underlay we could run the Oregon plant five days, three shifts. At first I wasn't sure my brash moves were right. The first week we ran the large floor insulators, I saw that it took thirteen people at the take-off end of the machine to de-plug and scalp the cutouts required for car cables, bolts, and seat stanchions to pass through. The people were new to this operation, so the start-up was euphemistically a training process, but in reality, chaos with a capital C. Pieces, arms, hands, cotton fuzz were flying everywhere. When I commented on this to the plant manager, his earthy remark was, "Yeah, it looks like three monkeys fuckin' a football." I tried to imagine this, but failed. I felt his answer, while humorous, reflected a non-analytical view of a problem. A few months later I replaced him.

In time, these parts became profitable because these workers needed a job and *they* solved the problems of de-plugging the parts. On my second trip to the plant, I spent fifteen minutes with them, helping them to pull out die cuts, getting my Brooks Brothers serge suite covered with linty cotton fibers. As we worked together, I shared that if we could make these parts economically, their jobs would be guaranteed. On my third trip, two weeks later, we were at ninety percent efficiency and the scrap was below a very acceptable three percent. This was achieved by these sincere hourly workers solving the problems of de-plugging the insulator. This "victory" told me that employees, when empowered by management, will bring to bear one of America's greatest, but often buried assets, the *mind* of the American Worker.

In my fifteen years with Globe, the Oregon plant was never shut down again—it only grew—from a hundred employees to over four hundred. That group was dear to me and their morale was the highest in the company, so what did I care when some of my staff hid their sniggers while I hugged a hard-working Polish lady (with a Kielbasa breath that would knock over a horse), or the African-American girl who needed this job to make monthly payments on the secondhand mobile home that housed her and two fatherless kids. These were the folks who made the machines run. They were the flesh and blood essence of industry. True, we needed well-designed machines, good methods, and quality materials, but men and women, properly trained and motivated, are the nerve centers, arteries, and muscles of any company. Mingling with our operators always left my suit covered with lint and asphalt all over my shoes —but, hey, the dry cleaner needs work too.

*   *   *

As 1980 drew to a close the economy continued to slide deeper and deeper into recession. Car companies had scheduled long shutdowns of several plants, and roofing demand plummeted as winter came, stopping the construction of new homes. After a gut-wrenching analysis of our finances and January orders, which were almost nil, I realized there would have to be some layoffs a week before Christmas—one hundred from automotive and eighty in roofing. My conscience flogged me with the promises I had made to myself as a fired executive, about not laying people off. At three in the morning, in yet another fitful night, I rationalized about saving the whole by sacrificing a few. And to get personal, if we failed, I'd be out in the cold too. Squirming in my night-time reasoning I would seesaw from the dire to the hopeful and back again. It reminded me of a painting I'd seen by Francisco Goya, *The Sleep of Reason Produces Monsters*. I had a few chasing me as I tried to work out the best solution for the most. But I truly had no choice. I like to think that I did a tiny thing to give our employees hope. Every company family received a large turkey, including those who had been laid off. And their filing requirements for unemployment compensation were expedited. To myself, I vowed to get more business. I believe the pain I felt over those layoffs motivated me far more than my board of directors or any personal goals I could have set.

At a staff meeting, I stressed that we needed more business. Our plants needed to run at least five days, with a full complement of employees. There was skepticism. "But, Bob, demand is off."

"Yeah, it is. So we have to have a bigger share of what demand there is. How, you ask? We'll get it by taking business away from our competitors. And how do we do that? By offering the best price, most responsive sales and plant forces, and no bad parts shipped! We'll broaden our geographic coverage in roofing by picking up incremental business on the fringes of our freight cost range even if it's a little better than break-even, but a good burden absorber. And we'll add to our product offerings in both roofing and automotive. There are a lot of car parts that use our materials that we don't make...yet!"

This meeting established *what* our company would do. The other check questions of: who, when, why, how, and where are better answered after you decide *what* it is you plan. I was now in high gear by seeing the road I would follow.

Flying into Chicago, either Midway or O'Hare, I would see hundreds of flat-roofed commercial and industrial buildings. When the plane was in its final approach, we were skimming the tops of the thousands of square feet of potential flat-roof market. I knew from my Philip Carey days that these roofs took one or two plies of an asphalt-coated sheet, plus two or three of asphalt-saturated felt. I knew the "black-backed" cap and base sheet made at Perth Amboy was the best in the trade, so I took my roofing plant manager into the back door at Perth and asked Manuel Martin to show us the mechanics of manufacturing the raw asphalt-backed sheet. Back in Whiting, we designed revisions to our idle saturated-felt machine. I talked International Bank into a half-million-dollar capital expenditure, and in two months, we were running the new products, thereby creating thirty new jobs, and adding much-needed revenue. Our successful entrance into the built-up roofing market caused a stir in the industry with the immediate acceptance of this superior product, previously unavailable in the Chicago area. We also designed a shingle that brought in new orders and extended our shipping radius by a hundred miles.

To increase our automotive sales I did a lot of research on our competitors, particularly the one reputed to have the largest market share. In the postwar years, prior to the late seventies, sales to the car companies were handled by reps, who charged five-percent down to one-percent as volume increased. The industry-wide *modus operandi* had long been booze, broads, and bromides—with a lot of gifts to purchasing agents. This style of marketing was now giving way to a more technical type of selling, with the car company's engineers playing an ever-increasing role in the selection of products and vendors. As designs became more sophisticated, the technical aspects of a product were of the highest priority. Globe had a very ethical rep, but he was not as technically oriented as was needed.

With our team pulling together, giving their input, we launched a major shift in our automotive marketing approach. We were going to abandon the rep method of selling, and create our own sales force, as well as a prototype shop, acoustic lab, and sales office in Detroit—where our customers lived! I felt like Galileo when I proposed that Lowell, Indiana, and Hegewisch, Illinois, were not the center of the automotive universe. But in time, this paradigm shift was accepted, and I never had to recant!

With our Detroit-based facility, we would be able to invite automotive engineers into our lab and prototype shop and get them involved at the beginning of a part's design. I wooed the sales manager away from the competing company (with the number one market share) and signed him up with a five-year contract, which his former employer felt he didn't need. Within two months our sound-deadening business moved up fifteen percent. Our new sales manager was very canny at building loyalty with car company engineers and buyers—he came with us, they came with him!

Despite several positive moves, 1981 was a tough year. The country was experiencing high interest rates of up to twenty percent, a charge that crippled industrial investment. People were writing off "rust bucket" America—steel and automobiles. When Marty and I would take the Illinois Central from Flossmoor to downtown Chicago on a Saturday, we noticed from about 116th Street on into town all of the boarded up, broken-windowed factories that were no longer viable—no longer a provider of jobs. Up the street from my office was now silent Wisconsin Steel— gone forever—its workers hanging out in nearby dingy bars talking about when "Big Steel" would come back. Like Eugene O'Neil's characters in *The Iceman Cometh*, they lived a life of pipe dreams, never venturing out into the world of reality, or even beyond the doors of the gin mill. Fred Jaicks, former president of Inland Steel in Gary, Indiana, said, "If the government would have stayed out of the labor-management disputes of the fifties and sixties (repeated invoking of the Taft-Hartley) and let the two forces fight out or settle their disputes themselves, the industry would be healthier." Who knows? I say short term success and quick affluence usually produces apathy, laziness, and an open road to one's capture by competition. Just ask the Romans, the Spanish, the English, and the people of Gary and Detroit. Even the Swiss were prey to the status quo with their refusal to accept quartz technology for their hallowed ticking watches.

Everyone was talking about "The Japanese style of management," except yours truly. I knew the Japanese had learned what they were effectively employing from Charles Deming, from General MacArthur's rebuilding of Japan after Hiroshima, and from the millions of Nikon-snapped pictures of American Industry by Japanese "tourists" wandering through

American plants. I believed then, and still do, that we Americans have a fine style of management and motivation *when* we don't let temporary successes weaken our resolve to continually improve. We're at our best when we are just a pinch hungry.

Some industrialists called for fence-building tariffs on Japanese cars, but Roger Smith, GM's chairman who steered his company into recovery and growth, and our government wisely said no. As a result, American car makers, without the debilitating effect of tariffs, got off their collective industrial asses and started to make better cars, more efficiently. It was a painful progress, sort of like turning a battleship around in the *River Rouge*, but little by little, we began to see the improvements. Lee Iaccoca got on TV and said "Let's go America." People responded to his cry, even though his fabled K car wasn't the best. But it was a symbol, a rallying object. He also sold the U.S. government on making one of the smartest moves they ever made: backing the Chrysler Corporation's bonds. This action, often criticized by shallow thinkers, saved thousands of American jobs, saved millions in unemployment compensation dollars, and returned a profit to the government (a novel idea) when the bonds were redeemed. Investing in a job-giving industry seems like a wise investment versus patronizingly handing out a pure dole. I believe a job is always better than welfare—there's no dignity in welfare.

1981 was another loss year for Globe, but we had made progress in sales growth, product-diversification, and manufacturing cost reductions. During the year-ending, dark days of December, as I reviewed our sad P & L, and at the same time had to acknowledge all of the positive things we had achieved, I understood how Sisyphus must have felt as his rock came rolling back on him. To my surprise, I received a raise just before Christmas. I guess the brass in Washington, D.C. thought we were on the right track. General Taylor said, "Bob, just keep on charging forward the way you are."

1982 opened with two weeks of twenty-five degrees-below-zero weather. Not only was the climate in a deep freeze, so were our plants and our order files. I worked out a plan to mothball our roofing plant for a month or two, and reduce the automotive plants to every-other-week schedules. It was a sad time—more layoffs would be needed.

One Sunday in the Episcopal Church in Flossmoor, I prayed a long time after the service had concluded. I asked God to give me guidance on how to save our people. There was a life-size statue of Jesus on the wall behind the altar. It was affixed halfway between the floor and the ceiling, depicting His ascension to heaven. I hoped that my prayers were ascending to our Father, as had His Son. This church had become our spiritual and community anchor as we settled into the area, and into the challenges of the economy. I had become very active in it, serving on the vestry, heading a youth group, and serving as a lector and chalice bearer. Marty was president of the women's group and on the altar guild.

A week after my extended prayer session, the clouds cleared and a bright sun brought temperatures up. Almost miraculously our order files rose as well. We had been within a few days of carrying out our "mothball" plan, with its penalizing layoffs for workers. I can't explain what turned things around or why—maybe it was pent-up demand from the reopening of furloughed auto plants. I'll never really know, but I sure was grateful for the eleventh-hour save of our people. As 1982 progressed, many of the things we had developed and structured in dismal 1981 started to pay off. Sales increased, we were making a slim profit, and we were able to call back a hundred-and-fifty workers.

Not only were Marty and I dealing with the recession, but so were two of our sons, Jim and John. They were both in Oregon, where they had gone to college, and struggling with a lumber-based economy that was equally as flat as automotive. After doing all they could to support themselves and their wives, they called me for a job. I thought for two seconds about the effect of bringing family into the company, and said, "Yes, come ahead." I wasn't sure how I'd work them in, but they were our kids, and I knew they'd work. To avoid conflict I placed John in Lowell and Jim in the Whiting roofing plant.

I tried to monitor their work to be sure they earned their way—they were. Actually, they had to work harder than others to prove they weren't riding on their dad's position. After a trial period, they were accepted and became valuable employees. Marty and I loved their proximity to us, particularly when they brought children into the family.

*   *   *

Japanese Invade American Homeland:
Columbus, Ohio, First Target!

No, this was not an invasion by helmeted soldiers firing Nambu rifles and shouting *Bonzai*. The "invaders" were Western-dressed Nipponese industrialists, armed with the latest robotic welders and meticulously designed production lines and cars—the Accord for one. The years were 1980-83, and the Honda car company was the first wave, soon to be followed by Nissan, Toyota, Mazda, and Mitsubishi. Honda was building an automotive assembly plant near Columbus, Ohio, heartland America. What had not lasted for the Japanese on Guadalcanal, Tarawa, Iwo-Jima, the Philippines, and Okinawa in 1942-45 was going to be a permanent beachhead in Ohio, with others in Tennessee, Kentucky, Illinois, Michigan, Indiana, and California. The Japanese, in order to protect their 25-to-30 percent market share, knew wisely that they would not alienate the American consumer if they used American workers and suppliers to manufacture their cars with a minimum of 60 percent American content (half a loaf is better than none!)

What did the presence of Japanese-owned car plants in the U.S. mean to American car makers and to Globe? It made Detroit think and work harder; in time better cars started to roll off American assembly lines. I always felt Ford led the pack on quality with their slogan, "Quality is Job One." To Globe it was a bit of a windfall. Was it luck, coincidence, or divine intervention? Imported cars created no market for American suppliers, but the Japanese cars being made in America opened up a new portion of the market to American parts manufacturers. Another break: Honda's largest acoustic supplier in Japan was the NTT Company who, like Globe, had a technological license with the same

European company. Globe and NTT were put together by the licensor. NTT took me literally by the hand to Honda headquarters in Tokyo and announced that Globe was an ally of theirs, and that we could supply the Honda plant in Columbus. After several stringent quality reviews and endless telexes that demanded more and more from us, we became the designated acoustical supplier.

Three years after we began supplying Honda, several other Japanese plants were either operating in the U.S. or were under construction. The owner and chairman of NTT, Mr. Nakanishi, a very honorable man, came to me and proposed that we form a joint venture in the U.S.—half Globe, half NTT. The venture would have its own plants and sales force, and be governed by a board with five members from each company. I would be CEO, in addition to being CEO of Globe. I loved the added responsibility and controlling authority. There were to be only five Japanese employees out of three hundred at United Globe Nippon (UGN), our name for the new company. It took a year to work out the details, sign agreements, and equip a former roofing plant I had bought for a song in Chicago Heights.

In 1985, Roger Smith led GM into a joint venture with Toyota to manufacture cars at an old GM plant in Fremont, California. It was a redone assembly plant, now highly efficient, and making a moderately priced, quality car. I saw Mr. Smith and Mr. Toyota drive the first two cars off the line three days before Easter—an industrial resurrection! I guess Mr. Smith with his huge corporation, and me with my small one, saw the wisdom in the old cliché, "if you can't lick 'em, join 'em"—at least partially.

We soon acquired ninety percent of the acoustic business from the Japanese plants now operating in the U.S. In staffing the joint venture, we placed our son Jim in charge of production, and son, John, in charge of sales. The Japanese partner had to approve them, which I liked, because it eliminated any taint of nepotism. The boys performed well; our sales and profits improved every year.

Things were sailing along as 1985 neared its close. The economy was improving, and car production had doubled from its nadir in 1982. UGN showed sales gains every month. I had received several raises, bonuses, and a Cadillac company car. Even the lunchtime conversations improved; we shifted from our business to other subjects, but always "elevated" ones. We'd ask each other questions that took thinking and research. This mental exercise kept our brains moving—not decaying with sit-com drivel. In time I took twelve to fifteen managers and their wives to evenings of dinner and a classical concert. At dinner, three selected couples would give a short presentation on the featured composers or artists. These monthly get-togethers built trust and propinquity in our management team.

I was totally autonomous in my management of Globe and UGN. My only reporting requirements were to tell, once a month, the company man in Washington, now Marshall Austin, General

Taylor's replacement, "Everything's okay." Marshall was a prince. He had been a combat marine in World War II and Korea and one of the founders of the third industrial division at IB. He and I, as well as our wives, spent many a happy hour playing golf at his winter home in Florida. He took good care of us, and I gave him a good performance to report to General Olmsted at International Bank. He gave me total autonomy and a lot of freedom with expenses on customer-entertaining trips, as well as healthy year-end bonuses

So what could go wrong? Well, something did—at least I thought my parade was in for a downpour, when at a board meeting in October, I learned that the industrial divisions were to be sold off. I was told I could sell Globe, and myself, to any friendly buyer who would pay book value plus a reasonable premium. All I could think about was Yogi Berra's, 'This is déjà vu all over again.' "Damn, I got everything going right! Now what's next: a new owner; a change in our strategies, people changes—maybe even a change of CEOs." At fifty-six these were not good thoughts. But I enthusiastically pitched Globe to a couple of companies. Christmas brought a healthy bonus, but a dim personal outlook for 1986. The sale was in limbo over the holidays. I prayed a lot and tried to tell Marty that things would work out, but I wasn't certain. I'm sure she saw through my shell of bravado. "I've got faith in you, Chris. Any new owner would be nuts to throw you out after what you accomplished. And, God has provided for us ever since we got married!"

"So have you, Babe. So have you. Maybe there'll be a good buyer. I've got a good presentation worked up and some pretty dramatic sales and profit growth charts. I'll get it," I said as I ran for the phone on New Year's Eve afternoon.

"Is this Robert Christopher, the president of Globe Industries?"

"Yes it is."

"I'm Kingdon Gould. My brother-in-law, Guy Martin, is General Olmsted's assistant. He tells me Globe is for sale, and that you are doing a terrific job."

"Yes, sir, I know Mr. Martin, and thank you."

"Would you like to help me buy Globe?"

My mind spun, I took a deep breath. "Yes, sir, Mr. Gould, I certainly would. It's a great company, and we have a good future."

"Good. I'll come to Chicago next Tuesday, if you want me to."

I was impressed, and a little amazed, at the almost humble way in which he expressed himself. I sensed that this was a man of integrity, without any pretentious ways. He was successful, yet he did not emanate this in his dialogue with me. He talked to me as a full equal. When I hung up, I was aglow.

We couldn't believe this. It was a miracle. "And, babe, he was so low key, and polite, almost as if I was doing him the favor."

In some fast and furious research, I learned that Kingdon Gould was the great grandson of Jay Gould, the railroad magnate—MoPac, Union Pacific, and Erie Railroads of the Nineteenth Century. Kingdon had been listed in *Forbes 400*. Later I would find out he was a WWII Armored Cavalry lieutenant who had been wounded in France, had graduated from Yale Phi Beta Kappa, and was a lawyer. Settling in the greater Washington D.C. area, he devoted his business energies to developing commercial property and building a large parking garage network. He had nine children and had served as an ambassador to the Netherlands and Luxembourg under Richard Nixon. As I got to know him, I would describe him as a renaissance man of impeccable character, generosity, and integrity. It was one of the luckiest days of our lives when he called me. And, in time, meeting us turned out to be good for him too. It was a win win!

At last, the day of Kingdon's visit arrived. Thinking about his success and position, I prepared for our meeting—new white shirt with a maroon and black striped tie, my best Oxford-gray, three-piece suit, charcoal-gray overcoat with black velvet collar, and black Homburg hat—a reincarnation of every great industrialist I'd ever seen. After getting to his gate an hour early, I paced the bustling corridors of United Airlines trying to visualize what he would look like. Finally, his plane inched up to the jet-way. The last person off the plane was a man of slight build, wearing a tweed sports jacket with leather elbow patches, a tweed cap, and a Land's End, vinyl back pack. "Hi, I'm Kingdon Gould." I was amazed at the understatement.

We drove to my office, reviewed some slides, financial reports, and our 1986 business plan. We spent some time talking about our markets, the Japanese joint venture, which intrigued Mr. Gould, and a little about my background. After two hours he said, "Let's do it!" Then he said, perhaps after seeing the respect, enthusiasm, gratitude, and some humility in my eyes, "I'll give you a third of the company if you'll run it."

I was overwhelmed, which is an overwhelming understatement. My firings at Evans and Susquehanna flashed before me, and so did this sincere, unpretentious man who gave me so much trust and financial promise, all based on only three hours together.

I looked into his eyes, holding back tears of thankfulness, and said, "I'll give you everything I've got, Mr. Gould. Thank you."

"Kingdon, please."

We drove to Lowell, toured the plant, now running at full capacity, and drove back to Hegewisch, where I asked him if he wanted to see our other plants. "No, this is like looking at a menu in a restaurant, I've looked at it, and I pick you. Come to Washington next week and we'll make our offer."

We did and it was accepted—$23,500,000. Six weeks of due diligence followed and the arranging of a $23,000,000 *unsecured* loan. Kingdon put up $5,000,000 in cash, which gave us sufficient working capital to run the business. On March 28th we signed two hundred pages of legal documents and Globe Industries was ours! At the conclusion of the signing, I broke into tears. Kingdon put his arm around my shoulders and asked if I was okay. "Yes, sir, it's just your unconditional faith in me."

1986 was a banner year—record sales, profits, and employment. It seemed that since the takeover, we had the "green thumb," (green as in cash.) We beat out nine competitors for the sole acoustic treatment of GM's innovative Saturn car, acquired three more roofing plants, and added over five-hundred employees to produce our ever-increasing sales in both roofing and automotive. We also paid down three million on our bank loan, paid our employees a year-end bonus, and took one ourselves.

Marty and I developed a close relationship with Kingdon, his wife, Mary, and son, Frank, who served as a liaison between me and the Gould family. Kingdon was an expert in the analysis of people. He knew how to motivate me—he'd say, "Go get it, Robert," which he let me do in total freedom. His skills in negotiating deals were employed many times in acquisitions and our divestiture of Globe in 1995. He was the best at this.

Our nine-year ownership was typical of all business as we experienced the swings of the country's economy. Ever since Joseph interpreted the Pharoh's dream of "seven fat cattle, followed by seven lean cattle"—the first forecast of the business cycle—economies have had their oscillations. Globe was no exceptions, but managing cyclical businesses in periodic downturns was my forte. We survived the mini-recessions of 1987 and 1990, coming out of them, leaner, more efficient, and stronger. We became number one in automotive sound deadening market share, and very profitable in roofing.

I figured that automotive was our strongest suit, and our non-fiberglass based roofing would one day see its demise, say ten years out. So we sold the roofing division for $36,000,000—a fine markup on a division valued at $15,000,000 a few years earlier. The sale wiped out all of our bank debt, gave us $5,000,000 for investment in two new automotive lines, and several million to Kingdon and I personally as non-compete compensation. We also bought out the Canadian-owned half of the plant in Ontario.

As we continued to grow—acquiring three trim plants in Michigan, adding two new damper lines, and creating a plant to supply off-road equipment manufacturers—and me entering my sixties, I knew I had to train a successor, or at least an assistant to help manage our growth. A search produced Gerald Barefoot, an intelligent, automotive-experienced executive, with a fantastic talent for handling customers. "Jerry," became an invaluable aide and a close friend, as well. We spent many productive and educational hours together, sometimes with our wives, and many without. It didn't matter if we were driving to Oregon, playing golf, or in a formal meeting, we always produced something that helped the company. Jerry also lifted our luncheon conversations to a new level. We complimented each other—the well-educated, polished, and technically strong fifty-year-old alongside the sixty-plus, gut-feel, driven, night-school educated, commanding guy who clawed his way up corporate ladders from a track-side shanty in the Depression. Two plus two equaled five in this addition.

In 1989, Kingdon allowed me to sell some of my equity back to the company, for several million, which allowed Marty and I to enjoy second homes away from Chicago winters and do some meaningful charitable work. Putting back some of what God had blessed us with became a driving force in our lives. Many times Marty and I would talk about our days in our three-and-a-half room apartment when I worked at night as a foreman, and spent every spare dollar on night school tuition. "Chris, when I was ironing your white shirt or packing your lunch box at ten o'clock at night, I never dreamed we'd be able to do what we now can, thanks to God's blessings."

"Yeah, you're right. Sure, I showed up everyday, but my skills and work could have been bested by millions of other guys. No, it wasn't my puny efforts that helped us, it had to be something else—some guiding hand I couldn't see. It was uncanny how when I'd get a division or company doing good, something came along—politics, business cycles, foreigners, whatever—that would push me off the top of the wall like Humpty-Dumpty. Yet something or somebody would come along and put us back together in better shape than we were before. There's gotta be a higher power."

"Perhaps He led you to develop your plan to involve every one of Globe's twenty-three hundred employees in the total process of managing the company. There must have been a positive influence for such a fruitful plan to evolve."

She was right. It had taken awhile to get the program going, but now over ninety percent of our folks met weekly and brainstormed new ideas to make our plants more efficient, safer, employee-friendly, and satisfying.

My secretary, administrative assistant and family friend, Marlene Outerbridge, was the heartbeat of our Employee Involvement Program. Her superlative skills in communications and people handling were quintessential in the success of this program. She kept all two-thousand plus employees "tuned in" with her monthly newsletter, which always highlighted the hourly worker, not the management. Everyone waited each month for its issuance.

Each year we took the best team from each plant (now ten) to our Detroit facility and asked them to present the proposal they thought was their best one of the year. Some of them made videos, colored graphics, and well-articulated suggestions. They were responsive, enthusiastic, sincere, and devoted employees and family folks, and made our company stronger and a better place to work. We had management "of the people, for the people...."

*   *   *

As I approached sixty-five, I thought about retirement. I hinted at this to Kingdon, and knew I had struck a nerve. He didn't react positively, but I think he started, at least subliminally, to formulate an exit strategy. We agreed that I would meet with a Swiss company who had a strong presence in the European and South American automotive acoustic treatment markets. They were the same company with which we had had a technological license. It was to be an exploratory meeting. Two men from Switzerland, Jerry, and I met with them near our winter home on Hilton Head Island. When we put out the hint that Globe might be for sale, they were ecstatic. Their eyes flashed and their breathing accelerated, despite their efforts to be poker-faced—I guess poker isn't a Swiss game. This meeting was in October of 1994. In the early spring of '95, they made strong overtures.

Jerry was a big help in selling the company. I made sure that the Swiss knew he was my choice to run the company. They tried to play their cards close to the vest, but in their hearts they knew he was the man. I'll always admire Jerry for his professional integrity in serving Globe, Kingdon, and me in the pre-sale talks and plant inspections. He did this not knowing if he would have a job after the sale.

The chess game of the pre-closing negotiations was masterfully won by Kingdon Gould. He had a few good pieces: the team and I had given him to employ; annual sales of $250,000,000; an increasing automobile market; being number one in market share for our products; and profits of five percent, net after taxes. The tense drama of checkmating the final price was an end play of extreme skill. Kingdon, after many meetings, calls, and social outings with the Swiss, settled on $162,000,000. Not bad for a purchase price of $23,500,000, nine years earlier. My share of the proceeds arrived the next day by wire transfer.

Prior to the settlement we granted every management person a liberal bonus, some of them in six figures.

At last, the deal was done. Globe threw a black-tie retirement party for me, gave me several fine gifts and a lot of teary-eyed hugs and shakes from fifty people I had worked with, agonized with in tough times, and had grown to both love and respect.

So what does a sixty-six-year-old industrial veteran do after he's worked for forty-seven years from foreman to CEO-Owner? Who had been a hero and a bum? Who had been a top dog and a fired has-been? Is he like an old general who never dies, but just fades off? Or, does he find a new niche, a niche of service, of continued growth, and of learning through reflection, the true values and the meaning of life? Does he leave a legacy for his family and for his Silent Generation and its heirs? What path does he follow?

~

C H A P T E R

15

"Tisn't life that matters! 'Tis the courage you bring to it…"
Hugh Walpole – 1913 – *Fortitude*

If you've ever watched a horse race, in the "The Sport of Kings," after the frothing, panting horse has crossed the finish line, the jockey and trainer walk the animal for several furlongs. Induced by surges of adrenalin and the jockey's crop, the supreme effort that pushed the horse past the wire is suddenly and abruptly stopped. Where does this super energy go; how is it calmed to normal? Is it cooled down only by doing the same thing at a slower pace?

And, what of the hard-driving CEO, who with the tick of a clock and the tearing of a calendar page, has suddenly come to the finish of his industrial race? Who walks him for the cool-down? Will the adrenalin start flowing whenever he picks up the *Wall Street Journal*, or sees a former employee at the supermarket checkout? What does he feel, when at a charity board meeting, he hears about the ongoing careers of his fellow board members? Does his mental ROM image his past glories, his perks, and position?

All of the mental electricity, the endocrine secretions, personal motives, drives, and needs are still there. The forces that carried him to the top of competitive ladders have to be channeled into new outlets—into meaningful endeavors, or he'll sputter like a broken high-voltage wire arcing futilely in disconnection from usefulness. Can he turn his psychological rheostat up another notch—from a non-stop drive for recognition to the nirvana of self-actualization?

I've heard stories about retirees who suffer depression, or turn to drink, fantasize over past sexual encounters, or pick up petty jobs on country club or homeowner association boards. Once ensconced with meaningless titles, they try, as in Shakespeare's sixth age of man, "in their big manly voices, now turned again toward childish treble pipes and whistles in their sound," to reestablish their former commands. Others drift off into dreaming about childhood times, "good old days," and sadly, "what might have been." Still, some I know see retirement as a new venue, a yet to be written chapter of their lives. I choose this route, and call this the Fall of my life, not the Winter…well, maybe the *late* Fall.

Faced with no need to hustle for the first time in my life, I pause to assess my wherewithall—my capital accounts of knowledge, health, experience, family, friends, and financial store. My business life has taught me, sometimes in harsh lessons, that no asset should ever lie dormant. It should always produce a respectable ROI (return on investment). I need to plan how to best employ my goods—spiritual, mental, and physical.

*   *   *

Soon after June 16, 1995, I started the walk in my labyrinth of retirement and came to a signpost. It showed up in Psalm 116, which Marty and I recited often in church:

> "How shall I repay the Lord
> for all the good things he has done for me?"

The more I thought about my life, the more I realized how little was due to my efforts, and how much to the providence of a higher power. Maybe I could put back some of what we had been blessed with—repay the Lord for all the good things he had done for me. I didn't want to be a bubbling "do-gooder," flitting around, forcing my great works on people, whether they needed them or not. I recalled a couple of lines from T.S. Eliot's *Murder in the Cathedral*, when Thomas a'Becket is being tempted as the knights of King Henry II approach to kill him. The tempter says,

> "The last temptation is the greatest treason:
> To do the right deed for the wrong reason."

Right deeds must be done for the recipient not the doer. Not an easy task, since my whole cognizant life had been dedicated to achievement, with its accolades of recognition—a mandatory need of a kid who felt he was not equal to his peers. And, as I thought about my new directions, I reflected on those Depression days of the thirties, when as a small boy I had wrestled with the absence of my mother and father, and learned that we were "poor." *Yeah, you've overcome the material want side, but have you grown spiritually? Do you share what God has blessed you with? Or are you doing "right deeds for the wrong reason?" Buddy, you've got a challenge ahead of you in these "twilight years" greater than any ailing businesses you ever took on. You gotta sort out your soul, your motives, and whatever legacies you think you can leave. And you don't have a host of employees to help. You gotta do this from within, by yourself. Can you learn to do things just from the inner knowledge that they're right, not for recognition or glory? Have you got the courage that the old guy in Fortitude says is more important than life—to surrender yourself to God, to the needs of others? That's funny...courage "to surrender." I guess it takes more guts to do that than to charge, headlong, like the fully armored (and vision-impaired) knight at a jousting match.*

Without the sharp focus and demands of directing Globe Industries, I started to see other opportunities where I might contribute. The Illinois Philharmonic Orchestra, a Chicago Southside classical orchestra elected me president, where I worked with its maestro, Carmon De Leone. Carmon lived in hometown Cincinnati, where he conducted (and still does) the Cincinnati Ballet, and composed the music for the ballet *Peter Pan*. He'd travel to Chicago every month to lead our ninety-piece orchestra.

There is a true need to present classical music—it develops the creative and "soft side" of humanity, as do the other arts. These days a Beethoven symphony might have a hard time competing with a half-naked girl flaunting her feminine endowments to wild music, or with the false power of wielding a joy stick, killing countless "beings" in a video game. Still we must try to preserve the creative geniuses of art, music, literature, and drama. It's likely that in the era of the classics, school shootings were non-existent. With the ever-escalating and impersonal technology of war weapons, and the dehumanizing of our culture through more and more "machines over men," we believe that truly creative, artistic endeavors preserve the mental and moral health of our society.

My 50th Walnut Hills High class reunion filled some hours for me. For this gala event I wrote a skit; wrote, narrated, and produced a video about my class' school days; and wrote a book about school and our class, *The Reunion*. I have said many times that my six years at Walnut Hills was a very positive and directional influence in my life. Thankfully I had an opportunity to "pay back" a little to this hundred-plus-year-old college preparatory school. The alumni, 16,000 strong, agreed to fund a $12,500,000 new Arts and Science Wing. Marty and I traveled the entire country talking to regional alumni groups to raise the money. As of this writing, this modern, technologically updated building is in use and almost all of the funds have been raised. We see education, particularly the quality of what was imbued at Cincinnati's Walnut Hills, as the beacon of light that our country, our society needs to follow to solve the ever-present problems that human nature keeps alive, generation after generation. Alas, George Santayana, if we could only heed your advice—"Those who cannot remember the past are condemned to repeat it." Through supporting good schools, we keep trying, realizing that we have a tough task, for as Philip Roth said in *American Pastoral*, "Intelligence never got in the way of human nature," and as psychologists tell us: in a duel between emotion and intellect, emotion always wins.

A Flossmoor friend, Stewart Scott, introduced Marty and me to an organization called Pads. This group provides a bed (pad) for the night, plus supper, breakfast, and toilet articles to street people, euphemistically called "the homeless." Area churches donate their undercrofts for the weekend so that the homeless of the area can have shelter from the elements and from predatory individuals. Marty and I have worked with the homeless population in both Illinois and San Francisco. In SF the Episcopal Diocese has a two-story building called The Sanctuary, where thirty men and thirty women are given meals and beds as well as counseling and often even job placements. Marty, Bob, and I have served meals there, and were always impressed with the thank-you's that came from men and women in tattered rags, most of whom looked us in the eye, a sign of their sincerity.

There are so many homeless, jobless, and often hopeless folks on the streets. Why do millions of these wandering souls remain in the maelstrom of futility? Why do they stay at the bottom of the social status system, without resources or system support? They are forced into gleaning from garbage cans and selling themselves or their blood to eke out another day, maybe a week. Many have serious addictions—heroin, cocaine, or alcohol, whose demon-like cravings force them into crime, prostitution, and an ever-spiraling descent to a total loss of dignity.

Sadly there are not enough agencies or professionals to work with each and every person to get to the root of that individual's needs. So in America, we serve up a meal, hear a thank you, say a prayer, and move on thinking, "Isn't that a shame, those poor people!" Most religions teach us that in *every* human, there is a bit of an Almighty. What can be done to let this spirit shine through and restore that human to full being?

We have a lot of unfinished business to do in the social welfare area. True, hundreds, even thousands of good citizens volunteer to help the needy; but there are so many. Marty and I need to find more places where we can do something to help—or at least contribute funds.

*   *   *

After a couple of years of retirement in Illinois, with summers in Michigan and winters in Scottsdale, we decided to move the family homestead permanently to Arizona. Jim and John brought their families here, while Bob stayed in the Bay Area, working in the mental health field to earn a doctorate in clinical psychology. Bob has matured into a very caring man, who devotes his life to helping others. His experiences as an intern at Cook County jail in Chicago, coupled with his work with recovering substance abusers in San Francisco, qualified him to intern for his doctorate at the highly selective Jung Institute.

John seems to have followed his older brother's path. He is counseling parolees, substance abusers, and those unfortunate enough to have both a substance and criminal history. John is articulate, incisive in evaluating a client, and persuasive in helping the client to seek a road to recovery. As a youngster, he always wanted to please, and like Bob, is suited for work in helping others. Both men have compassion and caring for those in need, whether family, friend, or stranger. We are pleased with their outreach work and ministries.

Jim too shares the quality of immense compassion, which he demonstrates in the business community with our employees. He is quiet but effective in supervising large numbers of people,because he treats them fairly and personally with non-autocratic leadership. He is conscientious—almost to a fault—and loyal to his family and his employees, often helping them with their problems, both on and off the job.

Our three sons were raised in the throes of the social revolution of the sixties and seventies, and while they tried some of the diversions of that era, they have settled into responsible, family-oriented men, who take care of themselves, love their parents, and exhibit true concern for others. We doubt any one of our sons will become a U.S. president, but their desire to help others is a sterling quality. They have enhanced our lives. Yes we have, like most families, had our adjustment years, but we have grown together, we love and respect one another, and we help each other.

*   *   *

As I aged, a few medical tests—CAT scans, M.R.I.s, blood work, and x-rays—minor treatments, and some skin surgery led us first to the Mayo Clinic, then the Mayo hospital in Scottsdale. We encountered nothing life-threatening, but experienced some of the rewards for passing the biblical three score and ten. Marty and I were treated so well by the Mayo organization that we became volunteers, working at the hospital one day a week: Marty on records in the organ transplant area and I in patient transport.

One of my duties was to take a *USA Today* into each of the 178 rooms in the morning. I saw every patient, and was privileged to do small favors for them as I dropped the paper. And I saw the care that the patients receive from dedicated nurses and orderlies. We hear so much criticism of the medical profession—some of it justified—but my observations at Mayo tell me we are, as a nation, a lot better off medically than were previous generations. Life expectancy is so much longer, and life quality is improving yearly. I believe we must do more pooling of medical costs, perhaps through the nationalization of medicine, and not depend on HMOs and other organizations that limit what a doctor can do for a patient. More importantly, however, any national medical program must be run by people acquainted with medicine and its costs, not by politicians. Finally, we have to limit lawsuit awards.

In each hospital room, I see either folks who are healing and working to be discharged, or I see despair and suffering. And every so often, I encounter an extraordinary example of human nobility. In one of the east wing rooms, the bed was elevated to a forty-five degree angle allowing the patient to be very visible. I just stood there looking at her, one of the most beautiful women I have ever seen. She looked to be about fifty, her hair was raven black with silver strands woven throughout, adding perfect highlights. It was splayed on the crisp whiteness of the taut bed sheet. Her skin was perfect, smooth ivory with a translucent quality, reminding me of Japanese porcelain. Her cheek bones were symmetrical curves that set off a pair of jet-black eyes, which gleamed like rare black pearls. Her lips were full, hinting that a smile was soon to appear...and it did!

"Would you like a paper ma'am?"

Glancing at my name tag, she smiled, and I warmed all over. "Why, that's good of you, Bob, to bring me one." She extended her uncovered arm and open hand. I advanced with the paper, feeling a surge of blood to my face as she penetrated my eyes with hers. "Thank you, Bob, and bless you." Again, I felt warmth oozing through my entire being. I just stood next to her bed, my hand lingering on hers, thinking how lucky the guy must be whose wife or lover she was.

Reluctantly turning to leave, I realized she was not covered by a sheet, and that her lower body was exposed. I noticed her shapely thighs, which were of the same porcelain-like skin as her face. My eyes traveled down her legs, wanting to see her calves, and I gasped. Her left leg stopped just below the knee, and the right only several inches above the ankle. Both legs ended in smooth, neatly turned-under roundness of beautiful, ivory skin.

I knew not to stare, even though I already had for an eternal second, so I quickly looked back to her face, saying nothing. It had changed from a smile to a blend of pathos and understanding. She cocked her head to one side, signaling, "I know, but that's the way it is. Don't anguish."

I half-stammered, "Hope you enjoy the paper, ma'am. Anything I can do for you, while I'm here?"

"It's, Joyce, Bob. No, thank you, I'm fine. Please come by again," she said as an appreciative smile lingered on her smooth cheeks. Only her eyes reflected the sadness of what might have been.

As I exited her room, I blew her a kiss and said, "Thank you."

Walking over to the west wing, I felt both sad and humble, but I marveled at the great beauty and compassion she had extended to me. Her beauty was the richest of all—emanating from within—she suffered, yet she thought of the needs of others. Joyce had put my momentary embarrassment above her own unfortunate and permanent condition.

Part of the deep feeling that Joyce stimulated in me must have come from the painful memory of Grandmother Allan's diabetic-induced amputations. Grandmother wasn't the best at adhering to the discipline that diabetes demands, so at sixty she had one leg amputated at the knee, just like Joyce's. Six years later the other leg was amputated above the knee, which caused Grandmother to will herself dead while she was recovering. The thought of all she did for me, and relating Grandmother to what I had just seen in Joyce's room, tore at my heart. I guess seeing a person like Joyce, who was the same age as our son Bob, made her plight even more painful. If there is a holy spirit, then there must be a sliver of it in Joyce's room—I know I'll always pray that it be with her.

Through our volunteer work at Mayo, and visiting with thousands of patients, my feelings of humility increased. To see that many sick, injured, and diseased folks, forced me to wonder why I was allowed to be outside of the bed...outside of the room. Amputees, transplant recipients, cancer-ridden men and women bald from chemo, and many with mangled limbs, silently said to me, "Buddy, get down on your knees and thank God for every hour you have as a healthy being." To be blessed with health and well-being is to be blessed with the greatest of riches.

I share any thoughts or observations I pick up on my hospital rounds with Marty regularly. We are both grateful for our health, and we talk about the great amount of sickness in the world—the consuming spread of AIDS in Africa, the thousands of people killed in accidents, and the deaths of so many children from a host of "wrong reasons," such as malnutrition, neglect, and birth defects. Discussions like this can lead one to ask, "How can a merciful God allow this to happen?" It's a question that provokes both deep thought and a litmus test of our faith and creeds. In my struggles with this, I came across a passage in the apocryphal book *Sirach*, which reads:

> It was he who created man in the beginning,
> and he left him in the power of his own inclination.
> If you will, you can keep the commandments,
> and to act faithfully is a matter of your own choice.

Before man are life and death,
and whichever he chooses will be given to him.

I believe God gave us intellect and reason, and the ability to pray. However, free will (his own inclination) precludes the idea of a master puppeteer pulling our strings as we tread across life's stage. I feel God has entered my life in answer to prayer, but never as an overprotective parent. If we were not exercisers of our free will, how would our love of God or each other be real? How would we grow if all was centrally controlled and predestined? It's also true that free will brings with it both risk and pain. God has given man the ability to learn and accumulate his knowledge so that each generation can leave a legacy to its follower. We *can* leave legacies of better medical care, of better technology, and a better understanding of each other—that is if we only *will*.

In the last few years, Marty and I have also been working with our local Episcopal Coalition, where we build Habitat for Humanity houses. This is truly a worthwhile venture as it provides low cost housing, bought by the deserving family at half cost with an interest-free loan. Today Habitat is international, helping families all over the world to have a home with dignity, containing some of the family's labor along with the free labor of their fellow man.

*　　　　　*　　　　　*

Together, Marty and I are learning the three Rs of retirement: reflection, regret, and rededication. With more free time, it is hard not to reflect on the past. Despite my occupation with buying a couple of businesses in the greater Phoenix area, which son Jim manages for the family, being active in several charities, and a lot of church work, I "involuntarily" spend some time in reflection.

If I weren't so busy, thoughts about all things past in my life—childhood, family and friends who have died, and all that my life has been about, would seep into my brain unbidden, igniting it with all of the emotional fires.

Many of the memories, usually triggered by looking at family photo albums, are pleasant, of course, but there are always a few "wish we would ofs" and "wish we wouldn't haves." Without mistakes and searching there'd be no growth, no maturing, or annealing of character and beliefs in the heat of life. Regret is the indictment, punishment, and penance for things left undone. And usually regret is punishment enough for the omission. The knowledge that "The bird was in the hand and one let it go"—as Walpole, in *Fortitude* describes the fourth and toughest land that a sojourner of life must compass to reach the mastery of his soul—is as persistently vexing as Zeus's Eagle was to Prometheus. My regrets, in hindsight, are in not achieving a better balance between my industrial work and my family and not realizing that surrendering to God is an easier path than that of the rugged individual. But, as some say, "It's never too late."

Rededication occurs when one sees hints of the journey's end. By rededicating oneself to a cause or endeavor, one breathes new life into him or herself. A sense of "this can go on" prescribes a tranquilizer for the dread of the end. I admire people, real or fictional, who, as our British allies say, "Carry on," despite any adversity. I recall the main character in Neville Shoot's book, *On the Beach*, who, as the last living man in Australia after a worldwide nuclear holocaust, and just a few hours away from dying of radiation sickness, buys, leaving the cash on the counter of a vacant store, a lawnmower and cuts his grass.

My grandmother Christopher dedicated her widowed life to raising me until her very last breath. Each day that we awake is either the first day of the rest of our lives, or it is the last day at the end of our lives. We never know in advance. Each day then is a blessing to be used, enjoyed, and shared with others. The days gone by, which were not shared with others, or made meaningful, can haunt us when there are but a few future ones for us to embrace. Again, I am reminded of *September Song*, "…one hasn't got time for the waiting game/ Oh, the days dwindle down to a precious few…."

*   *   *

Retirement has brought another phase—what some call "senior moments." Can't say I like the term, but I guess I have them—usually during a short post-lunch nap, after an aggressive aerobic and weight training workout in the morning followed by a myriad of tasks, often involving a couple hours of stressful driving in a maniacal morass of "can't go fast enough" SUVs, pickup trucks, beaters, and semis. I have learned to enjoy these "moments," rather than fight them. In fact, many times I awake with a glowing image of myself, in my catcher's pads, pegging a ball to Dickey George at second base as we try to get a guy from Manny's Mobile Mart who's hoping to steal second. Or maybe I see myself in the fifth grade, trying to wheedle a couple of extra turns to kiss Patty Drexel in a game of post office.

Clinging to another piece of my past, I have several HO scale models of steam engines in our library, even one of a Baltimore and Ohio Mikado 2-8-2. It's just like the ones I'd watch as a youngster, huffing and puffing past our house with a hundred freight cars in tow. One sleepy night recently, I was sitting at my desk staring at the B & O steam engine model. The longer I stared, the more the model became real. Through heavy lids I saw the engine and me floating back into time, year after year.

I was eight years old, standing on Grandmother's porch, watching the real 2-8-2 passing, with its chuck-chucks, shrieking whistle, and click-click-clicks of flanged, steel wheels crossing track joints. "Hey, Bobby, come on in and let's set up your electric train," my dad called to me from the door.

Daddy and I worked for an hour setting up my train; then we played with it until Grandmother called us to dinner. This was the last time my dad and I did this because two weeks later he got sick and went to the hospital where he died. Through my tears I saw my train disappear down the tracks. The caboose came into view, and there on the rear platform was my dad, smiling and waving to me. Next to him was a black-suited, ethereal conductor hollering to me, "Board, all aboard."

I look often at pictures of my football days. I guess making the Walnut Hills team and helping to win the championship was a highlight. Football taught me so much. How to work hard to earn a berth on the squad, how to pick myself up after being knocked down, and how to play on a team, yet still strive to star as an individual entity. After playing several years and coaching the church team, I learned that the rudimentary basics of blocking and tackling are most important in winning. In the ultimate, if you always block the other guy from getting to your ball carrier or passer, you'll score. And, if you always tackle the other team's ball carrier before he hits the line of scrimmage, they'll never score. Oversimplified? Not to me. Blocking and tackling—these are the basics that win. A simple parallel can be drawn with how we humans treat and work with each other—using the basics of: please and thank you. Childish, a bit perhaps, but if we have the mindset to never take or assume without asking first—as in please, may I—we gratify the giver and give him/her recognition. And, to the same end, if we appreciate, sincerely and graciously what is done for us, or given to us—as in thank you, we again give grace to the donor.

Over the last twenty years I have tried to go back to as many as possible of the people who helped me, particularly those who gave me love, support, and a leg up in my dark days and when I was struggling to grasp the first rung of my career ladder. Some have died before I could get to them, but many I have found and have been able to express my gratitude. I have also found the answer to my dilemma about missing those who had aided me without reciprocal help or thanks. It was taught to Marty and me by a little boy in a movie, *Pay It Forward*. The boy, after both giving and receiving help said that if we receive help or succor from someone, but can't reciprocate, we should "pay it forward," meaning to do a good deed or give help to someone else down the road. In effect, good deeds are poured into the pool of humanity, to be drawn from by those in need.

One more thought. Good high school friends, whom I had not seen since graduation, have resurfaced in my later life. Jack Rose and Millard Mack, both from hometown Cincinnati, have re-entered my life along with their lovely wives. I mention this because, like a flower's seed or bulb, friendship and love can lie dormant for periods of time, yet be awakened to full bloom with a few kind words, a meeting, or a shared event. I feel so good about these couples, because it tells me that good seeds sown long before do not wither and die—love and friendship can endure distance and time. Even in separation, the seed of love—unlike hatred or distrust, which festers like a cancer and dies taking the owner with it—can live forever locked in the heart and in our warm memories. I ask myself, "Will we harvest the dormant seeds of love from our lives in the hereafter?"

E P I L O G U E

The alarm goes off, its penetrating jangle tweaking my nerves. As always when coming out of a sound sleep, I mentally grope for a handle on what day it is, and what I'm to do. This Friday morning I'm to go to Mayo hospital for carotid artery surgery. I lie still for a moment, remembering my doctor's edict. It has to be done, and I know it intellectually, but not emotionally. My intestines contract in anxiety. Fasting since six o'clock the night before has left me hollow.

I go through the motions of shaving and toothbrushing, dreading what is to be done. I mumble a few prayers and tell myself that what I'm facing is, as one doctor said, "Bread-and-butter surgery." Well, maybe to him. Oh, hell, Moose get on with it.

"You up, Chris?" Marty calls. I know she's been up for hours, probably had a bad night's sleep worrying about me and my consuming dread of being out of control. I'm glad she's going to be with me, or nearby during the whole procedure. Lord, what would I do without her?

An hour later I'm in the pre-op bed engaging the nurse in conversation attempting to shake my anxiety. She knows the drill. God, how many queasy people's hands she has held? Turning my arm to insert an IV, she says, "Why, Mr. Christopher, what lovely veins you have."

"What are you a lady vampire?" I snap back. *There's that false bravado. It comes so naturally.* She puts strange cotton

320

stockings on me, thigh to ankle. "Honey, I'm not into this kind of thing." *I just don't quit, do I?*

"Don't knock it if you haven't tried it," she smiles. Matching my efforts to "keep it light" is her way of supporting me in this stressful moment. I'm grateful.

Dr. Fowl, the vascular surgeon, stops by asking how I feel. He's in green scrubs complete with plastic head cap. I like him, and seeing him calms me a little.

Just before I go into the land of modern-day Morpheus, I realize that what is happening to me occurs every day of our lives—we are never sure how the day will turn out. Will I come out of this operation at least as well as I went in? Do we end each day with the assured promise of another? God gave us free will and the ability to control most of our actions, but not those of others. Even with the gifts Plato said we have—faith, reason and emotion—we do not have control over what may impinge upon us.

I am once again aware, just for an instant, as the orderly pushes my gurney down familiar corridors, that I am at peace. I am in the hands of Dr. Fowl, whom I trust, in God's realm, and in Marty's and our sons' hearts. I don't have to run this one. I just have to surrender. And if I don't come out, I muse foggily....